# Christian Family Living

## JOHN COBLENTZ

Illustrated by
David W. Miller

Christian Light Publications, Inc.
Harrisonburg, Virginia 22801

Attempt has been made to secure permission for the use of all copyrighted material. If further information is received, the publisher will be glad to properly credit this material in future printings.

ISBN: 0-87813-541-3
Lithographed in U.S.A.

# FOREWORD

Some of you have been waiting a long time for a book such as you hold in your hands. One of the happiest persons to see this in print would have been the late Sanford Shank, founder of Christian Light Publications.

As he and the other members of the Book and Tract Editorial Committee—John Coblentz (Minn.), Lloyd Hartzler (Va.), Fred Miller (W.Va.), and Leon Yoder (Va.)—discussed the need for providing more practical Scriptural help for Christian families, the idea of this book came into being. As a result, the Committee asked John Coblentz to write a series of books addressing family issues. *Christian Family Living* is the first and basic book of the series. After dealing with practical issues facing every Christian family, each chapter of this book closes with thought-provoking questions under the heading, "Thinking Together." This is followed by a section entitled, "Working Together," which encourages readers to put into practice what they have just read.

*Christian Family Living* is designed for use in Christian homes, high schools, Bible schools, and Bible study groups.

Reviewing this series and working with the writer and the other committee members in the combined efforts of the editorial process has been a special delight. That delight increases as this series goes out to bless and enrich families around the world.

Fred W. Miller

# CHRISTIAN FAMILY LIVING SERIES

The *Christian Family Living* Series also includes:

*God's Will for My Body—Guidance for Adolescents*

A workbook to help parents in teaching their children about adolescent changes.

*God's Will for Love in Marriage—Cultivating Marital Intimacy*

A study for engaged persons or married couples, offering practical, Biblical guidance for healthy intimacy in marriage. Includes a frank, Biblical approach to the controversial subject of family planning.

*Courtship That Glorifies God—A Biblical Approach to Dating and Engagement*

A reprint of Chapter 3 in *Christian Family Living*. Available as a booklet for study in youth groups, Bible schools, high schools, etc.

*Singlehood That Glorifies God—Living With Eternal Purpose*

A reprint of Chapter 4 in *Christian Family Living*. This booklet is for single people as well as for those willing to understand and respect single people.

*What the Bible Says About Marriage, Divorce, and Remarriage*

A Biblical approach to a battered subject, this study follows a question-and-answer format in showing what the Bible says and in offering practical help for resolving difficult situations.

# CONTENTS

# INTRODUCTION

So why another book on the family? There are already countless books from countless authorities on the subject.

Something must not be right, however, when with all the advice of the authorities, we continue to sh..t closer toward family chaos, not only in secular society, but in much of the church as well.

I have a rich and deepening appreciation for the Mennonite culture in which I grew up, partially because in it I have found a heritage of strong family life. But I likewise have a growing concern that the cancer which has so wasted the family in general society is eating at Mennonite families as well.

Still, this book is not sectarian. It is a call to remembrance, an attempt to verbalize many of the Biblical principles and practices which have guided Christian families through the centuries and to apply them to the issues facing us today. It reaches to the heritage of Scripture and calls all Christians to measure their families by those standards.

The authority of this book, then, is not popular psychology. Instead, it acknowledges the Authority above all of us who instituted the family and by whose principles the family must be guided if it is to survive this present age. While other authors are quoted at times, quoting an author is not automatic endorsement of all that particular author says elsewhere. But it is in recognition that others, many others, have contributed to the understanding and application of the Scriptures presented in this book.

I wish to offer special thanks to David E. Showalter, David L. Miller, Eli B. Yoder, Leon Yoder, and Lloyd Hartzler who reviewed the unpublished manuscript and offered their suggestions and criticisms, as well as to Fred Miller for his careful editorial work. I also wish to thank the many people who have asked me searching questions about the family and have challenged me to find God's answers in the Bible. The "snapshots" in this book reflect some of the wonderful people and families I have learned to know and love. The details are given as my memory has served me; names, of course, have been changed (except in the story of my father's handicap on page 251). Above all I thank God for the family He has given me. My wife, Barbara, and our six children continue to provide me with the richest education I could desire in Christian family living.

The scope of this book is broad—too broad, no doubt. But it is broad in recognition that the family is not an issue by itself. If we are to build strong families, we must be building on many fronts.

I pray that the lives of readers will be built up in faith, faith that God's ways are right, faith that God's ways are practical, and faith that no man is a fool who builds his home by God's standards. May our Lord have the joy of establishing many stable homes in our unstable world.

John A. Coblentz

**BASIC FAMILY CONCEPTS**

## INTRODUCTION

To say that the family is in a state of deterioration in Western culture is anticlimactic. Many have said it. Many are saying it. And the family continues to fall apart. In spite of the multitude of books, seminars, and experts, husbands and wives are still alienating themselves from each other, parents from children, and children from parents. Unfortunately, what many fail to realize is that the problem is not simply the Western family, but Western life. While millions are being spent on more programs, better methods, and clearer training for parents, the real problem is often unaddressed. The

1

way we Westerners live—the things we think are important, the attitudes we have toward life, the very structure of our home life—renders ineffective much of the good advice we hear.

One example will suffice. While many Christian parents are wondering whether the music their teens listen to is suitable listening, and sometimes arguing about volume and forbidding this or that tape, few modern parents ever consider that today's music industry, including the Christian music industry, has virtually destroyed certain Christian values. Silence. The sheer noise (even nice-sounding noise) in many homes today would have driven many of our great-grandparents out to the pastures for a quiet walk. Worship. Where, in all the hullabaloo of Christian music today and the idolizing of favorite groups and the scrambling for each new tape and the bickering over how loud to play it, is the reverent sense of God? And how many thousand-dollar music systems (which are not worth a nickel in heaven) have silenced the voices of families singing simple but heartfelt praise to God?

The point is simple. There are many homes which can never be wholesome until some radical changes take place in the home structure. It would be foolish to try to build a house in a swamp on straw bales. And it is just as foolish to think we can build godly homes on the values commonly accepted in Western culture. If in Christian homes we find straw bales in the foundation, we cannot correct the problem by hiring some interior decorator to counsel us on paint. The foundation needs help first.

This chapter is about foundational things. From the Scriptures we want to see just what God intended the family to be. We want to look at concepts which are basic to the family as a social unit. And later we want to look at some of the straw bales which our culture is pressuring us to use in our homes, and which we must reject if we are to have wholesome families.

## THE SOCIAL UNIT

"And these words, which I command thee this day, shall be in thine heart: And thou shalt teach them diligently unto thy children, and shalt talk of them when thou sittest in thine house, and when thou walkest by the way, and when thou liest down, and when thou risest up" (Deuteronomy 6:6,7).

"A wise son maketh a glad father: but a foolish son is the heaviness of his mother. He that gathereth in summer is a wise son: but he that sleepeth in harvest is a son that causeth shame" (Proverbs 10:1,5).

"Children, obey your parents in the Lord: for this is right. Honour thy father and mother. . . . And, ye fathers, provoke not your children to wrath: but bring them up in the nurture and admonition of the Lord" (Ephesians 6:1,2a,4).

From these and similar Scriptures, we can easily see that God intended the family to be the most basic social unit of society. It is the place where such activities as visiting, eating, instruction, work, and play have their center. God intended that we interact with family members more than with anyone else. And having ordained the home to be the primary place of social interaction, God laid down guidelines for proper interaction.

As a social unit, however, the family in Western culture is seriously deficient. Those who want to work go to the corporation. Those who want to learn go to school. Those who want to play go to the park or the recreation center. Those who want to eat go to McDonalds. Visiting takes place only in snatches. Many Christian families find it strange to have the whole family home for an evening. Monday night is practice. Tuesday night is a ball game. Wednesday night is prayer meeting (for some). Thursday night is office cleaning (second job). Friday night a social is planned. . . . Run, run, run! Such social chaos was virtually unheard of for the family 100 years ago. And so, fathers must be told to do things with their children. Parents need to plan a "family night" or "quality time" because as a social unit, the family is falling apart.

Some of the pressures of over-activity will be discussed more later, but for now, let's note that every child and every adult needs wholesome family interaction.

### The Family Should Work Together

Obviously the job scene is changing in our modernized society. The family farm is no longer the norm. Many Amish and Mennonite men have gone to self-employment in construction. In some ways, this is good—it still provides opportunities for fathers to work with sons. But it has its dangers as well—if the father operates his business at the pace of many American or European contractors, he easily becomes so engulfed in his work that he interacts little with his family. The answer, in other words, is not simply in starting a family business, but in valuing family interaction.

Where the father can work with his family, he should. Where he cannot work with his family in his occupation, he should keep that occupation from swallowing all of his working energy and plan work at home with his family in his off time. Gardening is an excellent off-time work project. Where this is impossible, other projects can be chosen. It is good for children to see their parents work. It is good for parents to show their children how to work and to demonstrate the qualities of a good worker. It is good for families to figure out work-related problems, divide up responsibilities, and share the rewards of hard work.

### The Family Should Eat and Talk Together

Schedule clashing and hurriedness seem to have converged on the family table in an all-out effort today to stamp out family meals. It is true that some schedule conflicts cannot be avoided, especially as older teens begin to interact more in the adult world. It is also true, however, that much of the meal disruption today is simply the result of overinvolvement. Many of the activities that call for family members at mealtime are good activities. And it is not wrong to be busy, but something basic is wrong when the unhurried family meal is the rare exception. And something basic must be done about it.

In evaluating activities which keep the family apart at mealtime, it is well to consider the difference between service activities and self-serving activities.

Service activities are love's responses to the needs of others. People who are serious in their commitment to Jesus Christ will often find themselves busy in service activities. Jesus found mealtime with His disciples being cut out by such activities, and He took steps for relief. "And he said unto them, Come ye yourselves apart into a desert place, and rest a while: for there were many coming and going, and they had no leisure so much as to eat" (Mark 6:31).

Self-serving activities, on the other hand, are things we do primarily for our own enjoyment, pleasure, or interests. This kind of activity is not altogether wrong, particularly as a means of refreshment or enrichment, but any life filled with such activities is certain to be shallow, empty, and unfulfilled, no matter how exciting it may appear on the surface. Western culture is glutted with self-serving activities (and thus with unfulfilled people). And, unfortunately, many of the families being torn apart at mealtime are running off to these kinds of activities.

Consider the following list of typical activities which crowd out the family meal. Which are service activities? Which are self-serving activities? Which, depending on circumstances, might be either?

- ball game
- shopping
- singing
- socializing
- working
- visiting
- committee meeting
- practice
- driving/riding with friends
- listening to a singing group
- attending a meeting
- working on a project

Families who find mealtime togetherness regularly crowded out should monitor their activities for a week or two, honestly assessing the nature of their activities. Where there is service busyness, times of refreshment should be planned. Where there is self-serving busyness, a reevaluation of priorities is imperative. The years of family time are simply too short to sacrifice on the altars of indulgence.

Cutting back on self-serving activities invariably meets with resistance. Nobody wants to stop going. Change comes best by discussing the problem together as a family, clarifying family priorities, setting reasonable guidelines, and then following them for a specified period of time, after which reevaluation takes place. The guidelines should include not only restrictions on certain activities, but replacement with more wholesome activities which meet the family's social needs. (For a more thorough discussion of family activities, see Chapter 6.)

### The Family Should Worship Together

While it must be recognized that collective worship

finds its center in the church, worship is a vital part of the family's social structure as well. Families should pray together, sing together, read God's Word together, and offer thanksgiving together. It is impossible to verbalize all the ways in which healthy family worship time provides security, stability, wisdom, and maturation for family members.

The same forces which rob families of mealtime together rob the same families of worship time together. The hurried life, especially the indulged hurried life, grows impatient with the quietness necessary for reading and prayer. There are far more exciting things to do. But as we noted before, the exciting things are seldom the fulfilling things in the long run. The family which is too fragmented for worship together is living by a value system which cannot build strong Christians. Rather, such a value system actually prepares children to yield further to the pressures of sin and worldly society.

### The Family Should Play Together

Much as recreation and fun have been overplayed in our society, play has a very proper and wholesome place in the family. It is good for the family to laugh together. It is good for children to see their parents in the informal and sometimes blundering and comical situations of playtime. Dad on all fours does something good to the hearts of his children which he can never do otherwise. Games can reinforce such principles as fairness, honesty, group effort, and courtesy. Unstructured play, such as building cities in the sandbox or tenting on the living room floor, can encourage creativity and cooperation. Reading or telling stories can be both enjoyable and informative. The point here is that all of these forms of recreation, in proper balance with the rest of family interaction, are socially healthy.

### The Family Should Interact Socially in the Instruction/Learning Process

God calls parents to be good teachers and children to be good learners so that they in turn can become good teachers of their children. This interaction between parents and their children begins even before verbal communication is possible. It continues in one form or another throughout life. The responsibility of parents teaching their children is one which for certain learning situations can be delegated, but it can never be unshouldered. Children need the experience of learning from their parents; parents need the experience of instructing their children.

As we will see later in this chapter, our culture is placing tremendous pressure on families with regard to education. The center of learning for children in our society is moving away from the home, and the source of learning is moving away from parents toward the "expert." Unfortunately, the expertise of man generally moves away from the fear of the Lord, and thus, often at the "best" of educational opportunities, there is least of that wisdom which matters most. This is not only robbing families of valuable interaction but is also robbing education of its enduring value and purpose.

To summarize this section, we would repeat that God ordained the family to be the basic social unit of society. It is the center around which its members interact in such common activities as work, play, worship, eating, learning, and talking. And we have raised flags of warning over that society which pressures the family to give up this social interaction.

## HERITAGE—BLESSING OR CURSE?

We live in the present. We face present situations. But the present time and the present situations can be traced back through time and countless other situations which have led up to the present. In the family, we refer to this background as "heritage." Any given family is in many ways a product of its heritage. It was produced by people and events from the past. The decisions and character of father, grandfather, and great-grandfather and the choices and influence of mother, grandmother, and great-grandmother have all flowed into making any family what it is. Anything from physical features to little habits to outstanding traits to guiding beliefs and values can be part of one's family heritage.

Fortunately, heritage is not the only factor in shaping families. The present is always adding its part to the family heritage. Our heritage is not only what our grandparents and parents were, but what we are. The choices we are making and the lives we are living are contributing their part. We will always have the influence of the past, but we are never fully controlled by it. And we must, both for our own good and for the good of future generations, be making those choices which leave a heritage of godliness.

Heritage can be either a blessing or a curse. David wrote, "The lines are fallen unto me in pleasant places; yea, I have a goodly heritage" (Psalm 16:6). By this, David was not saying that everything in his past had been godly. David had suffered and was suffering many troubles and injustices. But David had walked with the Lord, and in his walk with God he had found a rich heritage.

In verse 5, David introduces the most significant factor in heritage. "The LORD is the portion of mine inheri-

9

tance." The presence of God in one's life more than anything else determines the impact and worth of his parental heritage. He who walks with God can look back, even upon a heritage of sin and failure, and see the goodness of the Lord drawing him to Himself. And he gives thanks. On the other hand, he who walks in rebellion against God cannot find, even in a heritage of godliness, much good in his past. He does little more than complain.

From the human standpoint, we might even say that the presence of the Lord works retroactively in respect to our heritage. No matter what our past, if we turn in repentance and humility to the Lord, He is able to turn past troubles and injustices into unexpected present blessings in our lives. And in contrast, no matter how godly the parentage, when one turns in stubbornness and disobedience from it, he finds the very benefits of his past turning against him and even pleasant memories souring and becoming indistinguishable from his mass of troubles.

Thus we come to see that no one can confine the effects of his life to himself. He who lives righteously passes on an influence of righteousness. He who lives in sin passes on a heritage of sin. And in both kinds of heritage God is at work, on the one hand declaring, "The generation of the upright shall be blessed" (Psalm 112:2), and on the other hand, "visiting the iniquity of the fathers upon the children, and upon the children's children, unto the third and to the fourth generation" (Exodus 34:7).

All of this verifies both the importance of upright, godly families and the impossibility of having such families without the Lord. There is simply no way to enjoy the blessings of a godly heritage or to pass on a godly heritage without devotion to God.

### Honoring Parents

God's expectations for the family are based solidly upon Scriptural principles. We have already observed some of those principles in relation to heritage. but there is another basic principle which has suffered such neglect and abuse in Western society that we must pick it up here and consider it carefully. That is the principle of honoring parents.

Among the commands God gave to His people was one specifically related to families. "Honour thy father and thy mother: that thy days may be long upon the land which the LORD thy God giveth thee" (Exodus 20:12). Paul, writing to the Ephesians, notes that this is the only command of the ten to which a promise is attached. The promise has to do with well-being and long life. Inasmuch as life is a social existence, and inasmuch as the family is the basic social unit, it follows that our obedience or disobedience to a basic family principle will directly affect our lives.

What does it mean to honor our parents? Do Westerners generally honor their parents? Do Western Christians honor their parents? These are questions we must honestly face.

The Hebrew word for honor literally has the idea of heaviness. In verb form it means to give weight to, or to hold as significant or worthy in contrast to something light or frivolous. The practical outworking of such a high regard for parents is invariably associated with such things as obedience, helpfulness, and deference. Children do what their parents instruct them to do, help their parents with work and responsibility, and where there are differences of opinion about plans or desires, they yield to their parents.

Of course, the other side of the coin is that parents are to be honorable. That is, they are to be venerable, loving, and wise. The truth, however, is that all parents have faults and fall short of the ideal, and that some parents are actually unloving, foolish, and contemptible. Does a parent need to be honorable to be honored?

The direction God gives for children to honor their parents makes no exception for parents who are not honorable. In another authority relationship where God calls for honor, He says specifically, "not only to the good and gentle, but also to the froward [unreasonable]" (I Peter 2:18). Young children do not grapple with whether they should obey or not. They tend to respond as their nature dictates. Older children and youths, however, begin to analyze their parents' performance as well as their own reasons for or against obeying. Those with Christian teaching struggle with this command of God in view of their imperfect parents. Three things must be kept in focus for those whose parents may not be honorable:

*1. One must honor the position of a parent even when the parent does not seem deserving of honor.* All authority rests in God. The position of parenthood with its responsibilities was given by God, and where parents are unfaithful in their responsibilities, they are unfaithful not simply to their children, but to God. By honoring the position of parents, children can leave in God's hands the task of rebuking, chastening, and correcting. With this view, one can say, "Even though my mother screams at me, she is still my mother. And I will try by God's grace to do cheerfully what she says."

*2. The giving of honor is more dependent on the heart of the one honoring than the life of the one being honored.* To honor parents, one must have an honoring heart, that is, a heart with the qualities suited to honoring. Such qualities include submission, love, faithfulness, meekness, wisdom, etc. Without these qualities, one would find it impossible to find a parent he could honor. With these qualities, one will find grace to honor the parents God has given.

*3. Since God commands honor to parents, and God is perfectly honorable, obedience and honor can be given to imperfect parents as obedience unto God.* As long as we focus on the imperfections of earthly parents, honor will be difficult. But when we focus on the glory and perfection of our heavenly Father, we have no reasonable option but to honor Him. Since He told us to honor our parents, our honor and obedience to them can be viewed as honor and obedience to Him.

Many Christian young people struggle with practical questions about honoring their parents. They wonder HOW? Here are some specific suggestions for teens who are serious about giving honor:

1. Develop a conscious habit of expressing gratitude to your parents. When you begin to consider, you realize your parents have done, and continue to do for you, far more than you can ever calculate.

2. Discuss with your parents plans you are making. Share both short-range plans for the week and any long-range plans you may have for the next year, several years, or your life. Failure to communicate is one of the most common problems between teens and their parents.

3. Ask for advice. Even if you think you know what your parents will say, ask them what they think. Many teens complain about overrestrictive parents, but probably the biggest cause of overrestriction in parents is underaccountability in teens. Initial advice from parents may not be intended to be the final word on an issue. If you have other thoughts, their advice provides a basis for you to discuss your viewpoint with them. When it comes down to the final decision, of course, you will need to honor them. But even if this means you do not do what you had wanted to do, you will have gained respect and

13

the benefit of further openness with them.

4. Value evenings at home. This will mean, especially in some communities, that you will not go to every activity available to you. Discuss with your parents a suitable schedule and then ask for advice when faced with schedule conflicts. Believe it or not, there will come a time (and shortly) when you will think back to evenings at home as a teen and wish that you could roll back time and just for one evening return.

5. Look for opportunities to do what is not asked. It is hard to describe all that happens when a task is done voluntarily as a gesture of kindness. The work becomes lighter, the worker is changed, and the one for whom it is done is affected. Parents find immeasurable joy in those who honor them in this way.

6. Honor your parents when away from them. Those young people who are really serious about honoring their parents will find that their actions do not change when they are removed from their parents. Neither do their words. Neither does their appearance.

7. Involve your parents in any steps you take in acquiring a life companion. This is not saying we should return to the oriental custom of parents arranging totally for the marriages of their children. It is to say, however, that the notion that only "I" can ultimately tell who is best for me is a false notion in the other extreme. More specific guidelines for this will be given in Chapter 3.

The principle of honoring parents is a lifetime principle. Certainly roles change as a person moves from childhood to teenage to adulthood to old age. But all through life there are ways to show respect and honor to one's parents. As a person moves out of his parents' home, one of the foremost ways to show honor is to seek counsel. As one's parents move into old age and frailty, honor is shown by caring for them. Some of the difficulties associated with that care are discussed more fully in Chapter 8. Here we will simply note that the benefits which come from honoring parents in this way more than offset the difficulties. Furthermore, the practice of sending old folks off to care centers has left a vacancy in the family which convenience cannot replace. The separation and loneliness experienced by many aged parents is a tragedy they should not be required to endure.

### Learning to Forgive Parents

Because nobody's parents are perfect, everyone is able to see particular features of his heritage which have not been right. Wrongs in the past often show up as scars in the present. Some of these scars are slight, some are major, and some are still festering. The wrongs which caused these scars are many times real, but other times they are imagined. As one writer put it,

> Just as our parents are human and subject to error, so are we. As children we interpreted what our parents said and did. Well-intentioned behavior may have been cast in the worst possible light, thus making our parents' good efforts seem wrong. A critical remark made by a parent many years ago may be replayed and blown out of proportion and significance by a child who now blames his or her parents for personal problems.[1]

There are many reasons why we should forgive our parents. These reasons do not necessarily make forgiveness easy, but they do show the importance of forgiveness. Obviously, the most important reason we should forgive has to do with our personal relationship with the Lord. "For if ye forgive men their trespasses, your heavenly Father will also forgive you: But if ye forgive not men their trespasses, neither will your Father forgive your trespasses" (Matthew 6:14,15). There are other reasons as well, but here we will consider especially those which relate to the family.

Learning to forgive our parents for their failures is an important determiner as to whether we can honor them or not. Resentment and bitterness destroy our ability to honor. Forgiveness, on the other hand, gives us a freedom to honor our parents.

Forgiving our parents is necessary in order to keep us from perpetuating their errors. One of the strangest phenomena of heritage is that often those things in parents which are most detested are most commonly acquired by the next generation. Indeed, one of the surest ways to pick up your parents' faults is to resent them— the stronger you resent them, the more likely you are to pick them up. Somehow by focusing negatively on someone else's problem, we shape our own view of life. The alternative, of course, is to forgive. Forgiveness frees us from the bondage of reviewing past injuries, helps us to see our parents in a more objective light, and makes available to us the transforming grace of God.

We must forgive our parents for their wrongs and failures if our children are to have the security of a healthy relationship with their grandparents. Resentment and bitterness cut off relationships. Forgiveness, on the other hand, opens us to the possibility of building (or at times rebuilding) relationships. Grandparents need the laughter and play of their grandchildren. Grandchildren need exposure to the wisdom and dignity of old age. There are peculiar ties between grandparents and grandchildren which can be formed properly only when parents have right attitudes toward their past.

Knowing the reasons for forgiveness is not always enough to cause us to exercise forgiveness. Scar tissue can go very deep. The following pointers show more clearly just what forgiveness is and how it works.

*1. Forgiveness means release.* It means no longer holding others accountable for what they have done.

*2. Forgiveness is a choice.* We do not need to feel like forgiving in order to forgive. We must choose to forgive. Usually when forgiveness is most necessary, it is emotionally most difficult. The Scriptures do not say, however, we must feel like forgiving, but simply that we are to forgive. Choosing to forgive carries its own reward, and the act of forgiveness is often followed by emotional relief and joy.

*3. Forgiveness is costly.* It means absorbing the "debt" instead of retaining it on record. It cancels the account held against another. The cross of Jesus is the clearest example in all history of the cost of forgiveness.

*4. Forgiveness is usually purging.* Particularly with our parents, when we are willing to forgive, we usually find that they were not totally responsible for the problem. We come to see that our own negative responses to them may have contributed as much (sometimes more) to our injury as their initial wrong. "A big part of growing up is learning to accept responsibility for our own lives, which in this case means admitting that we may have created some of the problems with our parents."[2] This point about forgiveness is often one of the biggest obstacles in the whole process. Many hurting adults are hiding their own failures behind the failures of their parents. To forgive the past means to reckon with the present, and for some, that seems too painful.

*5. Forgiveness is an act of faith.* This is probably the most important concept of forgiveness presented here. The process of forgiveness involves a refocusing from the offender to God. Instead of looking any longer at what was done wrong in the past, we can look in faith to God who is able to work everything together "for good to them that love God" (Romans 8:28). There is an unspeakable difference in such an outlook! It is virtually impossible to forgive parents when we focus on their faults. It is virtually impossible not to forgive them when we focus properly on God. Many people live somewhere between extreme bitterness and complete forgiveness by simply trying to focus elsewhere (just forgetting about their parents), but they end up missing both the peace of forgiveness and the joy of honoring their parents.

Heritage is a powerful factor in all of our lives. Families in Western society, by disregarding God and the principles of honor and forgiveness, have generally turned heritage into a curse which is being visited on children, grandchildren, and great-grandchildren. Learning to live in accord with God's principles is the key to making heritage a blessing.

## CULTURAL PRESSURES

Throughout this chapter we have considered various cultural ideals and values which stand in contrast to Biblical ideals and values. This is not to present an attack on our society, but simply to see how forces in our society are directly opposed to principles which God has given for the family. We should now look at these forces more specifically.

### Authority Concepts

The society of the unconverted has always had the earmarks of rebellion. But we would be naive to say that attitudes toward authority in our society are the same today as a hundred years ago. The Roaring Twenties with its speakeasies and shorter skirts certainly flaunted authority, especially the laws of prohibition. But any historian speaks mildly of that era as compared to the rebellion of the '60s. No established order of conduct

.

18

escaped attack in the '60s. Art splattered, music pounded, hair flopped, and clothing dwindled until decency blushed. Even unconverted society gasped at the brazen looseness and coarseness of the hip counterculture.

But somehow after shock wears off, acceptance sets in. The older folks grew tired of gasping, and the younger folks grew tired of shouting. Society slowly swallowed much of the counterculture, and hippies eventually emerged as yuppies, accepting many of the very values they had challenged, albeit with less restraints.

Even "Christianity" attempted to swallow some of the concepts of the counterculture. "Christian" rock groups of that era began pounding out songs of love and freedom with connotations altogether different from historic Christian understanding. It never occurred to dulled Laodicean minds that the new "freedom" was only a mask for age-old rebellion.

In this whole process, society has come not only to accept but also to value the "let me do as I please" mentality. Words such as *authority, rules,* and *obedience* arouse negative connotations of harsh men and abused women and children. Equality, liberation, rights, and freedom of expression carry the day. It is ironic, however, that the society which scoffs at its rigid grandparents is actually producing more abusive family settings than ever before. This is not to say that the more authority shown, the better, but that the supposed freedom is many times nothing less than chaos. The family in Western society has suffered irreparable damage from the attacks on authority, the redefining of freedom, and the resultant looseness.

Parents who spank their disobedient children face the pressure of appearing brutish. Parents who set guidelines for their children's clothes, hair, and activities face

19

the pressure of appearing legalistic. Great-grandparents who shake their heads at all the coming and going and warn against newfangled entertainments and activities face condescending smiles and the assurance that their ideas were fine in a bygone age. The changing authority concepts are placing tremendous pressures on those who would order their homes according to the Word of God.

### Separation of Age Levels

Earlier in this chapter, we noted the importance of family interaction. Families, we said, should work together, play together, worship together, etc. One of the ways in which families face pressure to surrender this togetherness is in the streamlining of activities today. When the consolidated schools took over the one-room schools, separation into age levels became a practical necessity. Everyone in the room was in the same grade. Today the separation has spread. It must be recognized that efficiency has not been the only factor in making this separation attractive. Working mothers, emphasis on knowledge and the experts, and the overall rush of schedule push family members into classes, special centers, clubs, and activities where everyone can be "with kids their age."

Yesterday's mothers wiped tears the first day a child went to school at the age of six or seven. Today's mother breathes a sigh of relief to see her two-year-old trundled off to the Tot Center.

Certainly many Christian parents will view the last example as an extreme which doesn't fit them. And yet the separation into age levels has affected many Christian families by its emphasis in the church community. We seem to have lost sight of the principle that **there is health in the interaction of various age levels.** This is not to say that all separation into age levels is wrong and anti-family. But we must recognize the danger in too much of this organization according to age level. As an example, many Christian families today are feeling the pressure of highly organized youth activities, so much so that parents sometimes despair of having the family together at home even one evening a week.

Put a group of young men together repeatedly to play ball, and you will likely develop excellent playing—a "good game." Pull together several families and play a game of ball where Grandpa pitches, a ten-year-old plays third base, and Dad is at bat, and the quality of play will seem less than excellent. But in the long run, the latter is far more likely to have enduring good. Or take another example: Send a group of young people regularly to give a program at a nursing home, and you may well have enthusiastic singing and leave a good witness. But go as a family or as a group of families where Grandpa reads a Scripture, Dad leads some singing, and children pass out cookies, and you not only leave a good witness, but you demonstrate that everyone has a part in the church's outreach.

Again, this is not to say that youths (or any other age level) doing things together is all wrong, but to emphasize that there is health in the mingling of age levels. Separation may seem to specialize interests and make things go better, but in reality it may cut out valuable interaction.

### Knowledge Explosion

Many of the changes in root family concepts have come about through the rapid changes in our technological society. New inventions, and thus new ways of doing things, hit the market continually. The latest breakthrough is scarcely broken in until it becomes outdated with a new discovery.

21

Parents, particularly those who did not continue their education beyond high school, often find it difficult to comprehend what is going on. Their fifth-grade child comes home from school and asks for help with homework, and the parents end up saying, "I have no idea how to do that. We never had that in school." This all sounds incidental until we consider the magnitude of the situation. As day after day the concept of the "new and improved" is pressed upon society, people develop the view that old means outdated. The expert in every field is the one who is abreast with the latest discovery.

All this would not be so serious if it were confined to technology. But it is not. The effect is felt in the home and even in the church. The parent or minister who does not know the difference between a ruptured disc and a floppy disk, between mosquito bites and megabytes, is considered out of touch with reality and hardly to be trusted with giving advice to modern teens.

Thus modern knowledge has in many cases intimidated ancient wisdom. Parents are made to feel incompetent to guide their children and are encouraged to seek the advice of "experts" when in reality the children desperately need the wisdom of their parents.

### Materialism

Expanding technology has produced truckloads of goods for the family to buy. Toys, appliances, work machines, play machines, in every conceivable form call for the buyer's attention. These things, of course, take money. It surely goes without saying that the lives of most Westerners are consumed with making money and accumulating these things.

Christians know that Jesus said, "Take heed, and beware of covetousness [the desire for things]: for a man's life consisteth not in the abundance of the things which he possesseth" (Luke 12:15). But such advice is easily forgotten when day after day we are encouraged to buy, indulge, lay up, and acquire; when we are told that the good life is filled with entertainment and activity and fun and amusement, all of course at a modest fee; when sales are on and prices are right and money is on hand and credit is available. The pressure is tremendous!

This pressure pounds at the family, making Junior beg for a new bike, causing Sis to moan for a "real, talking doll," making Mom consider longingly the latest kitchen appliance, causing Dad to figure whether the family can afford another vehicle. Easily, how easily, the family gets sucked into valuing things above people, getting above giving, luxury above sacrifice. And soon, very soon, there is little to distinguish the values of the Christian family from the values of the non-Christian, neighbor family.

This is not to say that every modern convenience is a sin, nor that there is righteousness in poverty. But it is to say that riches are dangerous. And it is to warn us that materialistic values are robbing Christians of their vision for the kingdom of God, and robbing Christian families of the peace of contentment and the joy of sacrifice.

"Godliness with contentment is great gain. For we brought nothing into this world, and it is certain we can carry nothing out. And having food and raiment let us be therewith content. But they that will be rich fall into temptation and a snare, and into many foolish and hurtful lusts, which drown men in destruction and perdition. For the love of money is the root of all evil: which while some coveted after, they have erred from the faith, and pierced themselves through with many sorrows" (I Timothy 6:6-10).

The following pointers may be helpful for families who wish to counteract the pressures of materialism:

*1. Learn to live simply.* This is important no matter

what the income level. Simple toys, simple foods, simple vehicles, simple clothing, simple living quarters, with godliness, can still produce a contented family, even in a world of affluence.

*2. Practice cheerful giving.* A family does not need to be rich to give. Giving may be monetary, but does not need to be. A plate of cookies, fresh garden vegetables, verses or wise sayings neatly printed, notes of encouragement to friends, fresh flowers, an hour or two of help to a neighbor—these are all ways of giving. It is nice to give to friends, but Jesus said we should also give to those from whom we expect nothing in return (Luke 6:35).

*3. Live sacrificially.* This is closely associated with giving, but it is not necessarily the same. We can fairly easily give out of our abundance. Every Christian should experience the joy of consciously denying himself in the process of giving.

*4. Develop wise buying habits.* Avoid replacing that which is still serviceable just because you are tired of it, or for the sake of novelty or prestige, or to compete with others. Much money is squandered and unavailable for use in the kingdom of God because people are catering to their vanity and selfish desires.

*5. Avoid wasteful living.* Many toys and recreational vehicles consume resources unwisely. Sometimes the market for certain things seems purposely geared to the throw-away mentality. Disposable diapers, for example, are now so widely used that they pose a national disposal problem in the United States.

*6. Channel resources into kingdom-building activities.* Money, time, goods, and even skills should be viewed as the property of God. We have been commissioned to use these things in the interests of our heavenly Father. If we waste these things on pampering ourselves, surely we will need to answer as unfaithful stewards.

## Husband-Wife Roles

A later chapter will be devoted to describing the Biblical directions for husbands and wives. But a discussion of cultural pressures on the family would not be complete without recognizing the distortions which are taking place in this area of the family. The controversy seems to center around the mother's role. Every conceivable argument has been raised to show that mothering is a drab life of changing dirty diapers and washing dirty dishes and scrubbing dirty floors while the father gets to roam the green earth pursuing whatever suits his fancy. This is nothing but the reasoning of selfishness. The fulfilled life is not the life that can do as it pleases, but the life that serves. The father does not find fulfillment in pursuing selfish interests, but in serving his family. Neither will the mother find fulfillment in pursuing selfish interests. Mothering is one of the highest and noblest occupations a woman can have—it is a work that requires character, creativity, talent, intelligence, and commitment. The removal of Father as head and provider, and the emergence of Mother as a career woman has done irreparable damage to the family.

Under the pressures of society, many a Christian mother finds herself casting a curious or even a longing look at opportunities outside the home and letting her shoulders droop when asked by other women what her work is. Christian families should cherish the high calling of motherhood.

## The Diminishing Family

Changes in the average size of the Western family have been caused by various factors. Awareness that the world population is growing and the shift from rural living where more children mean more workers, to city living where more children mean more mouths to feed are two reasons commonly given for the diminishing family. But the factors basic to the hearts of Westerners seem more selfish than humanitarian.

They generally sustain a standard of living which is simply too expensive and a schedule of living which is simply too exhausting to include many children. The diminishing family better fits the materialistic values and the career mindedness of the men and women of today. Children are viewed as threats to personal interests and material prosperity.

While Christian families claim not to have the values of their non-Christian counterparts, the pressures are certainly there. To have one or two children is acceptable. To have three is borderline. Four raises the eyebrows. Five and over means you are careless and irresponsible, likely raising parasites of society. The family of ten or twelve is a phenomenon of the Dark Ages. So goes the reasoning.

The Bible says, "Lo, children are an heritage of the LORD: and the fruit of the womb is his reward. As arrows are in the hand of a mighty man; so are children of the youth. Happy is the man that hath his quiver full of them: they shall not be ashamed, but they shall speak with the enemies in the gate" (Psalm 127:3-5). God considers children a divine blessing to the home, and we must certainly acknowledge that the decrease in children today has not made for a happier, healthier family unit. Christian parents, who walk in step with God, will love children, will see them as a blessing, and will not succumb to the self-centered pressures of society.

## THINKING TOGETHER

1. Should a family's schedule be slow-paced? Busy? Hurried? What actually is a slow-paced schedule? What is

a hectic schedule?

2. What work or service projects could families do which would increase healthy social interaction?

3. Can children be overworked? Underworked? What are the results of either? What determines a proper balance of work and play?

4. When barriers exist between parents and children, what practical steps can be taken by the parents to resolve them? What steps can be taken by the children?

5. When persons from a former generation are not Christians (parents or grandparents), what guidelines can be followed to keep interaction wholesome?

6. Currently, what seem to be the most dangerous cultural pressures acting on the family? How can families withstand these pressures?

7. Which of the suggestions for avoiding materialism seems most important? Which is perhaps most neglected?

## WORKING TOGETHER

1. As a family, analyze the health of your interaction. Where is improvement necessary, and how might it be accomplished?

2. As a family member, consider honestly how well you are contributing to a healthy family unit. What is your personal problem area? Poor communication? Disrespect? Ingratitude? List ways in which your problem has been demonstrated recently. List some steps you could take to improve.

3. List specific ways you might practice the guidelines for avoiding materialism. Discuss them with your family and decide how you can carry through with them.

*Christian Family Living*

# 2

# LEAVING CHILDHOOD

## INTRODUCTION

In the process of growth and development, humans go through changes more amazing and complex than words can describe. Tiny babies become romping children. Romping children become gangling intermediates. Gangling intermediates become energetic youths. Energetic youths become responsible adults. Responsible adults grow older and eventually slower and eventually frail, and finally pass on. Human life in all its stages is never fixed. It is always in a state of change. Bodies change. Feelings change. Behavior changes.

This chapter is about one section of human growth and

development—the time between childhood and adulthood. It is an important period of life. Boys are in the process of becoming young men. Girls are in the process of becoming young women.

Many times the uncertainty of this stage in life is compounded by a lack of understanding or by misguided information. This chapter is intended to help young people understand themselves and the changes they are experiencing. It is not intended to replace the role of parents, but to assist parents. Hopefully, it will provide a base for discussing sensitive issues with sensitivity.

## WHO AM I?

Humans are the only products of God's creation on earth with self-awareness. We not only think, but we think about ourselves. We analyze and evaluate ourselves. We commend or criticize. Mentally, we converse with ourselves, sometimes even to the point of muttering aloud our private conversation.

This self-awareness undergoes growth and maturity. A one-year-old, for example, has very little self-awareness. We consider such innocence dear. A sixteen-year-old, on the other hand, may at times seem to be altogether absorbed in himself. Somewhere in the interim between one and sixteen, radical changes take place in one's self-awareness. Usually these changes in self-awareness are closely associated with the physical, emotional, mental, and spiritual changes that come with puberty.

To understand these changes, we should begin by noting certain characteristics of childhood which fade out or undergo change as one enters adolescence. The following Scriptures are basic to this discussion:

"And they brought young children to him, that he should touch them: and his disciples rebuked those that brought them. But when Jesus saw it, he was much displeased, and said unto them, Suffer the little children to come unto me, and forbid them not: for of such is the kingdom of God. . . . And he took them up in his arms, put his hands upon them, and blessed them" (Mark 10:13-16).

"And the Lord said, Whereunto then shall I liken the men of this generation? and to what are they like? They are like unto children sitting in the marketplace, and calling one to another, and saying, We have piped unto you, and ye have not danced; we have mourned to you, and ye have not wept" (Luke 7:31,32).

"Whosoever therefore shall humble himself as this little child, the same is greatest in the kingdom of heaven" (Matthew 18:4).

"Brethren, be not children in understanding: howbeit in malice be ye children, but in understanding be men" (I Corinthians 14:20).

From these verses and others we could note several characteristics of children:

*1. Children are dependent.* They look to others as responsible for their care and protection.

*2. Children accept spiritual realities readily in simple faith.* They love to hear about God, His ways, His works, and His laws. And they accept these things as true without question or resistance.

*3. Children have an innocence in their relationships.* They can be held and hugged without embarrassment.

*4. Children are uninhibited in expression.* They laugh, they cry, they say what they think or feel, with little reserve or evaluation.

*5. Children have a thoughtlessness about themselves.* While children are in many ways self-centered, they generally have a very low self-awareness. That is, they are not preoccupied with evaluating themselves nor with what others think of them. (Jesus referred to this as a humility to be admired.)

6. *Children are free from guile.* They do not generally harbor evil intent, carry grudges, or suspect evil. They live in a realm of sincerity.

7. *Children are less concerned about logic and the deeper elements of understanding.* They are curious and they ask questions, but with a view to learning, not with a view to evaluating.

While these are characteristics of childhood, they are unfortunately not characteristics of all children. Childhood can be marred. It can be disfigured. Those children who are exposed to evil at an early age can lose the freedom and simplicity of childhood. Unfortunately, we live in a society where evil is rampant and open-faced. Many children meet violence and murder regularly through television. They see sexual advances, unfaithfulness, and treachery. They watch heroes and heroines lie, drink, fight, and cheat their way through life.

The effects of all this evil on the childhood of children can hardly be estimated. Innocence is bloodied with sin. Sexual urges begin before the child is capable of understanding what is going on. As self-awareness is forced on children, the conscience is battered even before it is properly awakened.

One psychologist has coined the term "hurried children" to describe the pressures children face today to "grow up" early. The hurried children, he says, are "the youngsters in our society who are being exposed to gratuitous sex and violence through the media, dressed in scaled-down versions of 'designer' clothing, expected to excel in school even when it is impossible, and asked, as though they were adults, to cope with divorce and separation from their parents."[1]

This is not simply pressure to enter the adult world. It

is exposure to sin, and such exposure is destructive to the beauty of childhood. Jesus said, "Whoso shall offend one of these little ones which believe in me, it were better for him that a millstone were hanged about his neck, and that he were drowned in the depth of the sea" (Matthew 18:6). We live in a culture where adults wittingly and sometimes unwittingly are violating the childhood of children.

Even in the haven of a Christian home, the process of leaving childhood innocence and entering adolescent self-awareness can have its traumatic side. The body is changing, and the adolescent boy may ask himself, "What's wrong with me?" The inner feelings are changing, and he may ask, "Why do I feel this way?" He feels too big to be with children anymore, but too little to enter the adult world. The thoughts he has are new to him, and many times are such that he would never risk sharing them with anyone else. What is true for boys is generally true for girls, although girls seem more apt than do boys to talk to a trusted friend or parent about their deepest thoughts, feelings, and fears.

The first thoughts of self-awareness basically boil down to one question: Who am I? Personality is deepening. Beliefs and values are only beginning to take recognizable shape. Change is still in progress. The twelve-year-old boy is wondering why he is not growing faster, and how tall he will eventually be. The twelve-year-old girl is feeling the urge to appear attractive and grown-up. Both will soon be testing and discussing with greater intelligence the guidelines and ideas of their authorities. The changes are in some ways exciting, and in other ways they are scary. The identity of childhood is suddenly gone, but no adolescent is quite certain just what identity will be found in adulthood.

To further understand this challenging era of life, we

33

will consider some of the changes in greater detail.

## PHYSICAL CHANGES

Probably the most obvious changes in the process of leaving childhood are physical. Sometimes these changes can be the most traumatic too, especially since these changes have to do with male and female sexuality. In years past, a kind of muted secrecy was draped over this subject. To adolescents such secrecy regarding something so obvious simply created more fears and frustrations. The world's response was to lift the covers on the whole subject, so that today nearly anything can be discussed in any setting without blush. While this has made the young people of our world knowledgeable, it has not made them godly. The moral condition has never been worse.

The proper setting for discussing the physical changes and development of young people is not in the mixed classroom. It is in the home—father talking with sons, mother talking with daughters. The proper approach is not the light, jesting manner of joke-telling, nor is it the secretive, fear-producing manner of vague but ominous warnings. There is certainly a proper restraint and dignity in discussing male and female sexuality, but given the proper setting and timing, parents do best to discuss this subject with honest frankness and openness. As the authors of *The Sanctity of Sex* wrote,

> What then is God's method of dealing with sex? Now any casual reader of the Scripture will quickly become aware that God's way has ever been that of fearless revelation and discussion. No one who reads through the early chapters of the Bible can escape the conclusion that our heavenly Father has never been ashamed of His own handiwork, and has freely discussed the functions of sex.[2]

The writers go on to recognize, however, that such frankness must be coupled with the fear and love of God. Otherwise, knowledge becomes degrading, as our society so clearly demonstrates.

### Male Changes

What changes take place in the process of a boy becoming a man? First, during adolescence, boys often have growth spurts. A boy may grow six inches or more in one year. Sometimes there is an early growth spurt and a later one. Usually the adolescent boy develops a voracious appetite, eating as much as, or more than, a grown man.

Somewhere during this time, usually around the age of thirteen or fourteen, the male body begins to produce certain hormones. These cause other male characteristics to begin developing. The voice begins to deepen. Sometimes it becomes rather harsh or crackly. Many boys experience the frustration of sudden changes in voice pitch—out of the deeper sound (which they like) into an embarrassing falsetto. Because of this, boys may be embarrassed to talk much in group settings. Male hormones also cause hair to begin to grow on the chin and upper lip. Most boys are as pleased the first time they shave as they were the first time they were told they could mow the lawn. The novelty of shaving whiskers, however, like the novelty of mowing grass, eventually passes.

The changes which take place in a boy's body are God's way of bringing him to manhood. Many boys suffer needless fears because of ignorance or because they hear of such things through degraded stories or jokes. Every boy should have the privilege of talking honestly and openly with his father, or if the father is not available, with a Christian adult man, about his questions and struggles during this part of his life.

 **SNAPSHOT FROM LIFE**

*George was a sensitive young boy. His father was a devout Christian, but was reared in a setting where talking about physical developments created embarrassment. Wanting George to understand himself, but not knowing exactly how to go about it, George's father gave him a book which explained physical development in young boys.*

*Unfortunately, the book was written in a condescending, "Now my dear George" sort of tone, and the descriptions were cast in such vague and terrible language that George found it only added to his fears and misgivings. He dreaded to pick it up, and he dreaded to have his father ask him whether he had read it.*

*These fears would have been much alleviated had George's father discussed these things in a kind and open way with him. Nothing can replace good communication with parents during the adolescent years.*

### Female Changes

What changes take place in a girl becoming a young woman? Unlike the boy, the girl experiences very little change in her voice. Female hormones, however, do cause other changes in girls including growth spurts, often a year or two ahead of boys their age. While this sometimes makes the girl a bit self-conscious, it also gives her a deepening sense of becoming a woman, and most girls view it positively.

Some girls experience physical changes later than

others, and some to a lesser degree. Those who find these changes delayed or more slight need not worry that something is wrong with them. Fears or questions should be openly discussed with a girl's mother or a trusted Christian woman.

## EMOTIONAL AND BEHAVIORAL CHANGES

The physical changes which an adolescent experiences cause emotional changes as well. We noted earlier that children are generally quite free from awareness of themselves as male and female. But as physical changes take place, the young adolescent boy begins not only to be aware of himself as a boy, but to experience attraction toward girls in ways he has not before. Often boys attempt to cover this attraction behind bold declarations of no interest, or by becoming something of a pest to girls. Adolescent girls likewise find the changes in their bodies affecting their view of themselves and of boys. Their appearance becomes much more important to them. They hate to be seen with their clothes dirty or their hair unkempt.

Boys typically become interested in strength. They like to know who can run the fastest, jump the highest, and lift the most. While the adolescent boy sometimes does not talk as loudly or as much as he did only a few years before, his drive to be strong and manly is higher than ever.

Adolescent girls typically become more ladylike. They begin to dress more grown-up, sit more grown-up, and talk more grown-up. They no longer enter into activities of romp and tumble, and often prefer watching others do things rather than participating themselves, particularly if there is the possibility of looking foolish.

The transition from childhood into adulthood is

relatively rapid. The ten- or eleven-year-old who still plays and pretends suddenly becomes a fourteen- or fifteen-year-old who thinks and talks about the adult world. Whereas before, adults tended to communicate down to a lower level of ideas and values, suddenly they are being met at eye level. The suddenness of adolescent change can be difficult for both adolescents and adults. Adolescents hardly seem prepared for what they can suddenly do, and adults feel inadequately prepared to cope with what these young adults want to do. Without the wisdom of God, homes can easily become the scene of conflict between testy young adults and threatened older adults. The following sections provide helpful suggestions for both adolescents and parents of adolescents to make this transition from childhood to adulthood a healthy, wholesome time of life.

## SPIRITUAL CHANGES

Emotional and behavioral changes in adolescents are not caused solely by the physical changes. Spiritual changes are taking place which affect emotions and behavior too. As self-awareness grows, the conscience begins to come alive in new ways. Young children feel guilty for acts of wrong which they have done. But as adolescents, they become increasingly aware of themselves as persons, and they become aware that the sin problem has not to do merely with what they do, but with what they are. They begin to analyze not only actions, but motives. And they sense increasingly how impossible it really is to be what they have been told all their lives to be—good boys and good girls. This is not to say that they clearly realize these things. Spiritually, young adolescents do not understand themselves very well. But they begin to sense spiritual truths about themselves which they never before knew.

The emotional effects of these spiritual changes are often varied. Some young people become fearful, super-sensitive, and shy. Others are touchy, grouchy, irritable. And some, resisting this spiritual awakening without even understanding it, become argumentive and re-bellious.

It is generally during the time of adolescent change, with the awakening of conscience, that a person becomes ripe for commitment to Jesus Christ. Many evangelicals today teach and practice evangelism of children. This represents an unfortunate misunderstanding of the spiri-tual condition of children and adolescents. Note the following considerations on this subject:

*1. The Scriptures reflect childhood as a time of inno-cence and acceptance with God.* Jesus, for example, in speaking of children, said, "Of such is the kingdom of heaven" (Matthew 19:14). He warned adults against despising them and offending them, noting that "in heaven their angels do always behold the face of my Father which is in heaven" (Matthew 18:10).

*2. The Scriptures describe conversion as a time of repentance.* Nowhere did Jesus or the apostles call chil-dren to repentance. Repentance requires a self-awareness which has not yet developed in innocent children.

Samuel Yoder, minister and Bible teacher, has noted at least three stages in awareness which must take place before true conversion is possible:

a. God consciousness. Children certainly can be aware of God, and indeed childhood is the time to establish certain God-concepts which become foundational to salvation. "And that from a child thou hast known the holy scriptures, which are able to make thee wise unto salvation through faith which is in Christ Jesus"

(II Timothy 3:15).

b. Sin consciousness. As we noted earlier, a child's awareness of sin has to do with personal wrongdoing. Children should be encouraged to confess these wrongs as they are troubled by them. God will forgive, and children certainly can have peace. Until the awakening of conscience which comes with greater self-awareness, children will not have the awareness of personal sinfulness. To pressure children to accept Jesus as their Saviour without this sin consciousness is sure to confuse the issue of salvation both as a doctrine and as a personal experience. People will have trouble knowing what salvation is and when they actually were saved.

c. Choice consciousness. Everyone must come to the awareness of the personal responsibility for repentance and faith in Christ. A child will readily respond to teaching about God and salvation if he is told to, because his decisions as a child are based on adult guidance. True conversion, however, can come only when we are capable of personally asking the question, "What must I do to be saved?"[3]

3. *The Scriptures describe baptism as for believers.* The points above demonstrate that the faith required for salvation demands knowledge which is above the awareness of children. Children can certainly believe in God. They can believe spiritual truth. But how can they believe in Jesus as their Saviour before they are conscious of their sinful nature? The Anabaptists refuted the infant baptism practiced by Roman Catholicism and insisted on believer's baptism as practiced by the early church. The Ethiopian eunuch, for example (Acts 8:26-38), demonstrates the prerequisites for baptism—understanding (v. 30), faith (v. 37), and confession (v. 37). To baptize children who have not the capability of

meeting such prerequisites is but to practice a delayed form of infant baptism.

What children cannot understand and experience by way of spiritual conversion becomes a very real possibility for the adolescent. Self-awareness leads inevitably to sin-awareness. And the wise parent seeks to lead his troubled adolescent on then to a Saviour-awareness. Some of the most meaningful experiences in the Christian home are those where parents can lead their repentant children to a meaningful commitment to Jesus Christ.

Responding to the spiritual needs of children and adolescents requires wisdom and sensitivity. Understanding is important. We must understand the spiritual differences between children and adolescents. We must also take into consideration the particular personality and development of each individual child. Children vary. Adolescents are not always very predictable, and the best of parents feel the need of God's wisdom. The following pointers are based on the concepts presented in this section:

1. Teach children they are the objects of God's love.

2. Meet children at their level of understanding. When they come as young children, for example, and want to become Christians, ask them to tell you what they mean. Often, they are troubled with something they have done wrong. If you guide them to ask God for forgiveness, they readily find peace.

3. Show children from the Bible how God loves and accepts them. Show them also how He calls people to repentance. This is what He will do in their lives when they are ready. Explain that there will come a time in their lives when God will speak to them about receiving Jesus into their hearts. Assure them that they will know God's voice when He speaks, and encourage them to tell

God that they want to obey Him.

4. Pray with children about needs they have and about needs you have as a family. Pray in faith and pray in submission, giving God liberty to provide answers in His wisdom and time.

5. Lead children in giving thanks and praise to God for who He is and what He does. Children love to sing. They enjoy times of thanksgiving, remembering how God has answered prayer in the past.

6. As children approach adolescence, distinguish between true conviction of sin and emotional responses to God. A child may, for example, feel the emotional pull of an altar call in a church meeting and want to respond. Ask the child if there are things which the preacher said which spoke to him. If the child has not been moved by truth, his response is not a conviction of sin. Explain to the child that coming to Jesus includes both how we feel and what we know. When God talks to him (or her), he will not only feel it during an invitation, but will hear God speaking to him other times too. Pray with a child at such times and encourage him to tell God how he feels. Some children are more free to talk about their feelings than others. This is perfectly normal. Do not force doors of communication open from the outside. But beware of neglecting the quiet child by focusing all your attention and concern on the talkative one.

7. Watch for signs of conviction. This could be shown as moodiness, irritation, or resistance to authority.

8. Watch for the development of self-awareness. This inevitably comes with maturing sexuality. As noted earlier, sin-awareness usually follows self-awareness. How all of this is tied together may be difficult for us to fully realize. Note, however, that in the Garden of Eden, Adam and Eve came to an awareness of sin and an awareness of their nakedness at the same time.

**SNAPSHOT FROM LIFE**

*When Ted was nine years old, an evangelist held meetings in his church. Ted, along with others of his age, responded to the emotional appeals given each evening to receive Jesus. Having been raised in a Christian home, Ted asked his parents that evening if he could be baptized.*

*"Well," his parents counselled, "you are only nine years old. Baptism makes you a member of the church. Why don't you wait several years until you are a bit older?"*

*Ted waited, but wondered why a believer couldn't be baptized for several years. In the years which followed, he made several recommitments, and at age 14 he was baptized and became a member of the church along with several others his age.*

*When he was 15 and 16, Ted became quite rebellious, doing things secretly which his parents would not have approved of. In his late teens, he began seeking the Lord again and eventually became a committed Christian.*

*In reflection, Ted often pondered, "Just when did I become a Christian? Was it when I first responded? When I was baptized? When I finally gave my all to following Jesus?"*

*Some of Ted's confusion (and that of many others like him) is the result of not clearly understanding the spiritual condition of childhood and not keeping the requirements for salvation clear. Well-meaning adults only create confusion when they place emotional pressure on children to be saved.*

9. Never pressure or bribe an adolescent toward salvation. Conversion must be a response to God and truth. Conviction is a work of God's Holy Spirit, and parents must trust Him to do His part. Outside pressure will only limit His effectiveness.

10. When leading an adolescent to Christ, emphasize basics:

●Repentance: One must recognize his sinfulness, and must be willing to renounce his past life (Acts 2:38).

●Confession: One must with the mouth declare and with the heart accept Jesus as his Lord and Master who will save from all sin (Romans 10:9-13).

●Baptism: One must be willing to testify publicly to union with Christ and His people by baptism with water (Matthew 28:19,20; I Corinthians 12:13; I Peter 3:21).

## LAYING A GOOD FOUNDATION

Changes in adolescents are many and they are sweeping. We have described some of these changes. Physically, boys change into men, girls change into women. Spiritually, innocent children become accountable adults. Emotionally and behaviorally, there is a maturing, a coming of age. It is an exciting and sometimes traumatic time in life.

Making this part of life wholesome requires the joint effort of parents and their children. It does not begin at adolescence. Long before adolescence, parents and children are laying the foundation for how they relate to each other during these strategic years of change and development. In this section, we want to consider what adolescents and parents need for a wholesome relationship and then discuss some foundational guidelines for meeting those needs.

*1. Adolescents and parents need a healthy respect for one another as persons.* God calls children to honor their parents. But parents must also learn to respect the personhood of their children. Each child has a unique set of feelings and qualities which makes him an individual. Parents must know their children as persons, so that each child has the security which comes from being understood and cherished.

Knowing children requires spending time with them. Probably, fathers face the biggest challenge here because many fathers spend work time away from home. Doing things with children must be a priority. Probably the easiest way for parents, especially fathers, to create barriers with adolescents is to be out of touch with them as children. Every person has good and bad points. Every person has special areas of interest. Every person has emotionally "touchy" areas which need to be handled with sensitivity. Every person needs privacy. These are all part of personhood which parents need to understand about their children, especially as they move into adolescence.

Parents who respect each child's personhood will avoid negative comparisons with other children. In correcting a child, they will deal with misdemeanor, not attack personhood. They will lead, not simply dictate.

Parents who respect the personhood of their children are laying a good foundation for relating to them as adolescents. When children become adolescents, they begin to see their parents as persons. They begin to observe traits and evaluate character. Their ability to respect the personhood of their parents is much dependent on the respect their parents have shown them. If their personalities have been walked over roughshod, they will tend to walk roughshod over their parents as soon as they are able. If, on the other hand, sensitivity

45

has been shown to them, they will have a base for being sensitive to their parents.

*2. Adolescents and parents need open lines of communication.* The importance of communication has already been underscored in discussing the physical and spiritual changes during adolescence. But the foundation for this openness is laid in the years of childhood. Again, busyness often keeps parents, especially fathers, from talking to their children. Where parents find this occurring, they need to learn to plan for communication. Fathers should tell stories to their children (telling is often preferred above reading). Children love to hear about when you were a boy. Fathers should describe to their children how things work, how things are made, and how to make them. Parents should ask for and listen to the ideas of children.

Attention is necessary for communication. And full attention, someone has suggested, is possible only with full eye contact. How easily fathers bury their heads in newspapers so that the only communication with anyone else is the occasional, disinterested grunt. How easily mothers shoo children out of the house or downstairs when they talk too much or ask too many questions. Wise parents certainly will not allow children to dominate conversation, but they will recognize the importance of investing in the communication opportunities of childhood. Parents who turn a deaf ear to children will later find their adolescents turning a deaf ear to them.

*3. Adolescents and parents need a clear understanding of boundaries and expectations.* The subject of child training and discipline will be discussed more fully in Chapter 6. Here we simply note that many of the frustrations between adolescents and parents come from instability in parents as much as from upheavals in adolescents. In spite of what children and adolescents seem to be saying by whining, begging, and arguing, they find security in knowing clearly what they can and cannot do, and in having parents stand firmly by their word.

Parents who give in to the begging of children in order to please them have a very shallow understanding of approval. Likely they are insecure themselves. Not only does their inconsistency make them ineffective the next time they happen to oppose their children's desires, but it undermines the respect they will need in the years ahead. Children who beg turn easily into adolescents who manipulate.

Wise parents will teach their children they mean what they say. They will avoid scare tactics, threatening, shouting, and such shallow blustering. They will not be harsh one minute and smoochy the next. Parents will not work behind each other's backs in dealing with their children. Rather, they will unitedly aim for clarity and consistency, so that when their children come into adolescence, they can set reasonable guidelines and hold to them with kindness and understanding, but with firmness.

*4. Adolescents and parents need proper and wholesome touch practices.* We live in a society where the statistics of sexual relationships within the family are alarming and disgusting. In spite of this, we must say that all children need properly expressed affection from their parents. Only one thing can pervert the hugging and kissing of a child by his parent, and that is a perverted parent. Perhaps a simple guide to characterize proper touch is as follows: cuddle your babies, hug your children, put your arm around the shoulders of your adolescents. This is, of course, not to say that a parent should never hug his teenage son or daughter. But it is to recognize that changes in characteristic touch are necessary as children grow older.

Wholesome moral standards in the family certainly depend upon more than touch practices. Modesty should be taught and practiced in the family with parents setting the example and leading their children to a sense of modesty at home long before they reach adolescence. Guidelines for bathing and dressing should be established with a view to preserving the innocence of children. Those parents who demonstrate a sanctified affection for their children and teach a wholesome sense of modesty are laying a good foundation for the purity of their adolescents. This point leads us directly into the next section.

## LIVING A PURE LIFE

The subject of moral purity is especially relevant in discussing adolescence not only because this is the age of self-awareness, but because natural biological urges are often at their highest by late adolescence. Unfortunately, not all homes lay a good foundation for meeting the temptations adolescents face. Some parents make a lot of mistakes during the formative years of their children. On the other hand, some youths want to live for God in spite of poor home settings. Other youths with good home settings get drawn into moral problems ignorantly. The approach in this section, therefore, will not only be preventive, but redemptive. In other words, not only are we concerned about keeping adolescents out of moral traps, but freeing those who have been caught.

Before we begin to provide guidance in this area, we should note an important principle for those struggling with impurity in any form. Why you are where you are is not as important as your willingness to move on to where God wants you to be. Much damage can be done by over-focusing on situations or people who "cause" our problems. Instead of accepting God's grace for victory and moving on, people can easily slip into bitterness and self-pity and stay right in their troubles.

### Purity—What Parents Can Do

*1. Lead children personally to a proper understanding of their sexual development.* While the material in this chapter and a companion workbook, *God's Will for My Body,*[4] are designed to assist you in this, books can never replace you. Parents commonly ask, "How early should I talk to my children?" One minister noted that in working with youths, he has yet to hear the complaint that parents talked to their children too early about sexual development. That surely is NOT to say the earlier the better, but to note that the tendency of most parents is to wait too long. A safe guide for the first six or eight years of a child's life is to consider the kind of questions he asks. The behavior of family pets or livestock can be the basis for discussing general information about fertilization, gestation, and birthing. Children approaching ten years old are normally ready to hear about the physical changes they will face in the next few years.

*2. Screen input into the home.* Public entertainment media in the West seems incorrigibly corrupt. Children who grow up with television, radio, or videos as entertainment will invariably experience moral damage. Other potentially damaging input includes books, magazines, and music. Christian parents must recognize that entertainment produced by the world gravitates toward the sensuous. Even media for information and education sometimes caters to the immoral mind. The danger, however, is not simply from sources we call secular. Too many Christian young people are led into moral snares by music, magazines, videos, movies, etc., which profess to be Christian, but which contain the same sensual

49

appeal as the world's media.

The full answer, of course, is not simply in screening out the bad, but in providing that which is wholesome. Good books and magazines can build moral character and should be part of Christian homes. Good music is wholesome. Parents should consider the age and interests of their children and provide media which is morally upbuilding.

*3. Practice a healthy balance of trust and accountability with adolescents.* Young people need to be trusted, and at the same time they need to know that they are accountable. Parents can show trust by respecting privacy, by assigning responsibility, and in certain situations by giving advice but leaving decisions to their young people. Parents can require accountability by setting limits, providing options, asking questions, and giving advice. Communication is a key factor in the trust/accountability balance. Parents should beware of trying to force open doors of communication and of tactics which require secrecy or snooping. Generally young people respect elders who are direct and clear with questions and requirements, but they have trouble respecting elders who hint at things or fish for information.

*4. If you know or strongly suspect your adolescent has moral problems and you find communication difficult, arrange for him/her to talk about it with someone you mutually respect.* Ministers and their wives, grandparents, or Christian teachers can provide valuable counsel to troubled adolescents. Obviously, this should be with someone of the same sex, and preferably it should be voluntary. There may be times, however, when counseling should be required, particularly where severe or long-standing moral problems exist.

*5. Avoid teasing adolescents about interests in boys or girls.* Unfortunately, many adolescents struggle with misconceptions about sex and moral issues because their parents are yet immature in their understanding. Humor is a vital part of our lives and can be a nice way of breaking the ice on touchy subjects, but beware. Teasing, a form of humor, promotes infatuation, not love. It actually encourages misconceptions, pushing adolescents forward on the slippery path of romantic feelings. Teasing has the potential of starting adolescent relationships on an exhilarating toboggan slide that eventually crashes in heartache and ruin.

6. *Practice clean speech.* What we say reveals what we think and reinforces what we are. If you want to be clean and pure and want your young people to be clean and pure, think clean thoughts and use clean language. "But fornication, and all uncleanness, or covetousness, let it not be once named among you, as becometh saints; neither filthiness, nor foolish talking, nor jesting [witty in a vulgar sense]" (Ephesians 5:3,4).

### Purity—What Adolescents Can Do

1. *Honor your parents.* You may not understand this, but there seems to be a direct tie between rebellion and immorality. Those who resist their parents simply cannot seem to resist temptation. A Biblical example of this would be Eli's sons (see I Samuel 2:11-25).

2. *Fill your mind with good things.* We cannot keep out every wrong thought, but we can accustom our minds to right thinking. Read good books. Develop a practice of reading from the Bible each day. Especially if you have become ensnared in immoral thoughts or habits, use the Bible to cleanse your mind. "Wherewithal shall a young man cleanse his way? by taking heed thereto according to thy word" (Psalm 119:9). Memorize verses which you find especially helpful, or paraphrase them, writing them out in your own words with your name.

*3. Avoid sources of temptation.* The Bible often encourages us to stand against temptation. But we are told to "flee" immoral situations. "Flee fornication" (I Corinthians 6:18). "Flee also youthful lusts" (II Timothy 2:22). "And [Joseph] left his garment in her hand, and fled, and got him out" (Genesis 39:12). If a place or a person or a situation presents you with temptation, GET AWAY from that place or person or situation.

*4. Never follow your curiosity into what you know is immoral.* One of the biggest traps of Satan in this area is immoral literature. Like Job, we need to make a "covenant with [our] eyes" (Job 31:1) to avoid looking at what would tempt us. Another trap of Satan in this area is curiosity about our own body. God made us, and our bodies are not evil. But we must treat private areas of our body with respect. Curiosity leads easily to self abuse. Sometimes we are tempted to think, "If I try something, maybe I won't have so much trouble thinking about it." That is false. Involvement in immoral thoughts, pictures, movies, or actions always leads us away from purity, never toward it. Impure thoughts and actions easily become habits which are hard to break. When you are tempted to follow your curiosity about immorality, follow Proverbs 4:15 instead. "Avoid it, pass not by it, turn from it, and pass away."

*5. Have good friends.* Friends are important to young people. Popularity is important to young people. But having good friends is more important than having popular friends, and being pure is more important than being popular. The Bible warns, "Be not deceived: evil communications corrupt good manners" (I Corinthians 15:33). The simple meaning of that verse is that bad company will corrupt our morals.

*6. Work hard.* This may sound like an unrelated suggestion. But hard work is morally beneficial in a number

52

of ways. First, just needing to concentrate is good for our minds. Second, work can help to relieve sexual urges—the body channels its energies into the work at hand. Third, hard work is good discipline and thus strengthens character.

7. *Keep clean and neat in your appearance, but avoid decoration and immodesty.* What we see affects us. But how we appear to others affects both them and us. The Bible teaches modesty simply because immodesty invites sin. Both God and good people admire Christian character. Let a good Christian character be your goal.

8. *If you have become ensnared in thoughts or habits which you cannot seem to overcome, confide in a mature Christian.* Talk to your parents or minister about your problem. Make yourself accountable to them. For example, ask them to ask you periodically how you are doing. Be honest. Pray together. They can help you to find in Christ the strength to live victoriously.

## SUMMARY

Adolescence is a time of change. Young people often struggle with understanding themselves as they come to self-awareness, changing feelings, and spiritual conviction. Adolescents need a solid relationship with their parents during these years of their lives. The foundation for this relationship is laid already in childhood as parents interact with their children and provide for their needs. During adolescence, young people face the challenge of building moral character, a challenge which requires the cooperation of both parents and young people.

## THINKING TOGETHER

1. In view of the characteristics of children presented in this chapter, what kind of stories and activities are wholesome for children, and what kind may be damaging to their childhood?
2. What makes for good communication between parents and adolescents, and what tends to create barriers?
3. How can parents protect their innocent children from premature or needless feelings of guilt?
4. How should parents respond to a child who is troubled about having done wrong? How should parents respond to a child who demonstrates basic innocence but wants to "become a Christian"? How might parents discourage children by wrong responses to the above situations?
5. Why is it important for parents to trust the Holy Spirit to draw their children to Christ according to His timing? How can parents maintain a balance between indifference and anxiety regarding their children's spiritual welfare?
6. What are particular ways in which children may receive misguided information about sex, and what can parents do to protect and guide their children? How is temptation presented to adolescents today, and what must they do to avoid it?
7. How is a typical ten-year-old different from a typical six-year-old? How is a typical fourteen-year-old different from a typical ten-year-old?
8. What fears commonly arise during adolescent changes? How do adolescents often cope with these fears?

## WORKING TOGETHER

1. As parents, evaluate the modesty standards in your home. Are there areas needing improvement? What steps do you need to take? (Note: Consider also that too much ado about this for young children can actually be counterproductive.)
2. As a family member, consider how your spiritual commitment came about. When were you saved? Who influenced you? As you evaluate it now, did you respond early or late? What helped you and what hindered you in making right decisions? Did you have spiritual struggles as an adolescent which you would want your child to avoid? Write down your thoughts or discuss them as a family.
3. Considering your childhood, what are your fondest memories? List some. Someone was responsible for these good things. Express gratitude where you can. What are your worst memories? Do they continue to bother you? If so, maybe you should list them also. Take the list in prayer and read it aloud to God. Tell Him you are forgiving those involved because you trust Him to use these experiences for your good (see Romans 8:28). Burn this list as a visible sign that you will no longer hold others accountable for your problems. If you continue to struggle, discuss your problem with your minister.

# 3

# DATING AND ENGAGEMENT

## INTRODUCTION

A number of years ago a minister was teaching a series of evening classes on relationships in a congregational setting. One evening the subject was dating. The minister began by raising the question, "Is dating a good way to get a life companion?" After a few moments of studied silence, a well-respected elderly member who had been married twice said quietly, but with a twinkle in his eye, "Well, it certainly has been enjoyable."

This man's off-the-cuff humor reflects what too few of us have been willing to acknowledge—we've been enamored enough with the pleasantness of dating that we have not seriously considered putting it to any other test.

Perhaps it would be well to begin this chapter with the same question. Is dating a good method for choosing a companion? There are, after all, other methods. We never read of dating or courtship in the Bible. Oriental custom was for parents to arrange the marriage. The Law added the special feature of a year-long honeymoon, where the husband had no assigned work except to get acquainted with his new wife.

Merely raising the question about dating in this chapter does not mean we will attempt to abolish the practice. The Bible does not prescribe practice in this matter. It does, however, provide principles. And we need to consider the question because surely if we follow Biblical principles in the matter of dating, OUR DATING PRACTICES WILL DIFFER MARKEDLY FROM THE ACCEPTED DATING PRACTICES OF OUR CULTURE. And we might even say further that faithfulness to the Biblical principles may cause us to differ even from dating practices which have been accepted by much of the church.

Some who read this chapter may disagree with some of the practical guidelines and suggestions. Thousands of successful marriages, some may argue, have occurred without doing all that is suggested. Fine. These suggestions are offered, however, as possible ways of honoring timeless principles. Witness a thousand Christian homes today and see how many, disregarding God's principles, are in trouble! As the pressures toward selfishness and sin increase, the more important it becomes to build marriages squarely upon the foundation of God's Word and His timeless principles.

## WHY ARE WE DATING?

The question of motives for dating at first may seem obvious and unimportant. But our concept of dating seems to have suffered considerably from not weighing motivation honestly, Scripturally, and rationally. Let's begin with noting what the Bible says.

"And the LORD God said, It is not good that the man should be alone; I will make him an help meet for him. . . . Therefore shall a man leave his father and his mother, and shall cleave unto his wife: and they shall be one flesh" (Genesis 2:18, 24).

"Whoso findeth a wife findeth a good thing, and obtaineth favour of the LORD. . . . A prudent wife is from the LORD" (Proverbs 18:22; 19:14).

"There be eunuchs, which have made themselves eunuchs for the kingdom of heaven's sake" (Matthew 19:12).

"He that is unmarried careth for the things that belong to the Lord, how he may please the Lord" (I Corinthians 7:32).

"For this is the will of God, even your sanctification, that ye should abstain from fornication: That every one of you should know how to possess his vessel [acquire a wife] in sanctification and honour; not in the lust of concupiscence, even as the Gentiles which know not God" (I Thessalonians 4:3-5). (It must be recognized that there is controversy about the exegetical meaning of "possess his vessel." But even if it does not strictly mean "acquire a wife," as some translations suggest it does, we may paraphrase it so for our present subject, and find it is a true statement.)

On the basis of these Scriptures, we will briefly discuss three propositions about motivation for dating.

*Proposition 1: Pleasing God must always be our highest*

59

*motivation.*

It is only stating the obvious when we note that many dating young people allow lesser things than God's will to motivate their relationship. Some want companionship above all else. Some are after security. Some are merely following biological urges.

The Christian young man and woman will need to surrender their dating plans to the will of God. This does not primarily mean asking the simple (but important) question, "Is it God's will that I date Sue?" Rather, it means honestly considering dating and marriage in light of God's will for one's life. Can anyone make practical and specific decisions about dating until he has sought God's direction for life? Unfortunately, many dating young people have never seriously asked the following questions: What work do I sense God leading me to? How will my life best contribute to the kingdom of God? Is there preparation which I need in view of God's leading for my life? The answer to these questions will affect not only WHOM I should date, but WHEN I should date, and in some cases even WHETHER I should date at all.

As long as God's will is not given this kind of priority, marriage (and life itself) is certain not to deliver fulfillment according to our expectations. This point can hardly be overstressed. It speaks to many of the hollow marriages of our day, even within the church.

*Proposition 2: Marriage is the only proper motivation for dating.*

On the surface this may seem obvious and incidental. But it is likely the most overlooked point made here, and perhaps the most controversial as well. Where dating becomes merely a casual event, a pleasant way to spend an evening, a fun thing to do on a weekend away from home, or where dating becomes a way of helping someone out of spiritual, emotional, or social trouble, those involved have serious misconceptions about dating. This is NOT to say that from the first date, a couple must be convinced that they are for each other. It IS to express warning, however, against dating for motivations less than marriage.

Following is a list of four common ways in which this point is ignored:

a. Dating many partners. For a young man or a young woman to date numerous partners for present fun, expressly not wanting to "get serious" with anyone yet, erodes the foundation for his or her faithfulness in the future.

b. Dating one person repeatedly, simply "as friends." To date with this "no strings attached" mentality is but to ignore reality. Ties are being formed which, if broken, will inevitably bring hurt.

c. Dating to help someone with problems. Major violations of integrity occur when the appeal of companionship is mingled with the working of the Holy Spirit. Commitments made to God under the pull of infatuation are never genuine. What appears to be God-ward progress is so confused with girl-ward or boy-ward progress that spiritual growth is virtually impossible to determine. The only safe standard is never to date with the goal of helping someone out of his spiritual problems.

A related violation in a non-dating relationship can occur when friends of the opposite sex "counsel" one another about personal, spiritual, or social problems. As a result of the caring, the concern, and the time spent together, either the counselor or the counselee or both form emotional attachments for each other, often without intention or awareness. In the wake of such "help" are many hurting people.

All of this should warn us that there are proper and improper ways to help someone with personal and spiritual problems. Dating should not be pursued for that purpose.

d. Dating too early. This will be controversial, but people should not begin dating until they are ready for marriage. To begin dating years before one would want to be married inevitably puts unwholesome pressures on the dating couple. The common inability to wait in dating is responsible for much of the common inability to endure in marriage. Both reflect immaturity and self-centeredness. The years before marriage are years that are necessary for emotional, personal, and spiritual maturity. Dating during this teenage maturing time can actually sidetrack one from proper development. Where young men and women wait to begin dating until they are basically ready for marriage, they have the freedom to steer their courtship wisely toward marriage. (It is to be recognized that "ready for marriage" will mean different things to different people. What we mean by it will be clarified in the following pages. The point of concern remains: too much dating is being done too early.)

The second proposition, again, is that dating is for marriage. With that in view, date only someone whom you, through careful, prayerful discernment, would consider eligible for marriage. Date only when you are ready to allow the discernment process of courtship to move in wisdom toward marriage without either rush or undue delay.

*Proposition 3: The urge for companionship is an inborn motivation which must either be answered by God-directed marriage, or redirected to a higher motivation.*

God made us male and female. A man desires a wife; a woman desires a husband. As we noted in proposition 1, however, too much emphasis on this desire can actually undermine the enjoyment of marriage. Where marriage is not one's experience, either by choice or by circumstance, a godly man and a godly woman will need to channel the very normal urges for companionship into other pursuits.

We mention this under motivation for dating because failure to understand this can lead to extreme frustration for those who are not dating but wish to be. We are motivated by our very makeup to seek companionship. That drive is honorable and not to be despised, but it can be and sometimes must be superceded by higher motivations to keep it pure and wholesome. Many years of a person's life can be robbed of joy and fulfillment by yearning for what might be and ignoring what can be.

 **SNAPSHOT FROM LIFE**

*Some years ago a minister was sitting in a commuter plane waiting for takeoff. He had chanced to sit beside a talkative boy whom he guessed to be about ten to twelve years old. The lad had spent the summer in a town in Virginia and was returning to his home in Boston. In the course of visiting, he mentioned that he was leaving a girlfriend behind in Virginia. While the minister searched for an appropriate response, the boy cheerily remarked that it really wasn't so bad because he had another girlfriend in Boston that he was looking forward to seeing again when he returned.*

This point will be discussed in more detail in the chapter on singlehood, but unresolved companionship drives can actually have the effect of making one less and less eligible for marriage as the years go by.

## ARE WE READY?

We may smile or frown at the immaturity of ten- or twelve-year-olds. But of far greater significance is the eighteen- or twenty-year-old whose mentality is still on the ten-year-old level. This is not said in disrespect to older youths. It is simply to recognize that age itself is not sufficient preparation for dating. Just because a person is "old enough" does not mean he is ready.

To be practical, we will consider six prerequisites for dating and briefly discuss each of them: 1) A growing relationship with Christ, 2) Moral purity, 3) Submission to authority, 4) A Biblical concept of love, 5) Biblical values, and 6) A sense of responsibility. Young people who are contemplating dating should consider this list. Parents who are guiding their young people should consider this list. Obviously, these things are not as measurable as one's age or height or weight. They require discernment. But those interested in godly courtship will wish to consider them seriously.

*1. A growing relationship with Christ.* The young person who has not yielded his life to Jesus Christ has not dealt with the most basic issue in life and thus has not the base for dealing with the weighty issue of companionship. The same is true of a person who is spiritually backslidden. Courtship is a process of decisions; the decisions made during courtship demand wisdom. And to put the matter bluntly, those who are yet resisting God are fools on the most basic level of understanding. "The fear of the LORD is the beginning of knowledge: but fools despise wisdom and instruction. The fear of the LORD is the beginning of wisdom: and the knowledge of the holy is understanding" (Proverbs 1:7; 9:10).

In this light, it also seems wisest not to date immediately following spiritual birth or renewal. Those who have freshly yielded themselves to God normally need time to deepen their spiritual understanding and commitment before they are able to consider adequately all that is involved in dating. An ill-timed dating relationship has the potential of sidetracking young Christians, keeping them from spiritual development which they need specifically for such things as dating.

*2. Moral purity.* "Who can find a virtuous woman? for her price is far above rubies. The heart of her husband doth safely trust in her" (Proverbs 31:10,11). One of the deepest joys of marriage is the knowledge that the mutual intimacy (not only physical, but in thought and emotion as well) is exclusive. That is, it is unmixed with any other human loyalty—the love is pure. This purity in marriage is much dependent on purity ahead of marriage. The young person who feeds his mind on immoral imaginations, impure stories or pictures, or who enjoys immoral practices is not prepared for the fidelity required in dating and marriage.

Certainly, all young people are tempted with immorality. In our culture, it hits us at every turn. Thankfully there are those who resist temptation, but unfortunately, on the other hand, there are those who willingly follow their lusts, at least as far as they dare. The point here is that those who are following their lusts are not ready for dating.

What about those young people who have been ensnared early, not only in their imaginations, but in actual practices or relationships? Are they eligible for dating and marriage? We are not considering here all the guidelines for handling such situations. In passing, we should note, however, that the role of parents is extremely important in working through these problems. What we are recognizing is that previous immorality does affect one's preparedness for dating. The record of immorality itself, however, does not exclude one from dating, provided the individual has experienced honest repentance and purging. This purging surely includes experiencing forgiveness, but also needs to include the renewing of a right spirit and a clean heart. The experience of Psalm 51 is a must for those who seek moral purity following immorality. "Wash me thoroughly from mine iniquity, and cleanse me from my sin. . . . Create in me a clean heart, O God; and renew a right spirit within me. . . . a broken and a contrite heart, O God, thou wilt not despise" (Psalm 51:2,10,17b). Forgiveness can be immediate, but purging of heart and character can come only through continued fellowship with God, continued meditation in His Word, and a continuation of wholesome input.

The question often rises about whether or when past immorality should be discussed by a dating couple. The very practice of dating here presents something of a dilemma, because the first dates are usually characterized by a more casual get acquaintedness, so that to discuss something so personal as past immorality would be wholly inappropriate, but to introduce something so serious after the relationship has developed for some time can likewise be devastating, to say the least. A practical suggestion for handling this problem will be offered in the section on dating procedures.

Again, the point here is that moral purity is a prerequisite for dating. It is a prerequisite which ought never to be compromised.

*3. Submission to authority.* In the first two chapters,

66

we noted the importance of proper authority relationships. Inasmuch as dating is very much a decision-making process, and inasmuch as parents are primary, God-ordained channels of counsel, it follows that those youths who wish to make wise decisions in courtship should have a good, open relationship with their parents. The obedient son or daughter is in a place of safety, and conversely, the disobedient, rebellious son or daughter is in a place of danger.

To be even more specific, both Scripture and life itself confirm that rebels typically are unrestrained in fleshly appetites. The rebellious son or daughter is particularly vulnerable to immoral temptations, and thus, is simply not ready for dating. Unfortunately, some of the most rebellious are also the most eager to date.

In addition to the moral dangers of rebellion is the danger of allowing rebellion to be the basis for decisions in dating. Young people who live in reaction to their parents, without realizing what they are doing, will often carry that reaction even to the selection of a dating partner. As with clothes, cars, hairstyle, music, and all the controversies of the past, the dating rebel gravitates toward a partner who will set him against his parents. This is, of course, subconscious. The rebel thinks he is doing what he really wants. It almost goes without saying that spite toward a third party makes poor footing for building a lifetime relationship. Yet, two disobedient young people will inevitably be attracted more by their common complaints and negatives than by their common goals or commitments. And they will inevitably make foolish decisions which will affect not only them, but those who follow them.

Again, dating is a decision-making process. The only safe way to enter it is to be living in submission to God-given authority figures.

*4. A Biblical concept of love.* Daily we face distorted concepts of love. The songs, literature, and advertisements of our day, even many "Christian" songs and writings, describe love primarily on a sensual level. There certainly is the feeling side of the man-woman relationship. But it is so emphasized today that "love" has been turned into a feeling-seeking self-centeredness. Unfortunately, what the most clingy young couples love is not one another, but themselves. When every one of their nerve endings is inflated with 100 pounds of this wonderful feeling, however, they cannot be convinced that they do not truly love each other.

We need only to look to the Biblical account of Samson to see the workings of infatuation and the unfortunate results. There was the exhilaration of flirting, followed by the fireworks of lovey-dovey. Then there were the inevitable spats and troubles, and suddenly Samson found himself a blind, defeated slave in a prison house of the Philistines. Reading the account, we have to conclude that Samson was blind and weak and under bondage long before he went to the Philistine prison. These same symptoms follow anyone today who is smitten with woozy concepts of love.

Biblically, love is associated with sacrificial commitment. It is demonstrated in the willingness to give of one's time, abilities, and resources for the well-being, care, and support of another. Such a commitment to the lifetime good of another person requires wise and serious thought, and wise, serious thinking is something the feeling-seekers are simply too exhilarated to engage in. The commitment of genuine love also requires selflessness. It calls for giving regardless of the high or low of feelings. No emotional condition can be preserved endlessly, including the emotional thrill of love. Dating couples who equate love with supercharged feelings unfortunately tend to find their misconceptions confirmed by their dating practices, rather than corrected. Marriage turns into one immense emotional letdown. Love concepts, therefore, must be straight BEFORE dating begins.

When we understand love correctly, we will not view it as something we helplessly "fall into." Nor is it to be rushed after for all we are worth as soon as "the right one" walks by. While love between a man and a woman has its strong feelings, we must know that those feelings come and go. An enduring love does not operate primarily by feelings, but by a commitment that is both sacrificial and selfless.

5. *Biblical values.* In childhood, we live with a view to the immediate. In adulthood, we learn to live with a view to the future. In Christ, we are taught to live with a view to eternity. Much could be said about these three views of life and how they affect values. Modern culture has shifted toward a value system of the immediate, disregarding the future. In many ways it is a childish view. Many older folks warn against the instant demands of the younger generation. Much wisdom is in the view which reckons with the future. But it also has a trap. Hard work and thrift today can produce an affluence which easily turns into worldly mindedness. Jesus said we are not to lay up treasures on earth, but to invest our lives, including our material assets, in the kingdom of heaven.

Homes are regulated by values. Patterns of living, including work patterns, play patterns, purchasing patterns, giving patterns, and even sleeping and eating patterns, are based largely on our values. Because dating is ultimately taking steps toward establishing a home, understanding our value system is prerequisite to dating. Do I live for now? Do I live for the future? Do I live for eternity?

It is to be recognized that when our values are based on eternity, we will not ignore either the present or the future. But eternal values help us keep both present needs and future plans in perspective. Indeed, we plan the future and operate in the present with a view to meeting God and giving a faithful account of all He has entrusted to us.

*6. A sense of responsibility.* Marriage always presents people with problems to solve and needs to meet. Foundational to working through those problems and meeting those needs is a sense of responsibility. Parental training is basic here. Those parents who give their children whatever they want, who do not assign their children chores or teach them to work, who generally clean up their children's clutter and argue in behalf of their children's grievances and misconduct—those parents are damaging their children's sense of personal responsiblity, a life concept which is basic to their children's survival and well-being.

Young people who are contemplating dating need to know that working and saving precede buying, that work precedes relaxation, that mistakes call for restitution, that problems require solutions, and that privileges call for trustworthiness. Many homes are being wrecked today by husbands and wives who have a pattern of sidestepping both their personal and their united responsibilities.

## HOW DO WE GO ABOUT THIS?

In the following paragraphs, we want to consider principles which should guide young men and women in seeking a life companion and then look at practical suggestions for carrying these principles through in the dating/courtship procedure. The suggestions offered are just that—suggestions. Situations vary. Not all the suggestions would be practical or possible for all dating couples. But they are offered as practical ways to honor Scriptural principles. It is the degree to which we honor God and His laws for life that we will find His blessing upon us.

1. *Dating should have parental involvement from the beginning.* This principle is inescapable in the Scriptures dealing with marriage. (For example, Genesis 24:2-4, "And Abraham said unto his eldest servant of his house. . . . thou shalt not take a wife unto my son of the daughters of the Canaanites, among whom I dwell: But thou shalt go unto my country, and to my kindred, and take a wife unto my son Isaac.") This is not to say that parents should arrange totally for the marriage as in oriental custom, but it is to suggest that the general disregard for parents in Western culture (and even in Mennonite custom) has been the cause of many marital problems.

Parents should be the source of continued counsel both before and during the dating process. The reasons for this are numerous. Parents know their young people and their needs, usually better than young people realize. Parents can provide a far more objective view of a relationship and its potential for joy or trouble than can the son or daughter directly involved. They have the ability to stand back, as it were, and see more than the two compelling eyes of the potential mate. Parents also have the experience of their own relationship as well as years of observing other relationships.

Parents, of course, need to consider their own hearts and motives in the counsel they give. They must not be governed by ulterior motives, such as materialism, status, insecurity, or selfishness in their counsel. Christian parents should counsel their youths with a view to establishing solid homes, advancing the kingdom of God, and preserving a heritage of godliness.

*Practical Suggestions*

A young man who wishes to date a particular young woman might sit down first with his parents and discuss the matter. Discuss not only the girl, but such things as personal readiness, future goals, and possible procedure toward those goals. Pray together about the decision. Where parents raise objections, be open to discussing them rather than ignoring them. You might classify objections as strong or mild. Strong objections should be considered direction not to proceed, at least for the present. Mild objections might be worked through simply by discussion or clarification.

Where parents are in agreement to go ahead, the young man is ready to seek the girl's consent. Some prefer at this point to talk to the girl personally about a specific date, and if she is willing, to use this as a springboard for asking her parents' consent. Others prefer to talk to the parents of the girl first, securing their permission before asking the girl.

In any case, the goal of early discussion with the parents of the girl should extend beyond simply asking for permission to date. The young man should express to the parents his desire to follow God, let them know his desire to honor them, and open himself to hearing any concerns or guidelines they would have for their daughter and his relationship with her. It is also an opportunity to ask for their prayer support and to express an openness to their future counsel.

The foundation which this builds for the dating relationship can hardly be overestimated. Parents who know their young people wish to honor them are generally willing to show trust. Many fears and misunderstandings can be avoided by openness with parents from the beginning. On the other hand, where parents are generally not informed, one of the most common frustrations in dating is tensions with parents.

A young woman who is asked for a date should request to discuss this with her parents, or should suggest that the young man discuss it with her parents (or at least her father). This can be done congenially and even with warmth if the girl is open to the relationship. She could, for example, reply with a smile, "Well, I am open to considering it. Would you be willing to discuss this with my father first to see how he feels about me dating you?" If she is less than eager, she could still refer him to her father and meanwhile discuss her thoughts and feelings with her father. If the answer becomes a definite no, a father can likely convey this more graciously than his daughter.

The procedures suggested above may present problems in certain cases. We live in a highly mobile society. Boy may meet girl a thousand miles from her home. How can he talk to her parents when he wants a date that very weekend? Or boy may ask girl for a date on the spur of the moment and there is no time for him to ask her father.

Slow down. If a boy wants a girl a thousand miles from home, he can perhaps arrange for a phone call, a letter, or even a visit to her community. Why should dating be decided on the spur of the moment? A girl who faces this problem could suggest a group activity for that evening instead of a date. If he wants her, he can follow her suggestion to arrange to talk with her father. If he merely wants a date, he can have it with someone else.

73

**SNAPSHOT FROM LIFE**

*Sam prayed about a relationship with Krista for several months before he actually took steps to begin dating. When he felt he had weighed the matter before the Lord sufficiently, he talked to his parents about it.*

*They were pleased—Krista was a sincere Christian, and they gave their blessing for him to begin dating if she was willing.*

*Sam then arranged for a private talk with Krista's father. He presented his request, had a good open talk, and found her father was very agreeable to the relationship. They prayed together.*

*Sam then approached Krista and found she also was willing to start a relationship. Throughout their courtship, Sam continued to ask his parents and hers for counsel, and eventually Sam and Krista were married.*

*During the early years of their marriage, they experienced the sudden death of their second child and the unexpected deaths of Krista's father and brother. The strong relationships they had built with their extended family helped them not only in coping with the grief, but in arranging details for the funerals and in facing the adjustments which followed with such wisdom that it left a profound effect upon their community.*

*2. Eligibility for the marriage relationship should be clearly established.* We live in an increasingly immoral society. The general promiscuity ensnares many teenagers in demoralizing relationships and in emotional, psychological, and spiritual traps, the consequences of which can hardly be imagined at the time. The resultant truth is painful: not all single people are free from the consequences and ties of former immoral relationships.

Because moral problems continue to press upon the Christian community, this matter will need to receive continued attention. Some of the basic issues will be discussed here.

The Scriptures solidly support bringing a pure life to the marriage union. They also stress the importance of openness about one's past. Finding past impurity was grounds for breaking the engagement (Matthew 1:19). Finding it after marriage meant, in the Old Testament, death by stoning (Deuteronomy 22:20, 21).

Does this mean immorality in singlehood disqualifies one from marriage? Not necessarily. It does indicate, however, that one who has kept himself or herself pure might legitimately consider such a person ineligible, and further, that hiding one's immoral past is a sin against a marriage partner.

Where an immoral person becomes a Christian, questions often rise, such as: Can't the past be left in the past? When God forgives, why can't people? Why would Christians even want to discuss someone's past sins? Unfortunately, this thinking ignores several things. First, it ignores the jealousy innate to marital love, which asks that the love one receives is love given to no other (see Deuteronomy 22:14 and Song of Solomon 8:6). Those who close their eyes to the past immorality of a prospective marriage partner are being naive. The marriage relationship is too intimate, marital love too exclusive, to allow people to play such games with reality. The second error of the "forgive and forget" thinking is that it ignores the continuing consequences of immoral behavior. One may be forgiven and still suffer. God forgave David's sin with Bathsheba, but the consequences followed him for life. Discerning the impact of past immoral behavior upon one's future marriage must never be simplistic for the following reasons:

1) The more that sexual urges are gratified contrary to God's design, the less "normal" they will be. "Be not deceived; God is not mocked . . . He that soweth to his flesh shall of the flesh reap corruption" (Galatians 6:7, 8). This general principle has a specific application here and emphasizes the consequences of fleshly decisions. When the sex drive is gratified repeatedly in impure ways, it may bring a person's mind into the bondage of continual preoccupation with sex and on into perversions of sex. Abnormal sexual drives can be ruinous to the pure love God intended in the marriage union.

2) Where sexual relationships have been loose and immoral, there is the danger of disease. Sexual looseness exposes a person to other sexually loose people and whatever diseases they or other partners of theirs may have had. Venereal disease is rampant today among the promiscuous and strikes with venomous consequences not only at disregarding adults, but often at innocent babies as well.

3) Sexual relations, even immoral ones, create ties. "Know ye not that he which is joined to an harlot is one body? for two, saith he, shall be one flesh" (I Corinthians 6:16). While the Bible is clear that sexual relations do not equal marriage, this verse acknowledges the complications of the physical union. These two people can never look at each other in the same way as before. Neither can they look at themselves as before.

4) Fathering or mothering a child as a single person carries obligations which cannot be ignored in forming other relationships.

5) An immoral past, repented of though it may be, can bring memories to the marriage bed which hinder oneness.

Obviously, the matter of eligibility for marriage depends much upon the extent of involvement. Some people are so tangled in former relationships that even though they may never have married, singlehood is advisable. Others, with less entanglements, may be able to find more freedom.

The manner of dating in the Western world, however, by placing the responsibility for the relationship primarily in the hands of the dating couple, complicates the problem of working through previous immorality. As mentioned earlier, first dates are not very suitable for discussing such things, but to learn of this after the relationship has progressed for some time, is both devastating and unfair.

## Practical Suggestions

Parental involvement before dating is a practical way of working through the problems of previous immorality. For a young man to discuss with his prospective father-in-law that he has committed fornication in the past, or for a father to inform his prospective son-in-law that the girl he wishes to date is not a virgin may seem like a terrible way to begin. It is. But it is better than to experience a painful discovery later—a situation which inevitably has the flavor of betrayal.

Where disclosure of previous immorality comes to light during the dating or engagement process, it may be necessary to discontinue the relationship, at least temporarily, to more objectively determine eligibility and compatibility. Discussion of one's immoral past, however, should always include a third party, such as parents or a minister. Medical testing can verify freedom from disease. Such issues as past ties and responsibilities should be clearly determined. If babies are involved, one should consider not only responsibilities, but the possibility of later demands by the other parent. Will the real father come around in years to come and ask for visiting rights? Will the mother come at some later date requesting support or other rights? Implications of sexual sins for the succeeding generations must also be weighed. Will the nature of the past sins require explanation to children in years to come?

In working through these issues, one's private life need not necessarily become public information (although sins against the brotherhood require correction in the brotherhood). Honesty with the right people, however, is a must. The more honest people are in facing the realities of the past, the more possibility there is of working through the present and future implications. Conversely, where a person covers over sins of immorality, God has a way of bringing the consequences back upon him in terrible irony. Nathan had to tell David, "Thus saith the LORD, Behold, I will raise up evil against thee out of thine own house, and I will take thy wives before thine eyes, and give them unto thy neighbour, and he shall lie with thy wives in the sight of this sun. For thou didst it secretly: but I will do this thing before all Israel, and before the sun" (II Samuel 12:11,12). The Bible is clear that God hates immorality, and likewise that He despises cover-up.

Parents who need to work through these things with their children have their own set of problems. On the one hand they may struggle with revulsion, hurt, or anger if someone with an impure past desires their pure son or daughter. On the other hand, they may subconsciously be controlled by the fear of offending a young Christian if they require him or her to face and discuss the past. The guilt of causing a young couple pain may tempt them to cover over or to ignore what should be opened up and discussed. Sometimes parents feel the need of more objective help and wisely turn to a minister or family friend.

In working through traumatic situations, sometimes it is helpful to jot down the things which need to be resolved. This can help to clarify issues and to look at them more objectively. One might also make a list of positive and negative factors in order to weigh them both individually and as a whole.

Prayer puts Christians in touch with their heavenly Father. Ultimately, the wisdom in decisions comes as Christians seek God, as they honor the principles of His Word, and as they receive the wisdom from above.

*3. Dating should involve healthy, open communication in the process of discerning compatibility.* Learning to know another person is prerequisite to learning to love that person. We cannot truly progress in love, in other words, except by real understanding. Unfortunately, infatuation thrives on imagination rather than on real acquaintance. Just as unfortunately, some commonly accepted dating practices actually hinder the getting acquainted necessary for love and instead promote the unreal world of infatuation. Since learning to know another person is accomplished through communication, dating should be planned in the way which makes communication easiest and most effective. That which hinders communication should be avoided.

## Practical Suggestions

In light of the need for wholesome communication in dating, isn't it time to reevaluate the commonly accepted practice of nighttime dating? Late night dating is more suited to stirring feelings than to encouraging thinking.

79

Why not plan dates for afternoons or early evenings?

Sometimes couples find it difficult to know what to talk about, especially on the first few dates. Here are several possibilities for the early stages of getting acquainted: Plan a date with each family in turn. Family chatter, particularly centered around an event such as a picnic, can not only open up conversation, but can also bring you valuable acquaintance. You might also plan for relaxed forms of recreation—a puzzle, a table game, sight-seeing, etc.—all of which will open up conversation in the initial stages of acquaintance.

In a moment we will consider a diagram which shows that discerning spiritual compatibility should have highest priority in dating. To discuss such serious subjects as personal convictions and beliefs, however, most people need a certain amount of getting acquainted first, particularly if they have not grown up in the same community. Here is a concise guide to what to talk about and in what order—facts, interests, beliefs. The initials are FIB, but don't fib. Ask questions and talk first about who you are, who your family is, where you work, what you do, significant things that have happened to you, your childhood, your grandparents, etc. Move on to asking and talking about your interests—hobbies, work, foods, and activities (both positive and negative). This could easily extend into discussing goals, hopes, concerns, and plans. You should soon find you have a natural base for talking about your beliefs.

For the Christian couple, learning to know each other in dating should not be a random procedure. The Scriptures describe different levels of our being and also give us an order of priority as to their relative importance. Consistently, such terms as heart, spirit, and soul are given priority over physical features and attractiveness. The Lord told Samuel, for example, "Look not on his countenance, or on the height of his stature; because I have refused him: for the LORD seeth not as man seeth; for man looketh on the outward appearance, but the LORD looketh on the heart" (I Samuel 16:7). The following diagram, using the terms from I Thessalonians 5:23, suggests an appropriate order of priority for dating.

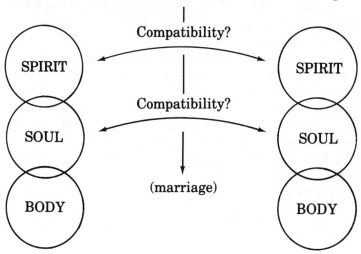

**Order of priority for acquaintance in dating**

Of highest priority is discussing and discerning spiritual compatibility. Do you have similar convictions, goals, values, and vision as relates to the kingdom of God? Secondarily, but also important, are you personally compatible? (The soul here is taken to include intellectual, volitional, and emotional characteristics which make up personality.) Just because two people's beliefs are similar does not always mean, however, they will work together easily as a husband-wife unit. While spiritual compatibility requires similarity, this is not necessarily so for personality. Personal similarities sometimes repel, and opposites sometimes attract. Two strong-willed persons, for example, may find it very difficult to live compatibly. A calm, steady man, on the other hand, may need a wife with a bubbling personality.

The purpose of dating is to discern spiritual and personal compatibility. When a couple has discerned this compatibility through prayer, wise courtship interaction, and parental counsel, they should be ready for marriage and physical union.

Here again we ought to see the wisdom of waiting to date until people are basically ready for marriage. Many youths see the value of giving a year or two in their late teens to serving the church. If during those late teen years young people also give themselves time for personal and spiritual development, dating could be reserved for the time when they are ready for the discerning process to take its wise and necessary course. There would be no need to employ delay tactics and face the dangers of an extended courtship just because "we're not ready yet for marriage." In other words, if we would look at dating as the process of making a wise decision about marriage and we would reserve dating for people who are basically ready to focus on that decision, there would likely be much more wisdom exercised before marriage (and perhaps less romance), and also a much more stable relationship after marriage (and a more enduring romance).

*4. Engaging in physical intimacies in a dating relationship distorts discernment and undermines the basis for respect and trust necessary for solid marriages.* The Scriptures are replete with both warnings and examples which stand against flirting with moral danger. "But fornication, and **all uncleanness** . . . let it not be once named among you, as becometh saints. Let no man deceive you with vain words: for because of these things cometh the wrath of God upon the children of disobedience" (Ephesians 5:3, 6). And yet, too many dating couples will actually arrange both the setting and the activities of their dates to get as close to this sin as possible. The truth is, young men and women who stimulate lustful feelings in each other, although they may not actually commit fornication, are nonetheless guilty of sin. Jesus said, "Whosoever looketh on a woman to lust after her hath committed adultery with her already in his heart" (Matthew 5:28).

Earlier we looked at a diagram which emphasized that acquaintance in spirit should have the highest priority for the dating couple. It is common in Western dating procedure, however, to completely reverse the approach suggested in this diagram. Many relationships are motivated by physical attractions, and these attractions keep the focus on physical acquaintance throughout the dating period. The tragedy of such a focus is not only that it leads to impurity, but it actually stifles acquaintance on higher levels. Couples whose dating includes physical intimacies such as kissing and petting, if they marry, will inevitably marry as strangers to a greater or lesser degree. Their focus of acquaintance keeps them from learning to know each other as persons. Not only do they neglect acquaintance on deeper levels, but they misinterpret what they do learn by viewing it through the eyes of their exhilarated feelings.

The following principles help to put in proper perspective the whole matter of physical contact in dating:

a. In dating, restraint is an expression of love. To NOT hold hands, kiss, etc., is to say, "I appreciate and respect you too much to place you in moral or spiritual danger."

b. Lack of restraint reveals selfishness. In effect, it says, "I am more committed to what I want and to how I feel at the present than I am to your well-being and the future stability of our relationship."

c. Physical contact is progressive. A little calls for a little more. Couples who allow certain intimacies almost invariably overstep their intentions. The only safe policy is to leave all physical demonstrations of affection for after marriage, and thus allow the focus in dating to be on discerning spiritual and personal compatibility.

d. Lack of restraint undermines respect. On the surface, physical intimacies in courtship seem to be saying, "I love you." The hidden message in such sensuous practices, however, is "I am not able to control myself to do what I know I ought." When the novelty and thrill of marriage wears thin, the shallowness of such "love," developed during courtship, surfaces with painful bluntness.

e. To arouse desires in another which cannot be satisfied is actually defrauding that person. Passion before marriage inevitably cheats someone. It cheats the individuals involved. It cheats the couple of true joy and peace. And if the couple should choose to discontinue their relationship, it cheats future partners.

f. Lack of restraint in courtship undermines fidelity in marriage. At heart, lack of restraint is not love but self-gratification. The more self-gratification is exercised in courtship, the more likely it is to be exercised in marriage. Self-gratifying marriage partners easily find themselves tempted to look beyond their marriage for stimulation.

g. Restraint is necessary to allow for proper evaluation. Courtship is a process of decisions. Wise decisions require careful thought. As we noted earlier, physical intimacies in dating destroy objectivity. This principle extends even beyond the matter of affectionate physical contact. A couple may be unrestrained in the amount of time they spend together. They may be unrestrained in the frequency of times they are together. Or they may be unrestrained in methods of communicating their affection other than actual physical touching. Any of this lack of retraint keeps them from being able to "stand back" from the relationship and reflectively, wisely evaluate, "Are we suited for a lifetime commitment to each other?"

## Practical Suggestions

In view of the preceding principles, Christian couples do best to practice "hands off" until after marriage. Further, they should arrange the time, the location, and the activities of their dates to encourage healthy acquaintance in spirit and soul, and thus fortify themselves against temptations toward physical acquaintance. Avoid late hours. Avoid having dates in dark or dimly lighted places. Plan for activities or discussions which will enhance spiritual and personal acquaintance.

To be even more specific, we should note that generally men are tempted through what they see and women through what they feel. It follows that in courtship the Christian woman will want to keep her appearance modest and the Christian man will want to keep his hands from affectionate touching, that both may avoid temptation.

Recognizing the need of restraint for objective evaluation, couples should by mutual consent and under counsel of their parents set limits on such things as the frequency and length of their dates, as well as on such things as phone calls and letters. If they find themselves repeatedly having "reasons" to overstep these limits, something is wrong. They need to develop more restraint.

Couples may also wish occasionally to set aside time blocks of several weeks or even a month when they have very limited interaction, using this time specifically for seeking the Lord and evaluating the relationship. Evaluation is our next point.

*5. Dating is a decision-making process which should have specific goals in view.* Throughout this chapter we have noted that courtship involves decisions, but we have not looked specifically at what decisions need to be made. A general observation is in order first: marriage is not simply the union of two people, but of two families. The decision making, then, involves more than personal evaluation. We can readily see this in the marriages of Esau. He married two Hittite women "which were a grief of mind unto Isaac and to Rebekah" (Genesis 26:35). These wives brought with them a mindset, a set of values, a heritage rooted in heathendom which was incompatible with the mindset, values, and heritage of Isaac and Rebekah. Whether Esau would have been able personally to live in peace with his wives, we perhaps cannot say. But his parents were not. And tension between in-laws makes for tension in marriage.

Esau and his wives demonstrate the most basic reason for incompatibility—spiritual differences. A man and woman who cannot be one in spirit will never be able to experience the union God intends in marriage. The Scripture flatly says, "Be ye not unequally yoked together with unbelievers: for what fellowship hath righteousness with unrighteousness? and what communion hath light with darkness? And what concord hath Christ with Belial? or what part hath he that believeth with an infidel?" (II Corinthians 6:14, 15).

*Practical Suggestions*

Following is a list of potential sources of conflict, which dating couples will want to consider. To aid discernment, these are listed according to the levels discussed earlier—spirit, soul, and body. This will help to assess their level of importance. Differences on the spiritual level should be taken seriously and should be discussed openly and kindly. Incompatibility (where differences cannot be resolved) on the spiritual level should be viewed as reason for discontinuing the relationship. Differences on lower levels may also be reason for discontinuing the relationship, but are more likely to be worked through to compatibility than spiritual differences.

## *SPIRIT*

☐ Relationship with Jesus Christ. A non-Christian or a backslidden Christian should be considered incompatible with a dedicated Christian for a dating relationship. Period.

☐ Differences in spiritual maturity.

☐ Differences in practical applications of faith. Couples who come from congregations with differing applications ought not to overlook those differences. They should seriously consider not only whether they can come to compatibility, but also whether that compatible position would enhance their spiritual goals, and further, whether changes they may make would alienate them from either family.

☐ Differences on doctrinal issues. (Separation of church and state, woman's role, church organization and discipline, end-time events, child evangelism, non-resistance in legal and economic affairs, etc.)

☐ Differences in calling or vision for service. The question should not be whether one is service-minded, but *in what way*. One person's concept of service may center around people, and another's concept may center around certain activities or perhaps around a certain location or only a certain group of people.

☐ Differences in values. Jesus taught us values which affect in very practical ways such things as work, leisure, spending patterns, investments, and indebtedness. Christians in the West demonstrate a significant variety of thinking and practice in these matters, and a growing number of marriages experience conflict over economics.

## SOUL

☐ Differences in likes and dislikes. This can be in simple matters such as colors or foods, or in more significant matters such as work or climate.

☐ Differences in educational background.

☐ Differences in culture. Mission work, service, and travel expose us to people of other cultures and thus to the possibilities of cross-cultural marriages. Such marriages are not wrong in themselves, but there can be tremendous hurdles to cross if one or the other partner is expected to leave his own country, people, family, diet, and customs and adjust to an altogether new culture. Frank counsel from missionaries, church leaders, experienced workers, and other cross-cultural marriages should be carefully sought even before courtship begins.

☐ Differences in customs. Customs have to do with social and behavioral practices and expectations within a group or a family. What may be normal and acceptable to one group may be considered crude or odd by another. A young man may think it silly that anyone would consider him crude to lick his knife after buttering his bread. But a girl reared by different standards may find his knife-licking and related habits too gross to stomach.

☐ Emotional differences. We noted earlier that emotional differences can be healthy. A vivacious, outgoing personality, for example, may find balance and compatibility with a subdued, reticent partner. Emotional compatibility, however, is not quite as simple as North Pole finding a willing South Pole. There is the matter of emotional norms. Some people view tears in a man, for example, as a sign of weakness, and others see it as something to be admired. There are also problems such as emotional instability and self-centered emotional patterns. Some people "fly apart" emotionally under minor stress. Some people are moody or sulky or depressed for days when something doesn't go their way. Others have developed patterns of bitterness or self-pity. These things ought not be viewed simply as emotional differences—underneath such emotional patterns are deeper problems which will not "balance" with any partner.

☐ Emotional scars or handicaps. All of us may experience insecurity, anger, guilt, and fear. But some people have been through abuse and/or sin to the point of serious emotional damage. Such damage can find healing in Christ, but *unresolved* scars or handicaps can place tremendous pressures on marriage.

☐ Differences in intellectual ability. All of us vary, but sizable differences in intelligence can create significant frustration post-marriage. Are you willing to coach a semiliterate partner through life? Are you able to accept not being able to explain your logic or share your discoveries with a partner who doesn't think on your level of thinking? Will you be able to cope with the problems of a partner passing on misunderstandings and intellectual errors to your children or other people?

☐ Differences in personality and temperament. Inasmuch as dating is getting to know someone else, it also includes self-disclosure. Communication and interaction, therefore, must be characterized by honesty, kindness, and respect.

*BODY*

☐ Differences in age. Generally, closeness in age is preferable, because a large gap in age increases the likelihood of other differences.

☐ Differences in race. Differences in skin color or appearance are not necessarily large items in themselves. But if they are associated with such things as cultural differences or differences in emotional norms, these need to be considered carefully. Furthermore, the expectations and opinions of others, fair or unfair, must be reckoned with. At heart, the key to compatibility here is discerning whether each can fully accept the other as he or she is in spite of what others may think.

☐ Physical handicap. Again, this does not automatically signal incompatibility, but it does require each knowing and fully accepting the other. Actually, every couple must recognize the limitations and needs of each other. Some couples must reckon, however, with meeting each other's needs at a point outside of the "normal" range. If this point is not recognized and accepted, it causes frustrations later.

☐ Close relatives. Biblical standards for not marrying close kin basically excluded members of the immediate family, uncles, aunts, and in-laws. Medical research today would verify the danger that marriage between close relatives, including cousins, increases the likelihood of mutations and genetic disorders.

☐ Distance between families. Our mobile society more

and more is making it possible to join two people across many miles. This is not wrong. It simply presents more to work through in the adjustments of a dating/marriage relationship. How will you cope with homesickness? Are you prepared to travel "home" at reasonable intervals? Although these are not the most significant adjustments, they must be reckoned with in the overall process of working through to compatibility.

If we view dating as a decision-making process, it makes sense to structure the time, the setting, and the activity of dates to enhance wholesome acquaintance. The more the dating couple understands one another, not only personally, but in the context of one another's culture and family, the better equipped they are for making decisions about their future.

All this is not to say that each date should be nothing but solid discussion of beliefs, values, and compatibility. It is not wrong to enjoy one another's company in leisure and recreation. But it is to say that communication is basic to wholesome dating. And it is also to warn that to make leisure and recreation the focus of dating may create emotional attachments which may leave couples largely ignorant of one another, rather than developing a true acquaintance.

To keep communication wholesome and productive, regular Bible study is appropriate. A couple might plan for specific Scriptures, topics, or questions to be discussed for the next date. This would give both parties freedom to offer suggestions and would likewise give both parties time to sort through what they believe.

*6. When a relationship needs to be discontinued, it should be done with respect to one another as persons.* For various reasons, not every dating relationship continues into marriage. Discontinuing a relationship can be painful. It is always more painful where proper respect is not shown.

*Practical Suggestions*

If it is clear that the relationship should be discontinued, it should be discussed promptly, honestly, and kindly. To delay the process is but to postpone the pain and likely to increase it as well. To skirt the issues or to use indirect methods of communication is likely to create misunderstanding. The most respectful approach is in person (rather than by letter) and with kind but clear wording.

The matter of wording is often a problem. We think sometimes that to give our real reasons will only hurt a person. Certainly, the wording should be thought through beforehand. Parental counsel can be helpful here. But a Christian young man or woman should have both the courtesy and the wisdom to state reasons for discontinuing a relationship. To give surface or hazy reasons will only foster unnecessary imagining. On the other hand, to demand reasons is not respectful either. While clear communication is desirable, it is not always a reality, and sometimes a decision must be accepted without knowing altogether the basis for it.

Reasons for discontinuing a relationship should be traceable to our motivations for dating. To be very practical, let's consider a possible situation and then contrast improper wording with respectful, clear wording.

Suppose the reason for discontinuing has to do with a strong-willed personality.

**Clear, but unkind:** "I don't like how stubborn you are. I think we need to break up."

**Vague:** "I just don't feel that God is leading us together."

92

**Respectful:** "There are many things I appreciate about you, but I have become uncomfortable with the tensions between us, particularly when we disagree about something. I've come to believe this would hinder us in building a home for God. I really think it is best for us to discontinue our relationship."

Sometimes in a dating relationship, the issues are not clear-cut. One or the other may have doubts about certain things but no clear direction to discontinue the relationship. An alternative to discontinuing is to put the relationship "on hold." A couple may decide, for example, not to date for three months to consider more carefully certain issues of difference or to more objectively look at certain personal decisions or doubts.

Where this route is chosen, several guidelines should be observed. First, the duration of the on-hold relationship should be agreed upon. One month? Two months? Six months? By agreeing on a time, the couple can more clearly consider their objectives. The time should be chosen with a view to the nature of the problem to be resolved. For example, one month may be adequate to personally study and clarify a personal position on some doctrinal item of difference. But suppose either a present or past moral problem comes to light and there is need for a time of personal purging. A wait of six months may not be out of order at all in such a situation. Generally an agreed time of waiting should not extend so long that the couple loses sight of their objectives.

Second, the nature of the relationship should be clearly defined. No dates? Limited dating? No letters? No extended discussions, unless mutually agreed upon? Without defining the relationship during the on-hold period, a couple may find themselves continuing to spend time together without intending to.

Third, an on-hold period should not be used as a means

of slowly breaking the relationship. That is, if one or both are convinced they should not continue dating, it is a breach of integrity to continue to hold out hope by postponing the time of parting. The on-hold agreement discussed here should NOT include the freedom to date others. Where that freedom is given, the relationship should be considered discontinued.

Obviously, not all the possible variations in breaking a relationship can be given here. The basic points to remember are to be respectful, clear, and kind.

## WHAT DO WE DO NEXT?

To this point we have emphasized that dating is a decision-making process. The bottom line of that process is the decision of marriage, and engagement is an affirmative commitment to go ahead with marriage. Hopefully the preceding pages have demonstrated that engagement is not a rash plunge, but that it can be and ought to be a rational commitment based on solid counsel, sincere prayer, and mutual faith and love.

In the Bible, engagement was considered binding; so much so, that the two were called husband and wife, and to break the relationship was called "putting away" (Matthew 1:19).

How should we view engagement today? Is it that serious? Is it ever right to break an engagement? We should note, of course, that in the Biblical view of betrothal, there were other safety factors including parental involvement, dowry, tokens of virginity, etc. Even so, it would seem that our present view of engagement could be much nearer the Biblical view if we were to emphasize dating as a time of decision making rather than a time of romance. Furthermore, inasmuch as the New Testament calls us to a trustworthiness that re-

94

quires no oaths, it would seem that a Christian ought surely to be true to promises he makes. Some would say, "Better to break an engagement than to ruin a lifetime." But is it not better yet to take the proper steps so that such engagements are not made? A high view of engagement is possible only when we maintain a high view of dating. Stated the other way around, lowered standards of dating will inevitably produce a lowered view of engagement.

In the following paragraphs, we will consider guidelines not only for how to view engagement properly, but for how to enter it and how to move from engagement to marriage.

We have already noted that engagement was viewed seriously in the Bible, and we have indicated it should be viewed seriously today. There are several foundation stones upon which this view of engagement is built. Let's consider them carefully.

First, a young man taking a Scriptural approach will view his prospective companion as subject to her parents. She does not belong to him, no matter how much he loves her, until she has been "given in marriage." It is proper and right, therefore, to view the first step in engagement as securing the approval of her parents. This means the approach should not be one of informing her parents of the engagement, but of asking permission and discussing the suitability of marrying their daughter. If a proper relationship has been formed with parents in the dating, this would be a very natural step.

Second, it is also Scriptural to view engagement as a commitment. It is not to be viewed as the final stage of discernment. As Ervin Hershberger wrote, "Engagement . . . should never be thought of as an experimental stage. The decisive testing period should take place before engagement."[1] Should a serious betrayal of trust occur during engagement or come to light during engagement (such as unchastity or deception about salvation), there is Scriptural basis for breaking the commitment. "When as his mother Mary was espoused to Joseph, before they came together, she was found with child of the Holy Ghost. Then Joseph her husband, being a just man, and not willing to make her a public example, was minded to put her away privily" (Matthew 1:18, 19). "Be ye not unequally yoked together with unbelievers" (II Corinthians 6:14).

Third, where engagement is viewed thus as a commitment to marry, the time between engagement and marriage can be viewed simply as a time to get ready. It should not be longer than the time necessary to make and carry out the plans for marriage. Prolonged engagements, except where plans are interrupted by unforeseen circumstances, demonstrate a misunderstanding of engagement and inevitably place unhealthy pressures on the dating couple.

Fourth, the commitment to marry does not give the couple the privileges of marriage. As Hershberger writes, "No matter how firm your engagement may be, the physical body of your friend is still private property which you do not yet possess."[2] According to I Corinthians 6:20, our bodies are not merely private property, but God's property, and to trespass is sin (see the setting of this verse). The principles given earlier against physical contact in dating apply equally to engagement. Pure, wholesome engagements serve to heighten the joy and strengthen the fidelity of marriage; whereas, physical intimacies in engagement will inevitably return to haunt marriages.

With the above view of engagement, just how does one go about it? Assuming proper acquaintance has taken place in dating, let's consider the following suggestions:

1. Prayerfully ask for God's wisdom and guidance.

2. Discuss your readiness for marriage with your parents. If they cannot be consulted, perhaps your minister will do. It is always wise to make life-changing decisions under the direction and counsel of authority figures God has placed in your life.

3. Think through the wording of your marriage proposal. You may even prepare a written proposal. The following is only a model. This can be attractively done in your own handwriting and wording suited to your relationship.

Dear _____,

God has blessed me with the joy of acquaintance with you. We have shared our faith, our goals, and our deepest thoughts. We have enjoyed many good times together. I love you, _____. I believe your commitment to God is real and healthy. Through counsel and prayer, I am ready to pledge my life to you and by God's grace to provide loving, Christian leadership in a marriage union with you. I ask you to consider prayerfully whether you are ready to join me in building a home for the glory of God. Will you be my wife?

With love,

_____

4. Approach the parents of your friend, seeking their approval and advice for your proposal. This approach to the parents should NOT be by letter or by phone unless a personal talk is impossible.

5. With the approval of your friend's parents, propose to your friend. Probably the best approach is to verbalize your request and then give the written form (if you use

one) so she can consider it more carefully. It may be that she has been in prayer and consultation with her parents about the matter and is prepared to reply immediately. Great. But if not, do not press for an immediate response.

6. If, as a young woman, you receive a proposal, you ought to consider not only your own thoughts, but your parents' approval before replying. If your suitor has not approached your parents, ask him if he would be willing to do so. You, too, may reply in writing. The benefit of a written, signed proposal and a written, signed response is that it clarifies the seriousness and authenticity of your engagement.

7. Seal your commitment to one another by prayer, together asking God to guide you both in your immediate plans and in your future home. In announcing to your parents your commitment, ask them to pray for you as well.

The practice among some people is to seal the engagement with a kiss. In view of the tendency of physical intimacies to progress once they are begun, the deep emotions associated with a love commitment, and the need of God's help to carry out that commitment, prayer would seem to be a much more appropriate seal for Christian engagement.

8. Verbally commit yourselves to moral purity in the time of your engagement. This will both fortify you against danger and will deepen your respect for one another.

9. Discuss together and with both sets of parents the time required to prepare for the wedding. Again, engagement should not be prolonged, but neither should it be hasty. Simply, move in wisdom toward the wedding. Engaged couples soon realize that the decision to be married opens them to the necessity of many more decisions. Openness in communication is a continuing

must.

10. Discuss with your ministry your plans for marriage. Ask them if they could arrange to give you premarital counsel. Discuss with them your wedding plans, both as to their schedule and any general guidelines they may have for weddings.

## SUMMARY

To sum up this chapter, let's review some of the most basic concepts. Dating is preparation for marriage. It should be pursued only by those who are eligible for marriage. Dating is an acquaintance process which focuses first on spiritual compatibility but also on personal compatibility. The decision making in dating is too important to become carried away by exhilarated feelings; therefore, physical demonstrations of affection should be postponed until after marriage. The counsel of parents and spiritual leaders should be sought as providing a larger base for wise decisions in dating. When the young man is fully convinced that he and his friend are ready for marriage, he should seek her parents' approval and then his friend's consent. Engagement should be viewed as a commitment which is not to be broken except where deceit or unfaithfulness are involved. The time of engagement should not extend beyond the reasonable time needed to plan and prepare for the wedding.

The pressures upon marriages and homes seem continually to be increasing. If ever the home needed a solid foundation, it is today. God has given us principles to follow, and if we honor those principles, we can still build solid homes. The shaky homes even in Christian circles today evidence man's tendency to follow his own way. If we are convinced that Psalm 127:1 is true, let's return to the ways of God. "Except the LORD build the house, they

99

labour in vain that build it."

## THINKING TOGETHER

1. What are some potential problems of dating too early in one's spiritual progress? What misconceptions common to new Christians could affect adversely one's view of dating or marriage?
2. The suggestion in this chapter for disclosing immorality in one's past is to work through parents at the beginning of a relationship. Are there other ways of handling this? What does one do when parents are not available?
3. What should young people do for counsel if parents do not give it; if even when asked, parents reply, "You are old enough to make your own decisions"?
4. Would God ever expect a young person to date someone for whom he has no attraction? How might a person with this idea be led to a proper understanding? (Consider such things as parental counsel, God's will, and the section in this chapter on compatibility.)
5. How can a dating couple be honest in discussing personal differences without hurting each other? How should embarrassing or annoying things in each other's speech, habits, or other conduct be handled?
6. How does a couple honor parental advice when parents want their child to remain in what the couple believes is an apostate church setting?
7. If a young woman recognizes signs of unresolved hurts in her boyfriend regarding his parents, but sees him as a growing Christian in other ways, how should she view this? (Unresolved hurts are indicated by a sense of blame, by a lack of freedom in showing forgiveness and love.)
8. What are the results of being too possessive in dating?

What are the results of being too casual?

9. Should Christians view engagement today with the same seriousness as in Bible times? Would the use of a written proposal/consent help to make engagement more meaningful?

10. What are the advantages of a couple agreeing on courtship standards early in their relationship?

11. What dangers are inherent in flirting? If a girl takes the initiative during courtship, with aggressive romantic overtures, what will she be like in the home?

## WORKING TOGETHER

1. As parents, discuss the kind of relationship you desire or expect of your dating children. Arrange to discuss this with them so they clearly know your expectations. If they are of dating age, be open to their input and feedback, especially if you are changing your expectations. Ask them what expectations they may have for you.

2. As a dating person, evaluate the acquaintance procedures you have used. How objective have you been? How well do you know the beliefs of your friend? The personality? The family? How well have you communicated your beliefs? How well does your friend know your family? Make a list of those things which are needing more clarity. Discuss with your parents or your minister how you might improve your communication in dating.

3. Make a list of the qualities you would want in a marriage partner. Then evaluate yourself according to the list—are there areas of weakness, and what might you do about them?

4. If you have not yet dated, what parts of this chapter

interest you most? Do you agree with the ideas? Do you need further clarification on certain points? Arrange to discuss these parts with your parents and see what they have to offer about your questions.

# SINGLEHOOD

## INTRODUCTION

Subjects such as dating, engagement, and marriage are generally more apt to be discussed by young people than singlehood. Perhaps this is because more people marry than stay single, and perhaps also because most young people want to get married. But it means, unfortunately, that sometimes people find themselves in situations they never have given much thought to, and just as unfortunately, situations which nobody else has given much thought to either.

Although this chapter is for single people, it is not for them alone. Single people are family members. Single

103

people are church members. Single people are neighbors and friends. The struggles and triumphs of single people need to be discussed and understood by everyone for several reasons. First, single people need to be understood because everyone in God's family is valuable. If we are to relate properly as Christian to Christian, we need to understand one another. Second, as we learn about single people, we often come to realize that some of their problems are compounded by unthinking and uncaring people around them. What may be thoughtlessly brushed aside as "their problem" is in reality sometimes "our problem." And third, the whole subject of singlehood needs to be considered more carefully by all because too much single talent and resource lie dormant or buried and go unused in the kingdom of God.

## WHY AM I SINGLE?

"Why" questions are not always profitable, particularly when they are asked in anger or discouragement. But "why" questions can be asked honestly. And with singlehood as with any other human condition, we usually function better when we understand ourselves. It is to that end we pursue the matter here.

Obviously, looking at why people do anything can be as varied as people themselves. The issue of why a person is single, however, is often confused in Christian minds because so many factors outside of our control bear upon it. True, some people choose to be single. For them, the matter of why is usually more clear. But for many, singlehood seems to be one's lot rather than one's choice, and here is where misunderstanding easily sets in.

Christians view God as sovereign. When they are willing to be married but instead find themselves single, they legitimately ask, "Is this God's will for me?" And the next "logical" questions are "Why? Is there something wrong with me? Am I not where God wants me to be? Have I just not found the right person?" At this point objectivity is easily lost. Personal feelings cloud the issues. And as Evelyn Mumaw points out in her book *Woman Alone,* "Frequently the real reasons and the felt reasons are not the same."[1]

If you analyze the above questions, they tend to fall naturally into three categories of possible reasons for singlehood—personal character, God's will, and circumstances. Let's look at each of these more carefully.

### Personal Character

In our hearts and in our minds, companionship is inseparably tied to love and personal acceptance. In reality, of course, companionship may bring hate and rejection. But in our hearts we want to be accepted, and in our minds we tell ourselves it ought always to be so in marriage. When we find that we are not married, we easily begin to assume that we are not because others have rejected us.

The feeling of rejection, left unchecked, can be destructive to say the least. It can damage relationships. It can sap one's spirituality. It can wear away at one's spirit and virtually destroy a personality.

In single people, the feeling of rejection may take a variety of forms. There may be anger at the opposite sex in general. The anger may turn inward and develop into a sense of personal failure, resulting in depression. On the other hand, there may be unconscious attempts to control others, particularly putting their love to the test—a person who feels rejected sometimes seems driven to prove that he or she actually is rejected. The feeling of rejection may also cause the single person to try to prove personal competence *as single.* Thus, he or she[2] may launch into work, hobby, education, or recreation with a drive that declares, "I'm quite capable of living life myself, thank you."

This rejection, however, may be much more of a felt reason than a real one. But whether it is real or felt, the reactions mentioned above invariably do not help, but only serve to alienate a single person even from those who could be true friends.

Having noted that the feeling of rejection, particularly as attributed to the opposite sex in general, is usually unfounded, we must acknowledge that character and personality do legitimately bear upon singlehood and marriage. They are foundational for companionship as well as for any other human relationship. Christian young men and women seeking companionship *should* be attracted to solid character and mature personality. And the same standard by which young people seek companionship should be used also to avoid companionship.

The ultimate One to approve character and provide acceptance, however, is God, not the ones we date or do not date. Those who feel rejected in singlehood must learn to come back to openness before God. What Paul wrote to Timothy could be applied here. "Study [give earnest diligence] to show thyself approved unto God" (II Timothy 2:15). We must recognize that people do not always approve or disapprove rightly. Some people who would make excellent marriage partners never marry, and some who are grabbed up readily in marriage make poor mates. The simple point is that the single life which has God's approval will inevitably be more fulfilled than the married life which has not God's approval.

So, is there "something the matter with me" if I am not married? There could be, just as there could be something the matter with me if I am married. But as we will see later, there are enough other factors involved that we are wrong to *assume* that singlehood is a matter of personal failure—either in assessing ourselves or others.

On the other hand, it can be healthy periodically to evaluate ourselves, not so much from the standpoint of whether we are eligible for marriage, but whether we are personally, socially, and spiritual healthy. Ask yourself: Am I continuing to expand my mind and skills? Am I gracious, thoughtful, and helpful in my relationships? Am I experiencing a deepening acquaintance with God, gaining insight into His ways and into His purposes for my life? As Mrs. Mumaw helpfully counsels, "Note your weaker areas, and set about to deal with these constructively."[3]

### God's Will

A second factor often viewed as a cause for singlehood is God's will. The whole subject of God's involvement in our lives is so much larger than the present discussion that we simply cannot do it justice here, and yet it is so basic to a proper understanding of life that we must consider it, although only in brief.

The Scriptures reveal truth, but the Scriptures do not always explain the truths they reveal. From the Scripture we know, for example, that God is sovereign. "Our God is in the heavens: he hath done whatsoever he hath pleased" (Psalm 115:3). The Scripture also reveals that sin is in the world and that things are not as they ought to be—there is pain, there is struggle, there is misunderstanding and betrayal, there is injustice and inequity, there is temptation and evil, there is hardship, sickness, and death. "God looked down from heaven upon the children of men, to see if there were any that did understand, that did seek God . . . there is none that doeth good, no, not one" (Psalm 53:2, 3). "I saw the prosperity of the wicked" (Psalm 73:3). "I have seen servants upon horses, and princes walking as servants upon the earth . . . time and chance happeneth to them all" (Ecclesiastes 10:7; 9:11). "For we know that the whole creation groaneth and travaileth in pain together until now" (Romans 8:22). "For all that is in the world, the lust of the flesh, and the lust of the eyes, and the pride of life, is not of the Father, but is of the world" (I John 2:16). The Scriptures further reveal that man has freedom of choice. "Whosoever will, let him take the water of life freely" (Revelation 22:17). "Your fathers tempted me, proved me, and saw my works forty years. Wherefore I was grieved with that generation, and said, They do alway err in their heart" (Hebrews 3:9,10).

But how does one reconcile the sovereignty of a holy God with the corruption in the world and the choices of man? Since it is God's will that everyone be saved (I Timothy 2:4), why isn't everyone saved? And why does God permit things to go on in the world which are not right? Is He running our world and our individual lives, or is He just letting things take their natural course?

Theological warfare has been waged over these very questions. Without shooting down all the arguments advanced by opponents, we will simply acknowledge that God's sovereignty, human events, and man's free will all combine to form the correct view of life. In His sovereignty, God not only created the world, but He oversees it and invades it with His power and purpose. But at the same time, God "lets the world run," as it were, within the boundaries of certain laws and principles which He has established—man can see cause and effect all around him, in other words, without any awareness of God's hand. And in that same framework of laws and limitations, God has given man freedom. Man can choose.

The awareness of a sovereignty so vast and wise as to permit sin, man's choices, and the flow of human events; and at the same time to work all things together for good in individual lives (Romans 8:28), is beyond human understanding. It can be accepted by faith. It can be experienced. But it defies comprehension.

Now, how does all this relate to singlehood?

First, such a view gives the single person freedom to evaluate and accept the unpleasant events of his life which are beyond his control as part of the flow of human history. Not everything in his life is "God's will" in the direct sense. He may be single as a result of betrayal, accident, misunderstanding, etc. And on the other side of the same understanding, he has freedom to evaluate changes in his situation with wisdom. If, in other words, after years of singlehood, he is suddenly in a situation where marriage is a real possibility, he need not view this as a "sign from heaven" so much as a situation in which he must exercise the same wisdom he has needed in his life to this point. God has not changed His mind; the situation has changed.

Second, this view of life gives us freedom to view God's Word, rather than our interpretation of human events, as the basic source of God's will. When we recognize that God's will is best revealed in the principles of His Word, we likewise must recognize our responsibility to study God's Word and to exercise wisdom in our choices. Many people, including single people, are caught in the confusion of trying to discern God's will primarily through life's events. They constantly face indecision because each new circumstance presents more possibilities to them, any one of which might be God's will. Decision-making to them is almost like a lottery system—when they decide, they hope they have hit the "lucky number" of God's will. What a relief to step out of that perpetual uncertainty onto the solid footing of God's Word. "For ever, O LORD, thy word is settled in heaven. Thy word is a lamp unto my feet, and a light unto my path" (Psalm

119:89, 105).

Granted, God sometimes impresses His particular will upon us in a given decision. He directed Philip, for example, to the Ethiopian eunuch. But far more commonly, God expects our decisions to be exercises in applying the wisdom of His Word to the situations at hand.

The third blessing of viewing God's sovereignty as large enough to permit the flow of human history and the exercise of human choice is that it gives us the freedom to trust our lives to His goodness. God is big enough to accomplish His will in the lives of His people even while permitting the flow of natural and human events. Specifically, singlehood may be our lot by causes altogether "ungodly" and still be one of the specific means of God accomplishing His purposes in and through us. The person who yields his life totally into the hand of GOD may have a thousand things "happen" to him which seem outside of God's will in their cause and yet find those very things arranged in indescribable symmetry, beauty, and purpose in his life. "**All things** work together for good to them that love God, to them who are the called according to his purpose" (Romans 8:28).

And so, is it God's will that I am single? It may be. The more important question, however, is "Have I yielded my singlehood to the hand of God?" And further, "Am I ordering my singlehood in accord with the Word of God?" If the answer is yes to the last two questions, any single person can with confidence say, "I am in the will of God." And should the possibility of marriage present itself at any time, this person has the proper premise for considering it wisely. Since he has taken each step in his singlehood according to the principles of God's Word, he will take no step out of singlehood which violates those principles.

## Circumstances

The third thing commonly viewed as a cause of singlehood is circumstances. Inasmuch as this is often associated with God's will, the former discussion has already laid much of the foundation for understanding it. A few clarifications, however, are in order.

First, for the person who experiences a growing relationship with God through His Word, circumstances serve as legitimate and important confirmations of God's will. Many can testify to the blessing of God confirming His direction and timing through circumstances.

 ── SNAPSHOT FROM LIFE ──

*Tina was a single young woman teaching in a Christian school. Considering her personality and her abilities, however, she felt that she may be more suited to the work of nursing than the work of teaching. She prayed about it and inquired at a local nurse's training program. For various reasons, the cost for her was simply prohibitive. Tina accepted this circumstance as confirmation that she should continue teaching and not take up nursing at the present time.*

*A few years later, however, Tina was teaching in another locality. There she learned of a small nursing school which was both more accessible and more economical for her. Furthermore, a Christian friend of hers was also wanting to take nurse's training. They were able to enroll together, and they found their mutual faith and friendship a tremendous support in the pressures of schooling.*

As we noted earlier, however, circumstances taken as a primary means of knowing God's will can be confusing. From our perspective, circumstances will at times seem chaotic, even contradictory to the promises of God. Consider Job. If a man so wise became confused in contrary circumstances, will not ordinary people also? Yes. And the best advice for single or married people in the whirlwind of confusing circumstances is to follow the testimony of Job himself. "Though he slay me, yet will I trust in him" (Job 13:15).

Apart from the circumstances which either confirm or confuse people in choosing singlehood, are those which beyond their control require singlehood. Evelyn Mumaw, herself single until quite past the "normal" age of marriage, lists numerous circumstances which may require singlehood.[4]

1. There may be a mismatched number of eligible marriage partners. Nationally there are fewer young men than young women. And so, nationally there are more single young women than single young men. Given Christian standards for marriage and other factors, however, any given locality could have a shortage of *eligible* marriage partners for either young women or young men.

2. Responsibilities may not permit marriage. The care of invalid or handicapped members of one's family may necessitate singlehood. Involvement in a service particularly unsuited to marriage causes some to remain unmarried. It seems as though the Apostle Paul was one who felt his responsibilities simply were not suited to marriage.

3. Handicap may rule out marriage. To quote Mrs. Mumaw, "It is amazing how many blind, deaf, crippled, or ill women [and men] have married, but even so, these have been limiting factors which have deferred or can-

celed out marriage for many."[5]

4. Distress of the present time has for some made marriage impractical. This seems to be the underlying factor in the advice given by Paul to the Corinthians. The general encouragment for everyone to "abide in the same calling wherein he was called" (I Corinthians 7:20) as well as the seeming preference for singlehood reflected in this chapter should be seen in the light of "the present distress" (v. 26). Through the centuries, Christians have found themselves in situations which reduced the occurrences of marriage. Sometimes the distress was persecution, sometimes it was poverty, and sometimes it was the latter as a result of the former. Although distress is not a general cause of singlehood in the Western world, at times it can be.

As we implied earlier, the outside factors which account for singlehood can lead to resentment. Help for avoiding this will be given later in this chapter. At this point we will simply emphasize again that turning our lives over to God is the basis for fulfillment and security for anyone, single or married. Why we are single is never as important as whether we are living in healthy union with God.

## WHAT CAN I EXPECT?

Attitudes toward marriage and singlehood have changed dramatically in Western culture in the past years. Decades ago, singlehood had the unfair stigma of eccentricity—shrill-voiced, straight-laced aunties whose company could not be endured long, or unsettled, roaming bachelors with an air of mystery. Today, society's image of singlehood for both women and men has turned into a classy, competent, 29-year-old with plenty of money, trained skills, and freedom to live life to the fullest.

While we could wish that such images in the world would stay out of the church, in reality, their pressures are usually felt. Besides, the church community can exert its own pressures, even unknowingly, upon singles. In addition to these factors from without are the intricate and sometimes misunderstood feelings, responses, and desires within the single person. It must not be assumed, however, that these inner feelings or even the outer pressures are all unwholesome. The single person faces struggles, true, but opportunities as well, which are the direct product of singlehood.

So what is it like to be single? What can a single person expect? We want to consider both the negative and the positive side of these questions, and we start with the negative in order to end on an upbeat. After describing singlehood, we will consider guidance for coping with negative factors and utilizing the positive opportunities.

### Negative Factors in the Experience of Singlehood

1. A single person will likely experience the expectations of others to marry. This is especially so in younger singlehood. While in itself it is not necessarily negative, it can at times turn negative, or it can be taken by single people as negative. The negative side of this intensifies the more a single person wishes to marry but cannot. If a person has younger siblings involved in dating while he or she as an older person remains single, there can be the uncomfortable feeling that others wonder what's wrong. Questions or remarks about the situation amplify the unwritten pressure—*I'm not meeting others' expectations.*

2. A single person will sometimes feel left out. As one single woman confessed, "I don't fit with the young people, and I don't fit with the married couples. I really

114

don't know where I belong." In an age when the family is under severe attack, and in a setting where most adults are married, and in a congregation where the leaders are concerned about families, there can be so many sermons, seminars, and recommended books directed to the family that single people not only feel left out, but indeed are.

3. A single person sometimes feels that nobody understands. Every person has a longing to be known, understood, and accepted. This is one of the strongest bonds of a solid marriage. Unfortunately, what many single people do not realize is that many married people have the same unfulfilled longing to be understood, and for them the feeling is intensified by the knowledge that they should experience this in marriage, but do not. Even so, singles often face the frustration of wishing they could bare their hearts to a fellow human and knowing they cannot.

4. A single person sometimes feels unneeded. This is really the flip side to one of the advantages of singlehood— "freedom." Because single people do not have families to provide for, they are often more free to come and go. The catch is that sometimes they feel too free. Nobody seems to depend on them in meaningful ways. A related problem which may occur in family settings is that singles sometimes feel others take advantage of them. Because they are "free," they are expected to do the things their married brothers and sisters don't want to do—they are needed, all right, but only for the dirty work. So it may seem, and unfortunately, sometimes so it is.

5. A single person usually experiences loneliness. Particularly where a single person has his own living quarters, he usually faces loneliness at some time or another. This is not to say that a single person should not live in his own quarters. There are advantages for some. Personalities vary. We simply are recognizing that loneliness is often a problem for singles.

6. A single person faces temptations for moral impurity. Everyone does. But in an age where temptations seem to be thrown at us at every turn, those who are single may at times feel overwhelmed. The problems are not simply from without, however. Inner urges are willing to collaborate with the temptations which come from without, and the tempted person sometimes seems to be at war with himself. This problem can vary in intensity from day to day, from one person to another, and from one period in life to another; but everyone faces it.

7. A single person will face a variety of struggles related to his personal identity. Marks of aging are rarely celebrated by anyone, but single people particularly often face the temptation to try to appear youthful and act youthful perpetually. A related struggle which some single people face is a drive to prove personal competence. This urge may be especially strong in a single person who has experienced a painful breakup in a dating relationship. The struggles with identity which single people face are always intensified if they resent their singlehood, and lessened if they honestly accept it.

More help for coping with these negative factors of singlehood will be given after we consider some of the positive factors.

### Positive Factors in the Experience of Singlehood

1. We have already noted that a single person normally does not have the responsibility of a family. This leaves him free, or "without carefulness," as Paul states in I Corinthians 7:32.

2. Because a single person does not have family responsibilities, he is normally more mobile and versatile. Changes in location and vocation are made more easily. A single person also is likely to adapt to conditions of necessity with less stress. For older single people, how-

ever, this adaptability often lessens. Particularly for older single women, major changes may appear threatening and may be very difficult to handle.

3. A single person is often able to give a high level of concentration to his lifework. In the chapter on dating, the suggestion was made to redirect sexual urges to other motivations. Often a committed, Christian single person is able to channel the energies and drives for companionship into his calling, or work. One day Jesus looked at His disciples and said, "Behold my mother and my brethren! For whosoever shall do the will of my Father which is in heaven, the same is my brother, and sister, and mother" (Matthew 12:49, 50). While Jesus perhaps had other meaning in focus as well, He seems here to reflect that His energies and goals for family and companionship had been redirected into His earthly mission. As a single person He could do that.

4. A single person is often able to help his family in ways married people would find very difficult. Elderly or invalid parents and handicapped siblings require care which single people often can provide. Sometimes, too, there is an economic or circumstantial need in a family which a single person chooses to meet instead of getting married.

5. A single person is often able to serve the Lord in ways which married people would find very difficult. Mission programs, Bible schools, and care centers often have positions which can be capably filled by single staff only, due to the nature of the assignment.

6. A single person generally has fewer material needs than a married couple with a family and thus is sometimes able to channel more resources, either of time or money, into the work of the Lord. Many Christian singles in times past have left an outstanding record of giving and sacrifice. Jesus and the Apostle Paul are two exam-

ples of singles whose simple material needs were an advantage for the kingdom of God. Jesus did not buy a house (Luke 9:58). Paul sometimes turned down reimbursement for his service (I Corinthians 9).

7. Single people sometimes gain insights into the Lord's grace and companionship which their married peers do not attain. Our needs often become the windows through which we see the glory of God more clearly. Joseph had been badly mistreated and was no doubt lonely as a single young man in Egypt. The Scriptures testify, however, "The LORD was with Joseph" (Genesis 39:2). In the strength of that relationship, Joseph resisted the improper advances of Potiphar's wife and demonstrated great wisdom in the ways of heaven. Whether our need is for wisdom, strength, companionship, or anything else, if we turn to the Lord, we come to understand and experience Him in increasing measure. Those who have no husband or wife have the potential for seeing the Lord supply their companionship needs, and with heavenly insight and joy they can say, "The LORD is my shepherd; I shall not want" (Psalm 23:1).

## WHAT SHOULD I AVOID?

Having looked at some of the negative and positive factors in singlehood, we will now consider some pointers for defusing the problems of singlehood and capitalizing on its potential. It is seldom enough to be told what to avoid in singlehood. We need also to know how to avoid these things. Along with each warning, therefore, positive suggestions are provided.

*1. Single people should avoid aloneness.* Single people certainly cannot always be in the company of others, but they should not withdraw from healthy social interaction.

- Develop and maintain a few close friendships with members of the same sex. David and Jonathan demonstrate this kind of friendship. If you have trouble having close friends, make a study of friendship. The Book of Proverbs contains many principles which will help you.
- Accept invitations to interact with families. Do not apologize or feel like an intruder in family settings. You need them and they need you.
- Entertain friends periodically, including families. This does not need to be for a meal if you do not consider yourself a cook. It can be for an activity such as a campfire singing time or for a picnic or cookout where others join in the meal preparation.
- Choose certain people whom you can look up to for counsel when you face major decisions. Aloneness in major decisions is one of the pitfalls single people easily fall into. In a healthy church community, this is unnecessary.
- Stay involved with your own family, when possible. Invite the nieces and nephews to a sleep-out or a cookie-baking day. You could deliver cookie plates to some elderly or needy families. One single lady who has no nieces or nephews does something special each year for her cousin's children or the children at her church. Also you might offer to help in the homes of your siblings with canning, gardening, housecleaning, etc.

2. *Single people should avoid becoming absorbed in themselves.* Single people face the problem of what could be termed "practical self-centeredness." This does not mean that they are more self-centered by nature than anyone else, but that the very nature of singlehood easily pulls them increasingly into themselves. Besides the danger of social isolation discussed in the last point are dangers such as self-centered goals in work, self-interest

119

in relationships, and self-indulgence in appetites and pleasure. Again, it must be recognized that anyone can have trouble in these areas. The point here is that where the single person does not have a family depending on him, such normal activities as buying, deciding, going, and doing are not as readily tested and tempered by the needs of others; hence, the potential is to become self-absorbed.

● Develop a practice of giving. This takes sensitivity. It requires a need-consciousness. And need-consciousness gets you to thinking of others. Giving does not need to be monetary. A single person can give by providing transportation, visiting sick or lonely people, sharing baked goods, or helping people with heavy work loads.

● Adopt certain children or older people to be special "family members." This is especially important for the single person who has no family in the vicinity where he lives. Beware of indulging them, however. Look for opportunities to help them in lasting ways. With children, for example, books are a better investment than candy. And the wise "foster" auntie or uncle will look for the neglected children to help, rather than those already well cared for.

● Ask the Lord to show you specific ways in which you can serve others in your work. Write down possibilities and make plans to carry out those which seem practical.

*3. Single people should avoid becoming bogged down in negative responses to their singlehood.* Some people choose to be single, and they generally have less struggles with negative responses toward singlehood than those who would prefer to be married. There are a number of pitfalls single people may fall into. Let's consider four specifically.

**a. Resentment.** Single people are sometimes angry about their "lot" in life. They seldom express this openly, but in their minds they are holding other people, themselves, life, or even God responsible for their unhappiness and frustrations as single people. They view themselves as victims. Many times their anger is not recognized as such. It may be suppressed or even denied. It may not feel like anger. It may not surface as anger about singlehood. It may surface as self-pity, as general irritableness, or as apathy.

This is NOT to say that all single people are angry. It is simply to recognize that resentment is a common human response when we do not get what we want. And it is also to say that resentment left unchecked has negative effects in our lives. Always.

We should note here that thoughtless remarks made by other people can trigger resentment. People may exclaim, "Haven't you *ever* dated?" Or, "How is it that someone as nice as you has never gotten married?" Such questions asked privately by a close friend may be fine. But asked in the presence of others, they may well cause embarrassment and stir resentment.

A single person who allows resentment to fester usually becomes less and less likely to marry happily, simply because resentment is self-focusing. Self-focused people are not attractive marriage partners.

●Accept the reality of your marital status. This does not necessarily mean saying, "I'd just as well face it, I'll never be married." It rather means saying, "I'd just as well face it, I'm not married."

●Make a list of positive things about your life. What do you have to be grateful for? What people have influenced your life for good? What do you enjoy which others in our world never will?

●Make a list of positive things about your singlehood. What has it enabled you to do? Where has it freed you to go? What has God taught you as a single person which you may not have learned as a married person?

●Honestly consider your thinking patterns. Are you resentful? Do you spend time thinking, "What if—?" Do you see yourself as a victim? Talk honestly to the Lord about this (you can be perfectly open with Him). Find characters in the Bible whom you can emulate. Study their lives. List verses which reflect proper thinking patterns about life. Read them. Memorize them. Put them in your own words. And then thank God for the change in perspective this brings to your mind.

**b. Purposelessness.** Another pitfall which may catch the single person is a lack of purpose or direction in life. This too is a negative thinking pattern—negative because it keeps single people in a frame of mind that breeds emptiness, discontent, and frustration.

Purposelessness can take several forms. Sometimes, especially in early singlehood where marriage is desired, the single person lives with a "waiting around" mentality. Work, living quarters, and even relationships are subconsciously viewed as temporary. This waiting around may easily cause single people to bypass opportunities for training, service, or learning because they are waiting for their situation to change before they make serious plans about life.

Unfortunately, a single person can spend years in humdrum. The waiting around settles into a scheduled but somewhat meaningless routine. And the single person begins to dread getting up, becomes bored with going to work, and overall, views life as dull and unfulfilling. Age only intensifies purposelessness.

●Learn to be a learner. Life offers a full curriculum in awareness and learning. Nature, people, relationships, work, and recreation present us with continued opportunities to broaden our understanding, test and strengthen our beliefs, expand our awareness, and develop our skills. For the Christian whose mind is continually being shaped by God's Word, this is not simply intellectual exercise, but growth in wisdom.

●Be alert for opportunities to increase your effectiveness. This is closely related to the above suggestion. But while learning can be a practice in all of life, sometimes we have specific educational or training opportunities. You should not necessarily take every such opportunity. You should, however, be alert to them and evaluate them, especially those which are in accord with your interests and would increase your effectiveness in the kingdom of God.

●Set goals. Short-term goals may include reading certain books or completing certain studies or projects. Long-term goals may focus more on such things as service or occupation. Your goals should be clear enough to keep you from floundering, yet flexible enough to allow for change as wisdom directs. Knowing what you are doing and where you are headed is an important part of avoiding purposelessness.

**c. Fantasy.** A third form of negative thinking is the unreal world of fantasy. Most people daydream at times. But some people daydream as an escape from reality. Single people may fall into this trap as a result of not accepting themselves, their situation, or life in general. Fantasy thinking at times is a form of compensation. If in the real world a single person feels rejected, he may create an unreal world where he is strong, intelligent, heroic, married, and well-liked. Even sensual fantasy may sometimes be a form of compensation—supplying in imaginations what seems to be missing in real life.

Fantasy, however, never fills the void of purposelessness. Where it is used as an escape, it occupies the mind with emptiness and allows it to grow more lazy. The gap between the real world and the imaginary only widens.

- The positive suggestions given for overcoming resentment and purposelessness apply here. You may wish to review them.
- Memorize Philippians 4:8. Verbally yield your mind to the control of the Holy Spirit. Set daily topics which you want your mind to be occupied with in its "free time." This takes practice, but it is rewarding as you learn to avoid being engulfed in fantasy.
- Identify distorted thinking. Wrong imaginations, particularly those which are self-gratifying, are built upon certain misconceptions. These misconceptions can often be identified by meditating upon Scriptures which address this problem.
- Expand your relationship with God. Underneath an enslavement to fantasy, a person usually is not finding the fulfillment in God which God intends. He is the rock bottom of purpose, meaning, and fulfillment in life.

**d. Denial.** A fourth negative thinking trap which single people are susceptible to is denial of certain realities. Sometimes a strong urge for companionship is denied. Subconsciously, the single person may think this is the only way to cope with it. The tendency to deny our true feelings is especially strong when trust has been betrayed and relationships have been broken. We may be tempted to pretend it doesn't hurt. Young women may try to "nullify their womanly responsiveness to men and develop a hardness or callousness that protects them from further possibilities of involvement and suffering."[6] Single men, too, may try to blot out their true feelings toward women and convince themselves that that part of them doesn't exist.

It does. Denial thinking only makes for cold spots in our relationships. When we try to safeguard ourselves from all hurt, we end up isolating ourselves from much joy.

- Be honest with yourself and with God about your inner feelings. Ask God to show you how to respond properly to your inner urges and desires.
- Look at your work, your calling, and particularly your service in God's kingdom as your "companion." Channel your energies, your abilities, and your commitment into God's service. Paul specifically describes this, apparently as his own experience. "He that is unmarried careth for the things that belong to the Lord, how he may please the Lord" (I Corinthians 7:32).
- Refuse to allow past hurts to keep you from present joys. There is risk in relating to others. But if we give ourselves to the main tasks of friendship—giving and caring—the risks are reduced.

4. *Single people should avoid chasing a potential partner.* Much as a man may want closeness of heart with a woman, he will tend to draw back from a woman who comes with her heart turned inside out. The same is true the other way around. It is not simply that love seeks the challenge of "winning" a heart. Underneath a pushy "love" is usually selfishness. Subconsciously, the person being chased senses this and fears the demands being made by the one doing the chasing.

- Focus on sincerity in your relationships. Talk, laugh, and interact with sincere interest in the well-being of others.
- Accept kindnesses from those of the opposite sex with genuine gratitude. Don't overplay the situation and don't flatter. A good way to test the sincerity of your gratitude is to ask yourself, "How would I respond if this were from someone of the same sex?"
- Keep in focus the reality that fulfillment and happiness in life do not depend upon one's marital status. We might paraphrase Proverbs 21:9 thus: "It is better to live singly in a small apartment, than to share luxury

with a companion I can't get along with."

●Respect the personhood of others. Really, being over-bearing is an invasion of privacy. If you feel interest in someone of the opposite sex, ask yourself honestly what attracts you. Try to describe the person objectively, considering both strengths and weaknesses. Develop consideration for how others feel, not simply how you feel about them.

5. *Single people should avoid using their friends to meet companionship needs in ways that violate healthy rules of friendship.* Single people who resent their sin-glehood are particularly susceptible to this pitfall. A single woman, for example, may unconsciously (or con-sciously) seek certain companionship needs in a male counselor—needs such as security, understanding, and personal closeness. Without understanding why, she may continually have a problem which she needs to discuss. Likewise a single man may seek to meet certain compan-ionship needs—needs such as acceptance and a sense of someone depending on him, by being a helper or defender of females. Without understanding his motivations, a man may continually find himself helping ladies out of their problems.

Using other people as surrogate companions can also occur in those of the same sex. Two single ladies or two single men may develop a dependence on each other and a possessiveness that actually hinders their freedom with others. Some single people have viewed the marriage of their single friends as a betrayal. Where this occurs, the former relationship likely had elements of compan-ionship substitution.

It is important to note here that these relationships can be unhealthy without there being anything overtly immoral about them. A woman may be finding compan-ionship in a man and he in her without realizing the emotional attachments involved. Either may be offended by any insinuation of impropriety in the relationship. The same may be true of friends of the same sex.

Where a relationship is motivated by companionship-seeking, however, rather than by healthy friendship-seeking, improper attachments may move from the unconscious to the conscious almost without awareness and catapult into sins which neither party intended. Countless heterosexual friendships testify to this danger, and it has also occurred in same-sex friendships.

- Where a personal problem requires repeated counseling, seek help from a spiritually mature person of the same sex, preferably someone older.
- Honestly assess the quality of your friendships. Have you made yourself dependent on one person in ways that are restrictive of that person? It is healthy to have close friends in which one can confide, but it is unhealthy to be possessive. And it is usually better to have several close friends than only one with whom constant closeness is sought.
- Build and maintain friendships on upbeat and positive interaction. You may wish to assess the topics you commonly discuss—are they characterized by those things which encourage and enrich, or do they focus on troubles and complaints? Proverbs 17:22 shows the effects of what we focus on in friendships. "A merry heart doeth good like a medicine: but a broken spirit drieth the bones."
- Seek the richness of God for your unfulfilled needs. "God is able to make all grace abound toward you; that ye, always having all sufficiency in all things, may abound to every good work" (II Corinthians 9:8). That is true for single people, for the widowed, for the fatherless, and for married people too.

**SNAPSHOT FROM LIFE**

*Mary was a young widow with four children. After living a number of years as a widow, she was again facing the possibility of companionship. Her perspective was noteworthy. She was seriously struggling with whether she ought to remarry because, she said, "God has become so precious in meeting my companionship needs that I am afraid I will lose that part of my relationship with Him when I don't need it anymore."*

*Mary did go on to remarry, but her words testify to the principle of God's all-sufficiency. "Ye are complete in him" (Colossians 2:10).*

## HOW CAN I SERVE?

Many of the positive suggestions in the former sections have reflected the potential which single people have. We have also noted that Paul, in writing to the Corinthians, recognized that single people can be special servants in the church. But now we want to consider more specifically some suggestions for capitalizing on the opportunities of singlehood.

Let's begin by putting the whole concept of service in Biblical perspective. A number of years ago an article appeared in the *Christian Focus* entitled "Here Am I— Serve Me." The gist of this revealing article was that the underlying motive in much Christian service today is to be ministered to. In various ways people want their "service" to serve them—to confirm their importance, to better their image, to satisfy their feelings and ambitions. The writer concluded the article by saying, "God gives us opportunity to devote our life to the glory of God.

We can go to our world for the same reason Christ came. As Christ lives his life in us, we are able to come fresh each day—not to be ministered to, but to minister."[7]

Such service is the product of love. Love for God first, and then commitment to the well-being of those we meet. It is the exercise of love, not the scope of our gifts or the position of our service, which gives us personal security and worth. "Though I have the gift of prophecy, and understand all mysteries, and all knowledge; and though I have all faith, so that I could remove mountains, and have not charity, I am nothing. And though I bestow all my goods to feed the poor, and though I give my body to be burned, and have not charity, it profiteth me nothing" (I Corinthians 13:2, 3). When love flows from our hearts, first upward and then outward, it frees us from absorption in ourselves and gives us the proper humility to say, "Here am I; send me" (Isaiah 6:8).

Given the proper attitude toward service, what can a single person do? Perhaps the best way to discuss this is to divide the possibilities into categories.

*1. Evangelism opportunities.* We could well wonder how the history of evangelism would be different had it not been for single people. Evangelism begins at home, but it moves out, and it must send out. Married people can go and do, but single people's flexibility and mobility have made them ideal to carry out many mission projects.

Missions in Third World countries continually need single staff. Single people often demonstrate easier adjustment to cultural differences than families do. Some assignments require travel, which for married people is restricted because of family needs. Some work includes sacrifice of comforts and conveniences, again more difficult for families.

Evangelism closer home likewise presents opportunities for single people. Singles are needed for street evangelism, including tract distribution, singing, and testifying. They also can be involved in follow-up work. In many areas, prisons are opening doors either for groups, or for one-to-one visitation.

We have already noted the impact of the Apostle Paul as a single evangelist. His work included travel and hardship in the extreme, but done as a service to Jesus Christ, it yielded joy and fulfillment. His testimony near the close of his life reveals no regrets or dissatisfaction. "I have fought a good fight, I have finished my course, I have kept the faith: Henceforth there is laid up for me a crown of righteousness" (II Timothy 4:7, 8).

*2. Care opportunities.* Many people in our world today need special care—old people, handicapped, sick, invalid, and bereft. Single people have opportunities here which many married people cannot properly fill.

Many of these care opportunities are inherently suited to women, particularly those women who have allowed their womanhood to be shaped by God's design. Qualities of "God's women" include quietness, meekness, faith, respect, reserve, wisdom, kindness, purity, and compassion, all operating with a modesty both in bearing and appearance. God's women are ideal for meeting the care needs of others.

Men can fill care positions, but women often have a special ministry here. Single women can find satisfaction in their womanhood in such care service. Marriage, in other words, is not the only end for which manhood and womanhood were created. Thank God for the countless single women who have given themselves as women to the nurture and care of others.

With this in view, it surely is no accident that the word for nurse, in both Hebrew and Greek, has female connotations. And it is likewise significant that even in modern times nurses in medical and care centers are predominantly women. Given the need for human care in a hurting world, single women have tremendous opportunities in providing care—opportunities which mothers with home responsibilities cannot provide and yet opportunities which bring fulfillment to the womanliness of many single women.

Not all care opportunities in our world are suited to the Christian. There are dangers both moral and spiritual in many professional nursing careers. God's single women who are interested in providing care as a service may well pass up money and prestige to offer their care where such dangers are minimized.

*3. Instructional opportunities.* A great area of need exists among God's people for competent teachers. In many ways it would seem that the vision for Christian schools has expanded far more rapidly than the vision for teachers. The day school, of course, is not the only teaching opportunity. Sunday schools and summer Bible schools likewise offer opportunities for teachers.

Both male and female teachers are needed, but various factors have seemed to accent the teaching role as a woman's work. Perhaps this has been because many of the teaching opportunities are for teaching children, and women do well with young children. But this emphasis on women teachers is in some ways unfortunate, not because women are incompetent, but because many men are forfeiting a privilege and a responsibility by not appropriating more of the opportunities to teach.

Seldom is teaching a high-paying work. This, too, may be a factor in not attracting many men. But even as care is in many ways suited to womanhood, so instruction is in many ways suited to manhood. The master/disciple relationship depicted in the New Testament (see, for example, Matthew 10:24,25) normally reflects a male master. Certainly women are not out of place as teachers, but

131

there is a special place for men to be teachers as well. They can find a tremendous sense of fulfillment, a fulfillment which no salary can buy, in leading the uninstructed to knowledge and the simple to wisdom. Teaching presents a wide open field for single men today who are committed to building homes for God and serving the church.

*4. Clerical opportunities.* God's work includes paperwork. Office workers are needed to a greater or lesser extent in virtually every organized effort of God's people. Writers, typists, coordinators, correspondents, and such workers can provide a tremendous service to the church, whether the work is evangelism, publication, aid, counseling, training, care, or any combination of these.

Where such work is going forward, it is usually being supported either altogether or in part by donated funds and volunteer workers. Sometimes "voluntary service" units are set up where workers' basic needs are provided for, with only a small stipend for personal use. Many single people have discovered the joy of sacrifice in such VS units.

Foreign missions, Christian publishing houses, Bible schools, disaster services, and counseling centers are all ministries which need personnel who value the opportunity of service above the accumulation of high wages. Many of these programs require other personnel in addition to clerical or office workers. Cooks, custodians, mechanics, pressmen, carpenters, production workers, as well as counselors, deans, and public relations personnel are often needed.

Sometimes the marital status of the worker is of no consequence. But there are other positions for which singlehood is highly preferable, if not a necessity. Some programs which work with troubled or delinquent youths, for example, use Spirit-filled single men or women to serve as role models. Some Bible schools and educational programs in missions have similar positions.

Having looked at many of the service opportunities available to single people, some may wonder, is it ever right for single people to hold normal jobs? Are they expected to view their singlehood as subject to special service? This matter has two sides to it. From one side, we might say, single people have the freedom to live as everyone else. But the other side is that we might well look at "everyone else" and question whether most people (most church members) are living with the kind of dedication to God and His kingdom which He asks of us, whether single or married.

Every child of God, whether single or married, ought to attempt to make his work a service to God and His people. This is so no matter how boring or trivial or earthly the work may seem. The farmer, the contractor, and the office worker, as well as the nurse, the teacher, and the missionary ought to be looking for the ways in which their work and their resources can serve the Lord and His church.

The service opportunities discussed here are not to say that the single person's opportunities are limited to these things, but to outline how single people can and do serve in ways which are unique to their singlehood. Further, these service opportunities are listed to show the richness that can and ought to be in the lives of the Lord's single people. There may be no legal wife or husband and no blood children, but "more [far more!] are the children of the desolate than the children of the married wife, saith the LORD. . . . For thy Maker is thine husband; the LORD of hosts is his name" (Isaiah 54:1, 5). When such a shout of joy comes from a single life, the Lord surely is imparting His life and having His way.

## HOW SHOULD THE HOME AND CHURCH RELATE TO SINGLES?

Earlier we noted that single people sometimes struggle with knowing just where they fit in. This occurs both at home and in the church. At home the single person often faces the following questions:

1) Should I continue to live with my parents or should I find my own living quarters?

2) If I stay at home, how responsible am I to my parents for such things as my schedule, my purchases, and my plans?

3) If I stay at home, should I have freedom to invite my friends, and on the other hand, if my parents invite guests or plan activities, am I always obligated to participate?

4) As my parents grow older and I begin to take over some of their responsibilities, do I always defer to them in times of difference, or should I begin to make decisions as I think best?

5) If my parents have need of care, am I more obligated than my married brothers and sisters to provide it?

Finding answers to these questions is not always easy. Situations vary considerably, and there are no pat answers for everyone. There are some general guidelines, however, that can help.

*1. Where single people live with their parents, there needs to be respect and consideration all around.* Single people need to respect their parents. While the parents are physically and mentally competent, they bear the major responsibility for the operation of the home, and singles living at home need to honor that. The other side of this is that parents need to respect the adulthood of their single children. Parents should counsel and advise, but they should respect the decisions and plans and needs of their adult children as they are able within the framework of their home.

When single people are living at home, boundaries of responsibilities and privileges should be clear. Parents can honor the adulthood of their single children in various ways—respecting the privateness of their room(s), turning certain responsibilities over to them, and being considerate in trying to mesh their plans and interests with plans and interests of the family. Families need to establish in practical ways who is responsible for what in the house—clothes, cleaning, washing, cooking, home decor, etc. If the single person is part of a family business, again, the lines of responsibility need to be clear. Kind, open communication is a must.

Single people living at home face special challenges when parents grow older and less competent. More guidance is given in Chapter 8 on this, but respect for the elderly includes understanding the struggles that accompany old age. Are single people more responsible than their married siblings at such a time? No. They may, however, be less tied to other responsibilities and thus be more available. If we view service as an opportunity rather than a chore, we are less apt to experience resentment, ill will, and inequity in such cases. Where the whole family, in other words, is service oriented—willing to help, sacrifice, and do good one for another—no one member will be as apt to try to compare his situation with another.

*2. Where single people move into their own living quarters, they should do so with vision and purpose, not in reaction to their home setting or simply to escape their parents.* Single people may feel the need for more quietness or more alone time. They may feel the need to learn the disciplines of operating their own living quarters. Or they may wish to be closer to other work or service opportunities. Repeated tension between single children and their parents does not always mean one or the other is in the wrong. It may be a signal that they should sit down and discuss options for more "space." To do this wisely and considerately can help all understand one another and, furthermore, may open doors to other arrangements which are good for both the parents and the single person. In such situations, parents should not view a single person's move to his own quarters as personal rejection.

*3. When a single person lives at home, both he and his parents should beware of unfairly assuming on one another.* Taking each other for granted is usually done subconsciously, and it is often related to the single person's emerging role as an adult. Parents sometimes forget that the single person is as much an adult as his or her married brothers and sisters and may give directions or assume control of the single adult's decisions and time and money in ways that seem demeaning and inconsiderate to the single person. A single person, on the other hand, may continue to relate as a dependent and irresponsible child—assuming that Mom will clean up the clutter and that Dad will fix whatever goes wrong, and that three meals and a clean bed will always be ready automatically, no problem.

Both the single person and parents need to consciously accept the adulthood of the single person. When a single person continues living at home, there is greater potential for ignoring the changing roles and taking one another for granted. It is wise periodically to talk about such things as plans (both short-term and long-term), expectations, financial arrangements, possible schedule changes, and work loads and responsibilities.

Understanding each other is basic for good relationships in the home. But single people also have relationships in the church, and they need to understand their role in the church and be understood as well. As we noted earlier, sometimes the "group" concepts in a church seem to take everyone into account except singles. There is the youth group, the young married group, the middle age group, and the senior citizens. But where does the single person fit in?

If congregations are going to tap the resources of single people effectively, they must operate in such a way that single people feel at home. Following are some pointers for accomplishing that:

*1. Maintain respect for singlehood.* The Apostle Paul referred to singlehood as a gift from God (I Corinthians 7:7). Jesus said that some remain unmarried for the kingdom of heaven's sake (Matthew 19:12). Both Jesus and Paul recognized that not everyone has the fortitude for such a calling, indicating that singlehood is to be respected.

Part of the responsibility for maintaining respect for singles comes back to the home—showing respect for those who are single and teaching children that respect. In a practical way this means refraining from joking about those who are unmarried and refraining from using derogatory names for them.

*2. Include single people in the normal functions of the church.* Within the church, singles should have the joy of participating in teaching, outreach, and work projects. A minister can help single people even as he helps married people by occasionally preaching messages related to their role, their needs, and their potential. He may do this by direct reference to singlehood or more indirectly by considering the lives of outstanding single people in the Bible.

Married people within the church can in very practical ways be the key to including single people in brotherhood. They can include them in the full range of congregational conversation—visiting, exhorting, discussing, and counseling. They can express appreciation for what singles do for the church. They can invite them to share in family activities.

*3. Single people should be included in church counsel.* Every church needs to make decisions, discuss plans, and set goals. Different groups have different procedures for arriving at a concensus. Some hold members meetings. Others have private interviews. Some have meetings with "heads of homes." Depending on the method used, single people are sometimes left out. If church leaders wish to fully harness the potential of single people in the church, they should see to it that single people (including widows) are somehow included in the plans and decisions of the church. If meetings are called with the heads of homes, various ones could be assigned to be in touch with the singles in the church, both to receive their input and to inform them of the outcome of meetings.

*4. Families may at times provide housing for single people.* Sometimes single people need to live away from home but are not necessarily wanting to have living quarters of their own. This is especially so for single people in service—their income may be minimal, and their stay rather temporary. Families and single people often find this arrangement a mutual blessing. The single person enjoys the benefits of a family, and the family enjoys the benefits of another adult.

Again, there must be mutual understanding and respect for one another. Furthermore, there needs to be discretion in relating to non-family members of the opposite sex. And there usually is need for flexibility in adjusting to those manners and customs which may vary from one family to another. While this sort of arrangement is normally temporary, there are times when it continues for an extended period of time and the single person becomes an "adopted" son or daughter in the family.

## SUMMARY

Single people have much potential. But the decisions they face and the responsibilities they carry are often not without struggle. In the Christian home and church, a person's sense of belonging and acceptance should not be based on his marital status. Every person is unique. Every person has his own strong and weak points. Every person is worth understanding.

Single people need to accept their singlehood and open themselves to those opportunities for service in the kingdom of God which are suited to their abilities and opportunities.

As the people of God understand single people and as single people learn to understand themselves, there can be a working together. Needs can be met both in singles and by singles as each finds his place in the family and in the church.

## THINKING TOGETHER

1. How are single people sometimes misread by their married peers?
2. To what extent should a single person discuss or acknowledge companionship desires? Where is the balance between being honest and being discreet?
3. What are some worldly concepts of singlehood which may be influencing Christians? How can these influences be counteracted? Does the church have unhealthy concepts of singlehood? Are singles in any way treated as second-class church members?
4. When a single person seems to be dwelling on the

negative factors of singlehood, what help can be given by friends?

5. When a single person is in a place of continued temptation, what is the best way to cope with it? How does one know if he should stand or run as Joseph did?

6. What are "chasing" tactics which single people should avoid? How can a single person be friendly and outgoing without being misjudged as wanting a partner?

7. When single people seem to be developing unhealthy ties in friendships, how can they be approached and helped without offending them?

8. How can the talent and potential of single people be used to greater advantage today? In what ways might we expect too much of single people?

## WORKING TOGETHER

1. As parents, discuss with your children the possibility of singlehood. Consider some of the single people in the Bible whom God used as His special servants. Make a list of possible ways of serving today as single people. Discuss also what the Bible teaches about fulfillment and happiness.

2. As a single person, do an evaluation of your singlehood. What particular sections of this chapter should you consider further? Are you allowing God to have your life? Arrange to discuss any unresolved questions or struggles with a trusted friend.

3. As a church or group, evaluate your use and acceptance of single people. Are they part of the church family? Are there ways in which single people are being neglected? List some possible steps the church could take for including single people more or for more adequately meeting their needs.

# 5

# MARRIAGE

## INTRODUCTION

The Bible refers to marriage as a mystery. As used in Scripture, of course, this word has nothing to do with clues and detectives. Rather, *mystery* refers to that knowledge which comes to us by revelation. There are some things about marriage which we know only because God has revealed these things to us.

Marriage, according to God's revelation, is a union. It bonds two people by invisible but real heart ties, so that in reality there is no such thing as detached love between man and woman. God intends that this principle be recognized and preserved by a lifelong commitment in marriage. This commitment, in turn, reflects the higher relationship of love and commitment between Christ and the church. Seeing it this way, we can readily understand why Paul wrote concerning marriage, "This is a great mystery" (Ephesians 5:32).

This also helps us to see why man, left to his own understanding, makes such a mess of marriage. Without God's revelation, men and women view marriage only through their own eyes and largely for immediate or at least foreseeable goals. Such things as personal happiness, need, and convenience guide them not only into marriage but out of it as well, as the situation seems best to them.

Against the flood of ruined marriages, Christians need to man the dikes courageously, both by word and example. What God has said is true. What God has instructed is right. Therefore, let what God has joined be lifelong.

## GOD'S PLAN—ONE MAN, ONE WOMAN, TILL DEATH

"Therefore shall a man leave his father and his mother, and shall cleave unto his wife: and they shall be one flesh" (Genesis 2:24). This is the first direction found in Scripture concerning marriage. After quoting this, Jesus added, "Wherefore they are no more twain, but one flesh. What therefore God hath joined together, let not man put asunder" (Matthew 19:6). And the Apostle Paul taught further, "For the woman which hath an husband is bound by the law to her husband so long as he liveth; but if the husband be dead, she is loosed from the law of her husband" (Romans 7:2). The Biblical direction is clear—one man, one woman, till death.

Such a union requires commitment. Both husband and wife are called to a self-sacrificing, faithful love in marriage which excludes all other partners. "Husbands, love your wives, even as Christ also loved the church, and gave himself for it. . . . So ought men to love their wives as their own bodies. . . . Let every one of you in particular so love his wife even as himself" (Ephesians 5:25, 28, 33). "And the wife see that she reverence her husband. . . . The aged women likewise . . . that they may teach the young women to be sober, to love their husbands" (Ephesians 5:33; Titus 2:3, 4).

Just what does it mean to love? The highly visible side of love in marriage is painted with bright colors, exhilarated feelings, and sweet dreams. Men and women are universally drawn to it because such love feels terrific. But underneath, there is much more to marital love than feeling. Love calls for commitment.

The surface of love looks not only attractive, but also easy, and it is. A husband easily loves his wife as long as she pleases him, and she naturally loves him in like manner. But nobody can always have his way. Life sooner or later presents tests which call for the deeper part of love—commitment. Plans go wrong, adversity sets in, sickness and accident register their demands, heavy responsibilities settle down upon them; and suddenly, newlyweds begin to see that love is not all floods of exhilaration. To be in love means giving, working, sacrificing, weeping, losing sleep, caring, forgiving, forbearing, adjusting, and then giving and giving and giving some more.

This is not to say that after the first year of marriage, love is no longer enjoyable. There is a depth of joy in a continuing love which is actually much richer than the first tastes. But the richer love is known only to those who are truly committed, to those who have been willing to move beyond the thrill of receiving love to the joy of giving love sacrificially.

And so it is only by practicing the principle of sacrifice that the true joys of marital love become a reality. And it is only by viewing love as a commitment that one is willing to sacrifice in love. It must be acknowledged, however, that the sacrifice and commitment of marital love are beyond the reason and power of fallen man. "Love is of God" (I John 4:7). Marital love calls both husband and wife to their knees in confession of their inability to love without the indwelling Christ. And it must also be acknowledged that Christ lives His life only in those who are emptied of self. In many ways, therefore, marital love becomes an exercise in brokenness and spiritual growth. Indeed, the richest dimensions of marital love are spiritual, for the source of an undying love is the undying Saviour.

## THE GODLY WIFE

We come now more specifically to the partners in the marriage relationship. A marriage, obviously, is made up of a husband and a wife, but what kind of husband and what kind of wife make for solid marriages? And must everyone fit the same mold? In modern times, the traditional image and role of the wife has been challenged to the point of a revolution in marriage concepts. We begin, therefore, by considering from the Scriptures a description of a godly wife.

"Who can find a virtuous woman? for her price is far above rubies. The heart of her husband doth safely trust in her. . . . She layeth her hands to the spindle, and her hands hold the distaff. She stretcheth out her hand to the poor; yea, she reacheth forth her hands to the needy. . . . She openeth her mouth with wisdom; and in her tongue is the law of kindness. She looketh well to the ways of her household, and eateth not the bread of idleness" (Proverbs 31:10ff).

"Every woman that prayeth or prophesieth with her

head uncovered dishonoureth her head: for that is even all one as if she were shaven . . . let her be covered" (I Corinthians 11:5, 6).

"Likewise, ye wives, be in subjection to your own husbands . . . whose adorning let it not be that outward adorning of plaiting the hair, and of wearing of gold, or of putting on of apparel; but let it be the hidden man of the heart, in that which is not corruptible, even the ornament of a meek and quiet spirit, which is in the sight of God of great price" (I Peter 3:1-4).

"The aged women likewise, that they be in behaviour as becometh holiness, not false accusers, not given to much wine, teachers of good things; that they may teach the young women to be sober, to love their husbands, to love their children, to be discreet, chaste, keepers at home, good, obedient to their own husbands, that the word of God be not blasphemed" (Titus 2:3-5).

That is the woman God admires. We can see just how far from God's ideal the modern woman has strayed by contrasting the popular ideals with a summary of God's ideals.

| By the world's standards, you are an ideal woman if: | By God's standards, you are an ideal woman if: |
|---|---|
| 1. You are pretty. | 1. You demonstrate a quiet and reserved manner. |
| 2. You have an attractive figure. | 2. You have a morally excellent character. |
| 3. You dress in a way that accents your feminine attractiveness. | 3. You demonstrate loyalty, support, and moral faithfulness to your husband. |
| 4. You have a suntan. | 4. You cover your hair with a veil and clothe your body simply and modestly. |
| 5. You have charm in speech and conduct. | 5. You demonstrate good economics and industry in |

| | meeting the food and clothing needs of your family. |
|---|---|
| 6. You develop an attractive smile, a quick laugh, and perpetual optimism. | 6. You avoid gossip and slander. |
| 7. You acquire education and skills above changing diapers and doing laundry. | 7. You bear children and provide a home atmosphere suited to godly training. |
| 8. You marry a man who is materially prosperous. | 8. You show hospitality and kindness, especially to the poor. |
| 9. You pursue a career of your own. | 9. Through life you develop a wisdom from which you can instruct and counsel younger women. |

One can readily see how the difference between the two sets of ideals affects home life in practical ways. Imagine home life with the worldly woman as the wife and you likely see schedules growing hectic, children becoming a nuisance, prepackaged meals, and the potential for arguments between husband and wife over cars, house furnishings, jobs, and a host of other things. Imagine home life, on the other hand, with God's woman, and you likely see more children, more love, more contentedness, better meals, more working together, and overall an atmosphere to which a husband loves to return at night and in which children feel secure.

## THE GODLY HUSBAND

What does the Bible say about the husband?

"Her husband . . . he praiseth her" (Proverbs 31:28).

"Husbands, love your wives, even as Christ also loved the church, and gave himself for it. . . . So ought men to love their wives as their own bodies. He that loveth his wife loveth himself. For no man ever yet hated his own flesh; but nourisheth and cherisheth it, even as the Lord the church. . . . Nevertheless let every one of you in particular so love his wife even as himself" (Ephesians 5:25ff).

"And ye fathers, provoke not your children to wrath: but bring them up in the nurture and admonition of the Lord" (Ephesians 6:4).

"Likewise, ye husbands, dwell with them according to knowledge, giving honour unto the wife, as unto the weaker vessel, and as being heirs together of the grace of life; that your prayers be not hindered" (I Peter 3:7).

"Let thy fountain be blessed: and rejoice with the wife of thy youth. Let her be as the loving hind and pleasant roe; let her breasts satisfy thee at all times; and be thou ravished always with her love. And why wilt thou, my son, be ravished with a strange woman, and embrace the bosom of a stranger? For the ways of man are before the eyes of the LORD, and he pondereth all his goings" (Proverbs 5:18-21).

Again, the Lord's ideals for a man are quite different from the ideals of the world. What sort of man is admired in the world today? What do men think is important for their happiness and fulfillment as men? Let's contrast the two views.

| By the world's standards, you are an ideal man if: | By God's standards, you are an ideal man if: |
|---|---|
| 1. You are handsome. | 1. You resist evil influences. |
| 2. You are tall and muscular. | 2. You show understanding, respect, and moral faithfulness toward your wife. |
| 3. You have a suntan. | 3. You show gentleness with children. |

147

| | |
|---|---|
| 4. You drive a sporty or classy car. | 4. You work hard and honestly to provide for the material needs of your family. |
| 5. You have plenty of money and can travel widely. | 5. You order your home with material simplicity, focusing on heavenly investment. |
| 6. You hold a position in business, preferably with a title. | 6. You give liberally to the poor, especially to widows. |
| 7. You can give evidence of economic success, such as extra vehicles, recreational equipment, etc. | 7. You lead your wife and children in the worship and praise of God. |
| 8. You are well-educated, well-dressed, and have plenty of long-term investments. | 8. You provide teaching and training whereby all in the family can grow spiritually. |
| 9. You marry a pretty woman. | 9. You demonstrate an understanding of God's ways whereby you can be a source of counsel and encouragement to others. |

Again, consider the difference in the home life of the man of the world and the man of God. With the man of the world, one can easily imagine plenty of money, but little family time and plenty of conflict and hurry. With the man of God, one senses love, leadership, understanding, and security.

For more insights, consider the man of the world married to the woman of the world described earlier. And for contrast, consider the godly man married to the godly woman. The relationship of the first couple will likely be full of things, but empty of joy, meaning, and fulfillment. The relationship of the second couple, on the other hand, will de-emphasize the material but be rich with love, security, and significance.

In considering God's ideals for husband and wife in marriage, perhaps the most controversial element for people of our day is the submission of the wife to her husband. Let's look specifically at what the Scriptures say. "But I would have you know, that the head of every man is Christ; and the head of the woman is the man; and the head of Christ is God" (I Corinthians 11:3). "Wives, submit yourselves unto your own husbands, as unto the Lord. For the husband is the head of the wife, even as Christ is the head of the church. . . . Therefore as the church is subject unto Christ, so let the wives be to their own husbands in every thing" (Ephesians 5:22-24).

The submission of the wife to her husband is commonly construed to mean she is of less importance, unequal, and under bondage. And this may well be the feeling of the wife where the husband is self-centered in his role, but it is far from true where he is godly and obedient to God's calling for him. The misconceptions about the husband/wife roles are rooted in misconceptions about personal fulfillment. In the mind of the world, freedom and fulfillment come in being able to do as we please, and thus, the position of the husband seems to be the position to be envied as the more fulfilling. In reality, freedom and fulfillment come in pleasing God and serving others. And thus neither husband nor wife has advantage over the other.

Is the husband free to do as he pleases? Never. He will be free and fulfilled only as he understands, loves, and provides for the needs of his wife and children.

Is the wife bound to cater to every whim of her husband? Is she obligated to support and encourage whatever he does in wisdom or in folly? According to the Scripture, a wife is under the authority of her husband.

149

She is to obey him, submit to him, and support him. The Bible does not make exception for things the wife disagrees with or dislikes or thinks unwise. There certainly is, however, a place for dialogue and appeals. And particularly if the husband is abusing his authority, she may appeal to authorities over him. But there are factors more important to the above questions than a specific yes or no answer. If a wife is willing to view her support of her husband as "unto the Lord," she can gain a freedom in her responses which cannot be brought into bondage. Furthermore, as she views her role as one of support— helping him to be the best husband he can be—and as her actions, words, and entire attitude enter into that supportive role, she will likely find her husband more considerate of her, and she will have a wisdom from which to respond to specific problems.

The arrangement of loving leadership on the part of the husband and loving support on the part of the wife is so important to the Lord that He has given opportunity for expression of it. According to I Corinthians 11, the wife's long hair and veiled head and the husband's short hair and unveiled head give testimony to his submission to Christ and her submission to him.

Many are the knotty questions and painful problems when husbands and wives do not honor God's instructions to them. Husbands feel threatened and manipulated, and wives feel misunderstood and bullied. Rather than discuss all the wrong ways to be husband and wife, let's look at four principles which must be understood in working through marriage problems.

*1. Only those who follow God's plan will experience God's blessing.* Man's reasoning tends to be pragmatic, geared to the situation. Certainly, we must consider situations, but with a view to honoring what God has said. The husband is to lead; the wife is to support. Where he is weak, she can help him to be strong, but she can never step into his place. Where she is out of place, he can instruct, encourage, rebuke, love, and provide for, but he can never step beyond the bounds of Christ's example. He never has the "freedom" to force his wife to support him. Again, honoring God's plan is the only way to have God's blessing.

*2. Where either the husband or the wife is not what God intends, it places pressure on the other.* An unloving husband is hard to honor and support. An unsubmissive wife is hard to love and show consideration toward. Any partner, therefore, who has a complaint against the other should honestly and prayerfully take personal inventory. "Am I being what God intends me to be?"

*3. The most effective way to help an out-of-place partner is to be for all you're worth the godly partner God calls you to be.* Seldom will an unsubmissive wife respond well to being told to submit. But a husband may well win her honor and submission by redoubling his love, consideration, and understanding toward her. Seldom will a harsh, dictating husband respond favorably to reminders from his wife that he is to love her. But a husband "may without the word be won" by the loving support and godly submission of his wife (see I Peter 3).

*4. Although mistakes may be made in choosing a marriage partner, eligible partners are bound by marriage for life.* We live in a world of haste and folly, and thus in a world of hurt and trouble. Too many today are waking up after the intoxication of the marriage altar and wondering how Cupid could have turned out so stupid. Their life hereafter is definitely for worse. What can be done about a bad mistake in marriage?

"When thou vowest a vow unto God, defer not to pay it; for he hath no pleasure in fools: pay that which thou hast vowed. Better is it that thou shouldest not vow, than that thou shouldest vow and not pay. Suffer not thy mouth to cause thy flesh to sin; neither say thou before the angel, that it was an error" (Ecclesiastes 5:4-6).

God calls us to faithfulness to our vows. Even though we may have made a mistake in choosing a companion, after marriage we must accept the reality that that companion is the only legitimate partner for us. By honoring our vows, we may well need to suffer, but God is willing and able to work mightily in behalf of those who commit their cause to Him.

## BASIC NEEDS AND HOW TO MEET THEM

When God created man and woman, He created them to complement each other. He indicated this when He said, "It is not good that the man should be alone; I will make him an help meet for him" (Genesis 2:18). God formed woman to round out man's incompleteness, so that physically, socially, emotionally, intellectually, and even spiritually, male and female would not be rivals, but mates.

Much of the tension and conflict in marriage today, as well as in other relationships, comes directly from an emphasis on rights and a de-emphasis on responsibilities. When the two are reversed, however, and marriage partners focus on personal responsibilities, they are less apt to fight and more free to serve. Instead of each being concerned with getting his way, each will be concerned about meeting the needs of the other.

This section focuses on some of the basic needs of husbands and wives. It is for those who wish to take seriously their responsibilities in the marriage relationship.

## Basic Needs of a Wife

The understanding of a wife's needs as opposed to her husband's will admittedly rest in the understanding of womanhood and manhood and the differences between the sexes. Cultural ideas about men and women have fluctuated over the years. At the present, equality has so carried the day that to suggest differences between male and female is rather unpopular. But to ignore differences is both unrealistic and unscriptural.

Not all the cultural ideas about male and female, of course, were correct before the twentieth century either. God made male and female, however, and they are not the same. Furthermore, their differences are not matters of worth or importance. To say that men tend to look at a project as a way of getting something done and that women tend to look at the same project as a way of building a relationship is not to say that one is better than the other. Rather, it is to recognize that men and women are different.[1]

What, then, are the needs of a wife?

*1. A wife needs someone who understands her.* "Likewise, ye husbands, dwell with them according to knowledge . . ." (I Peter 3:7). This Scripture speaks to the tendency of a husband to be preoccupied with interests outside of his home and marriage and to ignore things about his wife which are important to her. Every woman has habits, fears, tendencies, likes, and dislikes. In marriage, she feels the need to be understood, and the husband demonstrates his understanding of her by living with consideration toward her. Notice the Scripture does not say simply that a husband should know his wife, but that he should live with her according to his knowledge of her.

*2. A wife needs someone who accepts her as she is.* This is but an extension of the need to be understood. The

Scriptures speak of the intimacy of marriage as "knowing" one another. Marriage is disclosure, letting each other know the heart and mind—"the real you." Such disclosure can be either painful or wonderful, depending on acceptance. A husband sends clear messages of rejection to his wife by such actions as comparing her negatively with other women, ridiculing her personality, and overloading her with responsibility and then criticizing her for failure. Acceptance does not mean approving of everything a wife does or is, but it recognizes a wife's unique personhood and gives her the support to become all that God intended her to be.

*3. A wife needs someone who cherishes her.* This is again a step beyond accepting. Both accepting a wife and cherishing her depend upon understanding her. Cherishing is but another way of saying a wife needs to be loved. Love is probably the most basic need of a wife in marriage. And certainly it is no accident that repeatedly in the New Testament the instruction to the husband is "Love your wife." Paul wrote, "So ought men to love their wives as their own bodies . . . for no man ever yet hated his own flesh; but nourisheth and cherisheth it, even as the Lord the church" (Ephesians 5:28, 29). The word *cherish* here means literally "to warm, as a bird warms its young." A wife needs to be understood. She needs to be accepted as a person. But she needs also to experience the tender affection of her husband. She needs the security of being held close to the heart of her husband, not as a mere plaything, but because she is counted dear and priceless.

We should note here that meeting these first three needs is a cumulative process. Each depends on the former. A husband cannot accept his wife if he does not understand her, and he cannot cherish her if he does not understand and accept her.

*4. A wife needs someone who demonstrates strength and wisdom in leadership.* "Likewise, ye husbands, dwell with them according to knowledge, giving honour unto the wife, as unto the weaker vessel, and as being heirs together of the grace of life; that your prayers be not hindered" (I Peter 3:7). When the Bible refers to a woman as "the weaker vessel," it does not necessarily mean weaker in every way. And as noted earlier, it does not mean she is inferior. It does reflect, however, that women are drawn to strength in men, provided it is a considerate strength. The tendency of men is to flaunt their strength in ways that dominate women, and thus to exploit women's weakness. Such "strength" loses its attractiveness fast. A husband uses his strength as God intended by working for the protection of his wife and children, by shielding them from hardship and harm whether physical, emotional, or spiritual, and overall by guiding the home with consideration for them.

*5. A wife needs someone who is faithful.* "Set me as a seal upon thine heart, as a seal upon thine arm: for love is strong as death; jealousy is cruel as the grave: the coals thereof are coals of fire, which hath a most vehement flame" (Song of Solomon 8:6). Intimate love calls for the exclusion of all others. Thus, there is a very proper jealousy in love which says, "I belong to you, and you belong to me." A wife needs the security not only that her husband loves her, but that he loves no one else in the same way. Of course, there is an improper jealousy rooted in selfishness. This jealousy demonstrates itself in suspicion and fear, and in effect, puts a stranglehold on a husband. But nonetheless, a wife needs a faithful husband, and a husband who understands this need in his wife carefully guards her trust. He does not flirt with other women nor look at raunchy magazines. He guards his eyes, his humor, his heart. And he focuses his love faithfully upon the ONE woman in the world who is his wife.

### Basic Needs of a Husband

In many ways, the needs of a husband are the counterpart to the needs of his wife. God made the woman with a view to male needs (Genesis 2:18), and thus He equipped her with just the proper resources for meeting those needs. So just what are the needs of a husband?

*1. A husband needs someone who depends on him.* God has given to the man the responsibility of leadership in the home. There is something about the dependence of a wife which calls to the manliness of her husband. His very malehood wants to provide, to nurture, to care for, and to protect; and he finds satisfaction and fulfillment in meeting the needs of his wife. Even as the husband can misuse his strength to dominate, so the woman can misuse her weakness and dependence to manipulate. Many are the women who have used their tears, their headaches, and their whining to play upon the malehood of their husbands in order to get their own way. Such "weakness" gets old fast. A wise wife allows her husband to be her provider, but does not control him from beneath.

*2. A husband needs someone who accepts him as he is.* Everyone has a basic need for acceptance, and inasmuch as marriage is the deepest level of human friendship, it has the most potential for meeting that need. It likewise has the greatest potential for rejection. Nagging criticism and discussing a husband's failures with others are probably the two most common ways a wife signals rejection of her husband. Acceptance, as noted earlier, does not necessarily mean complete approval. It does mean recognizing a person for who he is, as opposed to fighting that reality, and supporting him in becoming all that God intends him to be.

*3. A husband needs someone who encourages and supports him.* In describing His intentions in making a wife for Adam, God said, "I will make him an help meet for him" (Genesis 2:18). The woman is a "help." This does not mean she is a tagalong, someone who comes in handy at times, but that she was designed to fill a necessary role as man's mainstay. Her mind, her will, her energies are hers to use, not in competition with him, but in union with him to complement his mind, his will, and his energies. Certainly, much of the wife's potential to encourage and support depends upon the husband's willingness to talk and work together. But a wise wife will recognize that every husband has weaknesses, and she will not allow her support and encouragement to mope continually at the foot of his failures. She will instead clearly ally herself with him so that both his strengths and his weaknesses are improved by her presence in his life. A very practical way in which a wife can encourage her husband is by her gratitude. Her smile, her expressions of thanks, her willingness to find joy even in difficult circumstances will fill one of the most basic needs in his life.

*4. A husband needs his wife's womanhood in the home atmosphere.* "Every wise woman buildeth her house: but the foolish plucketh it down with her hands" (Proverbs 14:1). "The aged women likewise . . . that they may teach the young women to be sober, to love their husbands, to love their children, to be discreet, chaste, keepers at home . . ." (Titus 2:3-5). While the husband is responsible for leadership in the home, he is inadequate by himself to build the home. He needs the womanhood of his wife to establish an atmosphere of order, beauty, cleanliness, and care. Contrary to modern thought, homemaking is not a dull, servile work for lower-intelligence women; it is a full-time, lifetime responsibility which demands creativity, intelligence, and management skills of the highest caliber. The womanhood of a wife is in many ways the heart of the home and, as such, is the fulfillment of her husband; and the career-minded wife leaves a void both in her home and in her husband which nothing can replace.

*5. A husband needs someone who is faithful.* "Who can find a virtuous woman? for her price is far above rubies. The heart of her husband doth safely trust in her" (Proverbs 31:10, 11). Fidelity is imperative on both sides of the marriage relationship. Even as faithful love stirs the sweetest emotions in human relationships, so unfaithfulness stirs the bitterest emotions. There is probably nothing so devastating to a marriage as the realization that a third party has invaded the sacrosanct realm of intimacy. Wives need faithful husbands; husbands need faithful wives. A godly wife will guard her manners, her speech, and her appearance, reserving her womanly charm and beauty for her husband alone. "In like manner also, that women adorn themselves in modest apparel, with shamefacedness and sobriety; not with broided hair, or gold, or pearls, or costly array; but (which becometh women professing godliness) with good works" (I Timothy 2:9, 10).

Understanding one another's needs in marriage is the first step love takes toward meeting those needs. If we focus on our needs rather than on those of our partner, we may easily stumble in self-pity rather than move ahead in love. Much of the success in marriage depends upon the willingness to give ourselves to meeting the deepest needs of one another. This is the exercise of love, and love is the cement of marriage.

## COMMON ERRORS IN MARRIAGE

The pitfalls surrounding marriage are many, and the pressures to fall into them seem to increase as life grows more mechanized and streamlined. Many are the mistakes marriage partners can make nowadays; we will consider a few of the more prevalent errors.

*1. Financial bondage.* The pressure is on to buy and have and consume. What is not affordable now is payable later. So we are told. All too soon, married couples find themselves neck-deep in debt and perhaps at the same time only ankle-deep in love. In the late 1980s, the average indebtedness of a 28-year-old in the U.S. was $66,000. Forty percent of Christian couples were paying at least $2,000 per year in interest, excluding mortgage interest.[2] One survey showed that 20 percent of "Christian" couples were on the verge of divorce and that 90 percent of these couples pointed to financial problems.[3]

What is financial bondage? It is when we cannot do what is right or proper for ourselves, for our family, or for the Lord because of overriding interests or obligations in financial matters. Bondage may come by the pressure of debt, unpaid bills, or business entanglements. It may, on the other hand, be the result of wrong financial attitudes such as desire for wealth, worry over investments (or the lack of them), or a willingness to fudge in dealing with others.

Staying out of financial bondage is possible only by a steadfast commitment to the principles of God's Word and by using common sense. Consider the following pointers:

- Seek God's kingdom above all else.
- Be honest, fair, and generous in all financial dealings.
- Value family togetherness and upbuilding activities above financial gain.

●Use finances as belonging to God. (You are manager, not owner.)

●Look for opportunities to invest in eternal ventures, not earthly.

●Avoid all material involvements which rival spiritual goals.

●Avoid partnerships.

●Avoid borrowing, especially for consumable or fast depreciating items.

●Do not use credit cards unless you pay accounts off each month.

●Never co-sign.

●Pay bills promptly.

●Pay taxes honestly.

●Work hard, live simply, give liberally, save wisely.

*2. Irresponsibility.* According to the Bible, the husband is responsible to lead out in the home and to provide for the needs of his wife and family. The wife is responsible to support her husband in his work and to keep (literally, be a guardian of) the home. Problems are caused in marriage when responsibilites are neglected. A husband who fails to hold a steady job, for example, or racks up unpaid bills, inevitably creates insecurity in his wife and problems for the marriage. A wife who leaves the house in a perpetual mess or who spends undue time visiting, hobbying, shopping, or otherwise running here and there causes frustration for her husband and children.

Problems are also caused in marriage by either partner attempting to fill the other's role. Some husbands attempt to dictate household procedures in a way that makes the wife feel her territory is invaded. A wife at times may try to control her husband, or take charge of his incompetence in such things as financial management and family worship. The problems in the long run always multiply by this role shifting, because at heart

**SNAPSHOT FROM LIFE**

*Dave and Janet had a shaky marriage from the start. Neither was truly a Christian when they were married, although they both had a religious background of sorts.*

*Shortly into their marriage, Dave was unfaithful. Janet didn't discover this until after they both became Christians and Dave wanted to clear himself. Insecure both personally and in their marriage, Janet nearly fell to pieces. She left the house in perpetual disaster. Meals were irregular, disorderly, and unsatisfying.*

*Dave, meanwhile, in spite of wanting to follow God, had his own problems with irresponsibility. He wanted to have family worship, but the time was never right and the mood was seldom suitable. He wanted to find steady work, but he had back problems, and things never worked out right, and Janet had developed such a jealousy that she felt insecure if he worked away from home.*

*Needless to say, the financial pressures added to their struggles.*

*By both focusing on the other's lack of responsibility, each was avoiding his own, and thus each was making it harder for the other.*

it becomes a working against rather than a working together. Many a child, when grown, will testify to the struggle of honoring a father or mother who is out of place.

Following are a few pointers:
- Talk about responsibilities. Ask each other to describe any areas of neglect. Listen. Ask for pointers in filling

personal responsibilities.
- If there is disagreement about responsibilities, talk *together* with a minister about the problem.
- Pray about your responsibilities.
- If there has been a pattern of irresponsibility, start with improvement on one thing at a time. Make yourself accountable to someone for regular checkup and encouragement sessions.
- Write out your commitment to your responsibilities. Be reasonable, but be specific.
- Where your partner is weak or neglectful, consider how you can be supportive without stepping into that responsibility. Make a list of suggestions.

*3. Lack of communication.* This problem is compounded by the hurried pace of the modern age. Husbands and wives rush in the morning, rush through the day, rush through supper, rush away for the evening, rush home, and rush to bed. Hurry always *increases* the possibility of misunderstandings and *decreases* the possibility of discussing them. It is unfair to any marriage to regularly let the problems of the day accumulate until bedtime and then try to resolve them. Unfortunately, some couples don't even try to resolve their problems. Married life becomes an existence in the same quarters, a place where communication is seldom deeper than hello and good-bye.[4]

While lack of communication is harmful to the total marriage, the wife generally notices it first and minds it most. A wife needs to hear the sound of her husband's voice; she needs to have the assurance of her husband's full attention. When a husband is uncommunicative, his wife feels insecure and left out. When he does not give her his full attention, she feels unimportant. The husband tends to respond to these feelings with *reason*—his wife is assuming things unfairly, she needs to relax and quit getting emotional. He is often right that she is assuming wrongly, but he is far from right in believing this is simply her problem. A wife's communication needs are often different from her husband's and he is responsible for meeting her needs. Sometimes this means setting a slower pace, sometimes it means missing the evening newspaper, and sometimes it means consciously taking time to talk about things.

On the other hand, a wife needs to consider her husband and his needs as well. Sometimes pressing duties mean a husband cannot talk immediately. Sometimes a husband is under the weight of a decision or responsibility in which he needs thinking time, and he may find it hard to keep his mind on his immediate surroundings. If talk time is needed in a full schedule, setting a time limit may be helpful. A husband's anxiety level may rocket out of control if his wife says, "Let's talk," and he knows he has only ten minutes.

Consider these pointers for bettering husband/wife communication:

- Keep work schedules trim. (Avoid jobs which demand prolonged absences.)
- Arrange for times when you can be alone other than nighttime (eating out on occasion, gardening, walking, etc.). Frequency of these activities should be mutually agreed upon.
- Refuse to harbor resentment toward one another.
- Commit yourselves to working through misunderstandings and disagreements.
- Be honest and open. Avoid communicating negative feelings indirectly.
- Do not make important decisions without openly discussing them.
- Postpone decisions where there is strong disagreement. (A husband should avoid overriding his wife's objections

in decisions, even when she has trouble stating her reasons. Many godly husbands have testified to God protecting them from a wrong decision through a wife's intuitive objections.)
•Never share information with others which betrays trust.
•Never belittle, rail, ridicule, or nag.
•Regularly express gratitude, commendation, and encouragement.
•Be polite and courteous. Say "please," "thank you," "pardon me," etc.

*4. Improper ties with the past.* One of the most painful problems in marriage is the problem of past relationships interfering with present loyalties. The most common example is where either husband or wife has parental ties which override loyalty to the marriage. The Bible describes marriage as "leaving" and "cleaving." For a husband and wife to join properly to one another, they must properly leave their parents. This does not mean forsaking parents in a hostile sort of way. It does mean that a husband finds in his wife what once he found in his mother, and that she gives to him the loyalty which she once gave to her parents.

In giving sons and daughters in marriage, parents must learn to release their children. While giving advice is proper, particularly when it is requested, interference in decisions violates God's order. The interference may come through emotional pressure, bribery, or visiting too frequently. Whatever the distance in miles between the two families, a proper distance must exist in loyalties so that there is freedom in decision making.

The following pointers may help:
•Separate living quarters should be maintained and respected.
•A wife should avoid regularly testing her husband's

164

ideas with her father's.
- A husband should avoid regularly suggesting that his wife check with his mother about how to do things.
- If counsel is sought from parents, a couple should go together.
- Both husband and wife should avoid saying, "That's not how my mom or dad used to do it." The husband should avoid a habit of saying, "My mom always. . . ." And the wife should avoid a habit of saying, "My dad always. . . ."
- Activities with in-laws should not demonstrate favoritism.
- A persistent problem with parents interfering should be discussed with them frankly but kindly.

## VIOLATIONS OF GOD'S PLAN

As we noted at the beginning of this chapter, the demands of marital love are beyond the power of fallen man. This helps us to understand why violations of love are so common in our world. Husbands get tired of self-centered wives, and wives get tired of self-centered husbands. Human love, however, has an underlying yearning for commitment, and therefore, people continue to get married. But many people are unwilling to pay the price of finding the deeper rewards of love, and so they skim what romance they can off the top of a relationship and move on to another. In the wreckage of their past relationships lie not only their own unfulfilled dreams, but the scarred lives of friends, spouses, and children.

### Adultery—Despising the Sacred

Both Old and New Testaments clearly describe adultery as sin. "Thou shalt not commit adultery" (Exodus 20:14). "And the man that committeth adultery with

165

another man's wife, even he that committeth adultery with his neighbour's wife, the adulterer and the adulteress shall surely be put to death" (Leviticus 20:10). "Now the works of the flesh are manifest, which are these; Adultery, fornication, uncleanness, lasciviousness. . . . They which do such things shall not inherit the kingdom of God" (Galatians 5:19,21).

Marriage was designed by God for our good, not only socially, but spiritually as well. To violate the covenant of marriage, therefore, is to despise that which is sacred. It does so in at least three ways:

*1. Adultery violates a sacred commitment.* The one who is guilty of adultery is saying in effect, "I don't care what I promised to you."

*2. Adultery tramples a sacred trust.* Marriage is not only what one is committed to, but what one has committed to him. Adultery, then, despises both a commitment and a trust. In effect, it says, "I don't care what you gave to me."

*3. Adultery pollutes a sacred union.* Marriage is not merely a covenant between two parties, but a union which God seals and records and for which He holds couples accountable. The marriage vows, in other words, are not only a matter between a man and a woman, but between them and God. Because of God's purposes in marriage, the union is precious not merely on a human level, but precious to God as well. Adultery despises what God considers important. In effect, it says, "I don't care what God thinks about my marriage."

Whatever the thrill of the moment, adultery in its full implications brings misery beyond description. Guilt, hurt, alienation, strain, heartache, and fear, like an enemy horde, leap into the adulterer's life. As one woman said, "Though you can find forgiveness, you pay and pay and pay." The proverb writer said it well. "Whoso com-

166

mitteth adultery with a woman lacketh understanding: he that doeth it destroyeth his own soul. A wound and dishonour shall he get; and his reproach shall not be wiped away" (Proverbs 6:32, 33).

## *Divorce—A Spirit of Treachery*

In the Bible, divorce is described as a "putting away" of a companion after having married or having been betrothed to him or her. Normally, the putting away is described as a man putting away his wife, but the reverse is also forbidden in Mark 10:12. Under the Law of Moses, divorce was permitted under certain conditions, but Jesus clearly said, "For the hardness of your heart he wrote you this precept" (Mark 10:5). Whereupon, Jesus just as clearly reinstated the original purpose of God. "But from the beginning of the creation God made them male and female. For this cause shall a man leave his father and mother, and cleave to his wife; And they twain shall be one flesh: so then they are no more twain, but one flesh. What therefore God hath joined together, let not man put asunder" (Mark 10:6-9). The divine directions are clear—one man, one woman, for life—no divorce.

Although God permitted divorce under certain conditions in the Old Testament, He clearly testified against the practice. "The LORD hath been witness between thee and the wife of thy youth, against whom thou hast dealt treacherously: yet is she thy companion, and the wife of thy covenant. . . . Therefore take heed to your spirit, and let none deal treacherously against the wife of his youth. For the LORD, the God of Israel, saith that he hateth putting away" (Malachi 2:14-16).

Why is divorce wrong? Following are seven reasons why.[5]

*1. Divorce is against the clear Word of God.* "What

therefore God hath joined together, let not man put asunder" (Mark 10:9)

*2. Divorce is against the character of God.* Notice in the above verses from Malachi 2, God calls divorce "treachery." God is faithful. What He promises, He does. Divorce is all in contrast to the faithful character of God. Love calls for loyalty. Those who divorce betray this sacred commitment of love, demonstrating, instead, unfaithfulness and treachery. The impact of Malachi 2, however, is not primarily broken marriage vows, but Israel's broken covenant with God. In graphic language, God demonstrated that covenant breakers with men become covenant breakers with God. Where the spirit of treachery is in human relationships, in other words, it will be in one's relationship with God. Small wonder that God says, "I hate putting away."

*3. Divorce demonstrates hardness of heart.* Jesus frankly declared that divorce was permitted "for the hardness of your heart" (Mark 10:5). To this could be added the witness of many marriage counselors. The underlying problem in marriage conflict is self-centeredness. Divorce is but the continued expression of a hardened heart. It takes humility, love, and brokenness to resolve marriage problems and to experience the oneness intended in marriage.

*4. Divorce hurts one's partner.* Treachery is a betrayal word. Where there is betrayal, there is hurt. Trust and loyalty are intrinsically bound up in love, and divorce knifes mercilessly through those bonds, causing hurt. Always. It is impossible to divorce a legitimate relationship between man and woman as an act of love and compassion. Attitudes of hate and hurt are always present.

*5. Divorce hurts children and scars their lives.* Following is the testimony of one daughter whose parents divorced:

"Please, please don't sign them! O, Daddy, don't sign those papers!" My pleadings must have added greatly to my father's burden, but the pen held firmly in his hand continued to write his name on the final paper.

Thus was my world destroyed and I with it, for on that day something died in the heart of a child. . . .

Bitter protests and tears were vain, for divorce courts do not consider human hearts when they collect their dues. Mother and Daddy were to be "free," but we children were not. I became a slave to despair. The quarrels? They ceased, to be sure, but cries of heartbroken children took their place, and I for one, longed to hear those quarrels if only it meant I could have my mother and daddy back! . . .

I wish I could take the hand of every parent harboring the thought of divorce and lead you back with me into the valley through which I have come. If the hurt of an innocent child's heart, the bitter shock of a tender life, the tears of the unwanted, misplaced child, the horror and gloom could be called to witness in the divorce courts, no child would again have to walk the dreadful road that starts with the signing of those final papers in the divorce courts. Instead, the tears would become your own and in the valley you would realize that the ones who suffer in divorce and remarriage are the innocent children.[6]

6. *Divorce creates further barriers in reconciliation.* In his first letter to the Corinthians, Paul warns against even separating from an unbelieving partner, but then says, "If she depart, let her remain unmarried, or be reconciled to her husband: and let not the husband put away his wife" (I Corinthians 7:11). While we are not discussing separation here, we can readily see that Paul

instructs towards reconciliation, not away from it, even with unbelieving partners. Divorce is like adding a padlock to the door through which an unfaithful partner has gone. Where reconciliation is the objective, divorce cannot be an option.

7. *Divorce perpetuates sin.* People choose divorce as an answer to their marriage problems. But it is impossible to correct problems through disobedience to God. Divorce always creates more problems. Jesus noted specifically that divorce is a cause of adultery (Matthew 5:32). No one can keep the consequences of sin to himself, and this seems especially true with divorce. Sin leads to sins, and those sins multiply in the generations to come. Studies have shown that those who come from divorced homes have a higher rate of divorce than those whose parents remained faithful. Sin simply snowballs.

### Remarriage—A Condition of Adultery

Much as divorce is sinful, remarriage following divorce is yet more sinful. It is a step further against the moral laws of God. The New Testament is consistent and clear in describing remarriage while one's companion is still living as sin. Consider the following verses:

"And he saith unto them, Whosoever shall put away his wife, and marry another, committeth adultery against her. And if a woman shall put away her husband, and be married to another, she committeth adultery" (Mark 10:11, 12).

"And I say unto you, Whosoever shall put away his wife, except it be for fornication, and shall marry another, committeth adultery: and whoso marrieth her which is put away doth commit adultery" (Matthew 19:9).

"Whosoever putteth away his wife, and marrieth another, committeth adultery: and whosoever marrieth her that is put away from her husband committeth adultery" (Luke 16:18).

170

"So then if, while her husband liveth, she be married to another man, she shall be called an adulteress: but if her husband be dead, she is free from that law; so that she is no adulteress, though she be married to another man" (Romans 7:3).

These Scriptures consistently describe remarriage as adultery. The Greek verb tense translated "committeth adultery" shows present continuous action, suggesting not simply an act of adultery, but a practice of adultery. The verse in Romans likewise shows that while a person's partner lives, remarriage is not a valid marriage, but an adulterous condition. There is an act of adultery—the sin of sexual union while married to another. There is also the condition of adultery—the sin of a marriage relationship with another while one's true marriage partner is living.

With such clear Scriptures, why would professing Christians attempt to justify divorce and remarriage? One lady who herself married a divorced man and later renounced her situation as an adulterous union described her downfall.

*Reasoning* is one of Satan's most effective weapons. How easy to reason away obedience to the Word of God. The eternal purpose for this life is not so much that we should be happy but that we should be holy. Yet there can be no true happiness apart from righteous living. . . .

I fasted and prayed a great deal, seeking God for an answer directly from Himself. But, although I sought a word from Him, no word was given. Nothing. Complete silence. Only later did it come home to me that it is vain to seek a *rhema* [utterance] from God when He has already so clearly spoken in the written Word. Yes, a word may come which contradicts what He has said in the Scriptures; but that word comes from the wrong source.[7]

It is impossible to remarry with integrity while one's partner is still living. The treacherous spirit which leads to divorce is the same spirit which leads one to remarry. It is a betrayal. In marriage, one can give his love and commitment to his partner, but in remarriage one can give only his treachery and broken trust.[8]

## CORRECTING VIOLATIONS OF MARRIAGE

Violations of marriage vary in degree and kind. Some violations may occur before conversion, some after. Cultural practices may confuse the issue of marriage—for example, common law marriage, contract marriage, annulment, polygamy, etc. This is simply to recognize that not all violations or their variations can be discussed here. Rather than attempting to do so, we will consider ten principles which should be considered in correcting violations of marriage.

*1. God considers the marriage of eligible partners as valid, whether they are godly or ungodly, and considers adultery, divorce, and remarriage as wrong no matter who does it.* "For Herod himself had sent forth and laid hold upon John, and bound him in prison for Herodias' sake, his brother Philip's wife: for he had married her. For John had said unto Herod, It is not lawful for thee to have thy brother's wife" (Mark 6:17, 18). "Marriage is honourable in all, and the bed undefiled: but whoremongers and adulterers God will judge" (Hebrews 13:4).

*2. Obedience is sometimes painful.* But as noted earlier, God is interested in our holiness above our present happiness. Describing the cost of discipleship, Jesus said, "If any man come to me, and hate not his father, and mother, and wife, and children, and brethren, and sisters, yea, and his own life also, he cannot be my disciple. And whosoever doth not bear his cross, and come after me, cannot be my disciple" (Luke 14:26, 27).

*3. The pain of obedience is never as severe as the consequences of continued disobedience.* With our limited understanding, we might think in some cases that obedience will only create problems and that disobedience will surely solve them. This is the reasoning of the flesh, not the direction of the Spirit. In the long run, disobedience always results in more pain than obedience. "There is a way which seemeth right unto a man, but the end thereof are the ways of death" (Proverbs 14:12). Discontinuing a legitimate marriage may seem less painful than a commitment to work through the problems. Continuing an adulterous marriage may seem to be much less painful than discontinuing it and finding God's solution to the resultant problems. But obedience always has God's support, and disobedience always has His reproofs. "He, that being often reproved hardeneth his neck, shall suddenly be destroyed, and that without remedy" (Proverbs 29:1).

*4. No amount of "righteousness" is good enough to offset willful, known sin.* When Saul tried to justify his sin by describing his righteous intentions, Samuel replied, "Hath the LORD as great delight in burnt offerings and sacrifices, as in obeying the voice of the LORD? Behold, to obey is better than sacrifice, and to hearken than the fat of rams" (I Samuel 15:22).

*5. Where there is sin, there must be clear confession (I John 1:9) and full repentance (II Chronicles 7:14).* This means naming the sin truthfully, forsaking it, and returning to God's standards of righteousness. "He that covereth his sins shall not prosper: but whoso confesseth and forsaketh them shall have mercy" (Proverbs 28:13). The most difficult application of this seems to be in the case of remarriage. But if indeed it is a condition of adultery, the only way to forsake it is to discontinue the relationship.[9]

*6. Sometimes living singly is necessary in one's commitment to God.* After giving instructions against divorce and remarriage, Jesus said, "There be eunuchs, which have made themselves eunuchs for the kingdom of heaven's sake" (Matthew 19:12).

*7. Where children are the result of a sinful relationship, the only safe course in raising them for God is to discontinue all sin and begin a legacy of righteousness.* Some object to separating an adulterous marriage where children are involved.[10] But in such a situation it is especially important to forsake sin because God visits "the iniquity of the fathers upon the children, and upon the children's children, unto the third and to the fourth generation" (Exodus 34:7); whereas, He "keepeth covenant and mercy with them that love him and keep his commandments to a thousand generations" (Deuteronomy 7:9).

*8. Though forgiveness can be received immediately upon confession and repentance, consequences of sin may be long-lasting.* Those who violate God's ways in marriage may find themselves in conditions of continuing hardship, pain, and struggle. Single life, one-parent child training, emotional scars both on parents and on children require the support, understanding, and counsel of spiritual brothers and sisters in continuing ways.

*9. The Christian should live above reproach from the world.* "Dearly beloved, I beseech you as strangers and pilgrims, abstain from fleshly lusts, which war against the soul; having your conversation honest among the Gentiles" (I Peter 2:11, 12). Sometimes Christians should avoid what may be allowable if it would bring reproach or raise serious question in the minds of others. For example, in our loose society, a person may have had one or several adulterous marriages, but no valid ones before becoming a Christian. As a single person, is he or she eligible for marriage? Since the relationships to this point have been adulterous and none a valid marriage, marriage may be legitimate. The Christian should consider not only what is lawful, of course, but what is expedient and edifying (see I Corinthians 10:23). Some people, in other words, including onlookers from the world, may have serious questions about such a relationship. In tangled cases where there is no clearcut answer from the Scripture, there is safety in opening oneself to the counsel and direction of a Spirit-led brotherhood.

10. *In working through violations in marriage, the principles of love and faithfulness between Christ and the church serve as a guide.* In Ephesians 5, Paul made the analogy clear, and solutions to marriage problems should be true to this analogy. Divorce, remarriage, and live-in relationships, for example, are all violations of the analogy of Christ and the church.

## SUMMARY

Marriages face tremendous pressures today. Viewing the heartache and pain people are experiencing as they choose their own ways, the rightness of God's directions becomes increasingly clear. Husbands and wives need to understand each other. Thus they need to communicate with and be loyal to one another. As a husband fulfills his responsibility in the marriage, his wife finds it easier to fulfill her responsibility. Each, therefore, must set to the task of doing what God has directed with wisdom, consideration, and faithfulness. To avoid common problems in marriage and to build homes for God, the Christian husband and wife will not fit the norm in modern society. The husband will not allow success in the work force to override responsibilities and loyalties to his wife. And the wife will not allow the pressures of the modern woman to pull her away from responsibilities and loyalties in the home. By working with each other rather than against each other, the husband and wife will experience the compatibility for which God made them male and female.

## THINKING TOGETHER

1. When Christians meet up with those who are violating God's standards for marriage, what should they say? Does it make a difference if these people are professing Christians? What Scriptural examples should guide our approach?
2. What are ways the church becomes responsible to support those who have been divorced and remarried but wish to return to God's standards for marriage?
3. How does a godly wife relate to an unreasonable husband? How does a godly husband relate to an independent, unsubmissive wife?
4. How can a husband make it easy or hard for his wife to submit? How can a wife make it easy or hard for her husband to love her?
5. What are some practical tips for living within one's income? What are some common ways people are drawn into overspending?
6. How often should a husband and wife go out to eat?
7. How can a wife make it easy for a husband to communicate?
8. What are typical ways a husband becomes absorbed in interests outside of the home so that his wife's needs are neglected?

9. To what extent should a husband help with household work—washing dishes, laundry, changing diapers, etc.?
10. If a couple lives on the same property as their parents, what practical guidelines should be followed to avoid in-law conflicts? Can couples interact with their parents too much? Too little? What are the signs of either?

## WORKING TOGETHER

1. As a husband or wife, meditatively read the Scriptures which speak to your character, your responsibilities, and your relating to your partner. Note the areas where you feel a need for improvement. Pray about them, and list any practical steps you might take for improving.
2. As a couple, sit down and discuss the sections "Basic Needs of a Wife" and "Basic Needs of a Husband." Are there any needs which are going unmet? Ask for specific suggestions of how you might begin meeting those needs. Are there any additional needs which are not being met? Discuss these until you are assured you understand each other and know how to respond.
3. As a couple, discuss your financial situation. Are you in bondage? Have you had arguments or friction specifically related to finances? Are there ways you are communicating or failing to communicate which add to the problem? If your financial situation or practices need to be changed, what practical steps should you take?
4. As a couple, evaluate your communication. Note specific habits which you find especially helpful or annoying. Discuss ways you could improve both the amount and the quality of your communication.

**6**

# PARENTING

## INTRODUCTION

The story is told of a single man who spoke to a group of his married friends on what the Bible has to say about child training. He was told, "You just wait till you have children. You will see things quite differently then." Some years later the same man, married now and with a few toddlers, again addressed the subject. "Just wait until your children are grown," he was told. "You'll learn a few things yet." Years later, after his children were raised, the same man spoke once again on the subject of child training. This time the response was, "Yes, well, times have changed!"

The humor of this little anecdote revolves around two rather important points on the subject of parenting. First, it is easier to have the right answers than to carry them out. And second, a parent, like anyone else facing a difficult task, is prone to evade responsibility with excuses.

This chapter is designed to reckon with the difficulty of parenting and to provide helpful, practical understanding. When we know what we are doing, we are less apt to feel the need for excuses.

## GOALS FOR CHRISTIAN PARENTS

The Lord has given to parents the responsibility of passing on a heritage of faith to their children. "For he established a testimony in Jacob, and appointed a law in Israel, which he commanded our fathers, that they should make them known to their children: That the generation to come might know them, even the children which should be born; who should arise and declare them to their children" (Psalm 78:5,6). With this responsibility, parents must have goals which extend beyond the present life and material things. Indeed, God never intended two people to find sufficient fulfillment in themselves or in the things of this life to live happily ever after. Parenting is serious work. Christian parents must enter wholeheartedly into the business of the kingdom of heaven if they want their children to be with them in eternity.

Following are five goals Christian parents can set as they order their home with a view to placing children in heaven.

*1. We want our home to be a house of prayer.* Christian parents should plan for regular times of prayer with their children. They should also pray at unscheduled times.

Every home faces crises, needs, problems, and conflicts. These needs should be brought to the Lord as they rise—they are opportunities to train children to seek the Lord and to find in Him the supply, the answer, the help needed.

2. *We want our home to be a house of praise.* Opportunities for praise follow opportunities for prayer. As the Lord works in response to prayer, parents need to point their children to what He has done. God will not lead every generation through the Red Sea, but He will "establish a testimony" in every home in every generation as parents come to Him in faith. And as the psalmist says, "He hath made his wonderful works to be remembered" (Psalm 111:4).

A very good way to develop a practice of praise is to sing as a family. Some parents may feel inadequate in their singing ability, but children will not be impressed so much by how well parents sing as by the singing itself. If attempts at family singing turn into musical disaster, perhaps the family could begin by singing along with some recorded singing. But beware. Recorded music has unfortunately been a mixed blessing to many Christian homes. Not only has it let in unwholesome "Christian" music, but it has silenced many families' active singing. Do not get caught in the trap of letting others do all your singing. God wants to hear praise from your lips. Sing!

3. *We want our home to be a school of truth.* As a tribute to Timothy's home, Paul wrote of "unfeigned faith . . . which dwelt first in thy grandmother Lois, and thy mother Eunice . . . and that from a child thou hast known the holy scriptures, which are able to make thee wise unto salvation through faith which is in Christ Jesus" (II Timothy 1:5; 3:15). Children do not come to parents as finished products. They need teaching, discipline, and training. Unfortunately, modern thought is to turn chil-

dren over to the "experts" for much of their training. They are sent to the nursery for child care, to school for their education, to church for their salvation, to technical schools for job training, and to the counselor for their problems. There is a legitimate place, of course, for education and training outside the home. But there is no getting around the reality that parents are responsible. Furthermore, the primary place for educating and training children is in the home. More will be said about this later.

*4. We want our home to be a haven, protecting our children from evil.* Sin and trouble abound in our world, and children cannot be completely shielded. Eventually they hear and see and experience things which beat upon their consciences and smear their memories with evil. A Christian home, however, can be a haven, a shelter, a protection. But it will be so only if parents plan it to be so. Parents must beware of the media of sin. Christian parents are working directly against a heritage of righteousness if they bring into their homes entertainment designed by the world—through television, radio, VCR, magazines, and music. The entertainment of the world is polluting. It is not geared to producing men and women for God. Christian parents will keep the world's "fun" out of the home and will provide instead wholesome literature and activities.

*5. We want our home to be a base for service.* We read in I Corinthians that the house of Stephanas had "addicted themselves to the ministry of the saints" (I Corinthians 16:15). Children tend by nature to be self-centered. They want things for themselves. They want them now. Wise parents will involve their children in the practice of giving, serving, visiting, and helping others. Children must be taught by example and involvement the joy of sacrifice. This may mean mowing a yard, baking cookies, raising produce, or cleaning for others. It may include deciding together to give monies to a relief project or an aid program. All of this, however, is only preparation for the time children leave the protective walls of home. The training in service in the home becomes the platform from which children move into life. They go as servants. They move into callings and vocations for which the home training has prepared them. They do not leave by accident. They are sent forth with vision and purpose. "As arrows are in the hand of a mighty man; so are children of the youth" (Psalm 127:4).

## WHEN IS THE QUIVER FULL?

How many children should we have? Young parents ask the question and generally answer it on the basis of their circumstances and generally go to their doctor for methods of control. Is it right to plan?

Before we consider the question, we should trace some of the modern mindset concerning children. As noted in Chapter 1, the typical family size in Western society is diminishing. Why? If we honestly examine motivations, the following reasons come into focus:

- The cost of having children is high.
- The cost of clothing, feeding, and educating children continues to rise.
- Children take a great deal of time.
- Children take a great deal of care—daytime and night-time.
- Children try parents' patience, especially when parents are already under other pressures.
- Having more children requires having larger means of transportation.
- More children make travel inconvenient and expensive.
- A large family requires larger housing.

Looking at the above list, we have to recognize that having a large family cuts right across the living standard and pace of Western culture. But we also should recognize that it is only a short step from the above reasoning to the reasoning that children are a bother, an inconvenience to be endured but sparingly.

The smaller family, however, certainly has not been the secret to happier families, nor the secret to less stressful family living. Considering the general attitude toward children today, it is likely that the modern mother screams at her two "brats" far more than yesterday's mother did at her eight or ten children. This is not to suggest that modern parents could decrease their stress level simply by having six more children. It is to recognize, however, that the real stress culprit in modern living is not children, but materialism. As we noted in Chapter 1, the standard of living is simply too expensive and the schedule of living is simply too exhausting to include many children.

The modern mindset toward children becomes alarming when we realize it has produced the horror of abortion. Behind the smokescreen language of "removing fetal tissue," surgeons and parents are guilty of mass murder—more than twenty-three million up to 1990 in the United States alone. And the gas chambers of Hitler were mild compared with the methods of abortion. The unborn are regularly snipped apart and removed in pieces or submitted to a saline solution which causes them to writhe and twist in pain until they die and are removed.

Christians should abhor abortion. The fact that these babies are not fully developed and that they have never been seen and held does not diminish the stark reality of their death. They may be tiny, but they are alive. And as living human beings, they are being killed.

But Christians may, without realizing it, be swept into the abortion mentality. The emotional and mental framework of abortion is an unwanted pregnancy. A woman comes to be with child, of course, through sexual relations with a man, but the abortion mentality says, in effect, "We want the privilege of sex without the responsibility of it. We want to be able to act as husband and wife without becoming parents."

This same line of thinking pervades the birth control industry. "Safe sex" is advertised, underscoring the idea of unwanted pregnancies, of privilege without responsibility, and of reduced families. Christian parents in the Western world cannot help feeling the pressure toward reduced families and higher standards of living. And so we come around to the question again, Is it right to plan?

On this issue, the Scriptural view is learned more through observation of principles than through direct teaching. The principles which guide us, however, are relevant and enduring. Consider the following:

*1. The Scriptures consistently hold a high view of children.* Upon both Adam and Noah God pronounced fruitfulness in terms of a blessing (Genesis 1:28; 9:1). Sarah, Rachel, Hannah, and Elisabeth considered their childlessness a disgrace and rejoiced for their children (Genesis 21:6; 30:1; I Samuel 1:1-11; and Luke 1:25). The psalmist describes children as "an heritage of the LORD," as "olive plants round about thy table," as "arrows . . . in the hand of a mighty man," and says, "Happy is the man that hath his quiver full of them" (Psalms 127 and 128). And Jesus rebuked His disciples for turning children away. "Suffer little children, and forbid them not, to come unto me: for of such is the kingdom of heaven" (Matthew 19:14).

*2. The Scripture nowhere gives instruction for methods of avoiding conception.* In the case of Onan (Genesis 38), who avoided having children with Tamar, God brought swift judgment. There were, of course, factors other than the matter of avoiding children—he was sinning against his father, his brother, and Tamar—yet what he did is clearly portrayed negatively, not positively. In another instance, we are told that Leah "left bearing" after having four sons (Genesis 29:35). Later she had two more sons and a daughter (Genesis 30:16-21). This "spacing," however, occurred in the context of marital rivalry, and Leah's words, "Is it a small matter that thou hast taken my husband?" (v. 15), indicate this was not her desire.

*3. The mentality which considers children a bother and which wants the privilege of sex without the responsibility of parenting is detrimental in marriage.* One German writer, assessing the birth-control and abortion mentality of our day, spoke of a growing *Kinderfeindschaft*— an attitude of hostility toward children.[1] Couples who postpone childbearing in the interests of temporal goals develop subconsciously (or sometimes consciously) resistant, negative attitudes toward childbearing, children, and parenting. Such attitudes are not only detrimental in the way parents view children but also have a robbing effect on the marital relationship.[2]

*4. Every married couple should be aware of natural cycles of fertility.* God gave specific directions for His people in the Old Testament regarding these cycles (see, for example, Leviticus 15:19-33 and 18:19). This awareness helped the Israelites to be both productive and healthy. The same knowledge is used today by those who consider it necessary to space children or leave off bearing but wish to use methods natural rather than artificial.

*5. The Bible regards human life as sacred, even in the unborn.* "Thou shalt not kill" (Exodus 20:13). "I will praise thee; for I am fearfully and wonderfully made. . . . Thine eyes did see my substance, yet being unperfect;

186

and in thy book all my members were written, which in continuance were fashioned, when as yet there was none of them" (Psalm 139:14, 16). "Before I formed thee in the belly I knew thee; and before thou camest forth out of the womb I sanctified thee, and I ordained thee a prophet unto the nations" (Jeremiah 1:5). "Thy wife Elisabeth shall bear thee a son, and thou shalt call his name John . . . and he shall be filled with the Holy Ghost, even from his mother's womb" (Luke 1:13, 15). Tampering with human life, therefore, is a moral issue. Willfully exterminating it, early or late, amounts to killing. On the basis of this principle, all birth control methods which permit conception but prevent fruition should be considered morally wrong—for example, the IUD. Some would place the pill in this category also because some kinds prevent implantation in case the anti-ovulation mechanism of the pill fails.

6. *The principle of restraint beautifies and preserves love in marriage.* Genuine love in marriage is not some uncontrolled urge which makes people helplessly lovey toward each other. Genuine love is considerate, and in that consideration, it exercises restraint at times in the expression of marital love. This restraint does not dampen love, but actually deepens it. The give-me-now generation is not of the restraint mindset, but for that very reason, many marriages run aground. The balancing instruction comes to us in I Corinthians 7:5 where married couples are warned not to defraud one another by total abstinence except by mutual consent for brief times and noble reasons. This shows that conjugal love is a responsibility not to be withheld.

7. *Couples should not base permanent decisions on changeable conditions.* With the aid of modern medicine many couples today make decisions which permanently keep them from having more children. There may be

legitimate reasons for this decision (for example, where pregnancy is life-threatening), but some couples have made such decisions according to the feelings of the moment. Later they found themselves in situations which completely altered their former view. They may, for example, experience the tragedy of losing their children. Or they may simply gain a heightened appreciation for children which causes them to want more. For such, how true the proverb, "He that is hasty of spirit exalteth folly" (Proverbs 14:29).

Christians are not agreed on the matter of birth control. Some feel there should be no planning. Others feel no artificial methods of birth control should be used. Others feel they can have a high view of children and the family but use either natural or artificial means to space children or even to limit family size in extraordinary circumstances. Unfortunately, many professing Christians have not given the subject serious thought and have heedlessly accepted the birth control practices and mentality of the day.

While certain issues and decisions must be left to individual conscience, every Christian couple must realize that the thinking of modern society stands contrary to the pro-family, pro-children, pro-fruitfulness emphasized in the Bible. Decisions which ignore these Biblical teachings and principles for fear of making us appear odd to the world will lead the family and church worldward. Conformity to the world always results sooner or later in tasting the world's cup of sorrow.[3]

## TRAINING CHILDREN FOR GOD

"Train up a child in the way he should go: and when he is old, he will not depart from it" (Proverbs 22:6). How meditatively and prayerfully Christian parents need to shoulder the responsibility of that verse! God wants parents to follow Him. He wants their children to follow Him. He wants those children's children to follow Him. A heritage of faith, however, is never automatic. It requires planning, prayer, and training; and because no parent is perfect, it requires a lifetime of learning from one's mistakes.

Before we consider the subject of child training, however, a word of caution is in order. The textbook can never be as real as life. Woe to the parent who reads the textbook and presto knows all about training children. The tender little three-year-old who is supposed to respond in such childlike faith to Bible stories may without warning throw his half-eaten cookie right into the middle of "Daniel and the Lions' Den." Besides spoiling the mood of family worship and disturbing his parents' patient composure, he may shatter their favorite textbook theory.

Parents should not despair. There is help beyond the books. While books can give valuable advice, they can never describe all children perfectly. And the wise parent must lean upon the Lord daily for understanding in how to put principles into practice. "If any of you lack wisdom, let him ask of God, that giveth to all men liberally, and upbraideth not; and it shall be given him. But let him ask in faith, nothing wavering" (James 1:5, 6).

Note carefully the emphasis on faith. Child training is not only a passing on of faith. It is also an exercise of faith. Sometimes in the blur of several preschoolers, God's ways look unrealistic, or even downright wrong. Parents must ask for wisdom. But they must believe God even while they ask! God's ways are right (Psalm 119:128). Often it is the willingness to obey, in spite of not fully understanding, which later yields the greatest insights.

189

What, then, does the Bible say about training children? A lot. But perhaps the Biblical teaching could be summarized in three words: teaching, example, and correction.

*1. Parents are responsible to teach their children.* "Hear, O Israel: The LORD our God is one LORD: And thou shalt love the LORD thy God with all thine heart, and with all thy soul, and with all thy might. And these words, which I command thee this day, shall be in thine heart: And thou shalt teach them diligently unto thy children, and shalt talk of them when thou sittest in thine house, and when thou walkest by the way, and when thou liest down, and when thou risest up" (Deuteronomy 6:4-7).

Note that it is parents who are responsible to teach their children. They are responsible to teach them the ways of the Lord. And they are responsible to teach diligently.

By clear teaching, parents show their children the standard of behavior which they expect. The children then not only know what is expected, but they also know when they have done wrong. Clear teaching, in other words, has prepared them to do what is right, but if they do wrong, it has prepared them to feel the sting of their conscience and to accept the justice of the consequences.

Teaching continues through all the stages of a child's development to adulthood, but to teach effectively, parents need to know children. They need to understand the mental, emotional, and spiritual characteristics of children at different age levels. Without this knowledge, parents may end up scattering very good seed on soil that is unprepared.

*2. Parents are responsible to be an example to their children.* In the same passage where parents are instructed to teach their children diligently, they are told,

190

"Ye shall diligently keep the commandments of the LORD your God, and his testimonies, and his statutes, which he hath commanded thee. And thou shalt do that which is right and good in the sight of the LORD: that it may be well with thee" (Deuteronomy 6:17, 18). Diligent teaching is ineffective when coupled with careless living. Parents cannot *send* their children into the ways of kindness, patience, and unselfishness. They must *lead* them. As the adage goes, we teach some by what we say, more by what we do, but most by what we are.

The quality of parental example comes to the forefront particularly when children reach teenage years. Children admire their parents; teenagers evaluate them. The idealism of youth tends to make them react to inconsistencies, and their yen for independence tends to make them super-react when those inconsistencies are in authority figures. Where a parent's example lags behind his teaching, a disobedient youth will commonly use the inconsistency as an excuse for even worse behavior. No parent, of course, can be perfect. But parents must have integrity. They must be honest and humble. And they must not set a standard for their children which they themselves are unwilling to follow.

Parents should appreciate the challenge of being an example, because it is a safeguard against slipping into spiritual complacency. The importance of their example becomes but one more reason to serve the Lord in sincerity and truth.

*3. Parents are responsible to correct their children.* Because this part of child training has come under such attack in this day, we should pause to note the clear direction from the Bible. The Biblical instruction for the use of the rod is founded upon the truth that fallen man has a bent toward sin, which evidences itself early in childhood, and which unchecked, leads the soul directly to hell. The modern objection to the use of the rod, on the other hand, rests on the error that man is inherently good and that children need only the proper promptings to discover and develop their hidden potential. Consider the following principles from the Bible concerning the use of corrective discipline:

*1. The rod delivers the child from the path of death.* "Foolishness is bound in the heart of a child; but the rod of correction shall drive it far from him" (Proverbs 22:15). "Withhold not correction from the child: for if thou beatest him with the rod, he shall not die. Thou shalt beat him with the rod, and shalt deliver his soul from hell" (Proverbs 23:13, 14).

The word *fool* as used in Proverbs refers to one who chooses his own way in spite of instruction. It is the nature of obstinancy, the root of disobedience. This "foolishness" is ingrained in the heart of every child, and the rod is to be used specifically against it. No amount of scolding, threatening, or teaching can replace the rod in bringing the rebel in each child to terms of surrender.

*2. The rod is to be used in love.* "He that spareth his rod hateth his son: but he that loveth him chasteneth him betimes" (Proverbs 13:24). It is partially the failure to understand and practice this principle which has given credence to the anti-spanking sentiment of our day. Without love, the rod becomes a medium of abuse and humiliation.

A study done by several college students underscored this very clearly. They wanted to find out why some parents were successful in raising their children while other parents were not. In their study, they grouped parents in four categories: authoritative, authoritarian, neglectful, and permissive. They rated the success of the parents by how well their children were socially adjusted, how well they followed their parents' ideals and values, etc. Both the authoritative parents and the authoritarian spanked their children, but the authoritative parents used the rod in love, whereas the authoritarians used it in slam-bang, kid-whacking anger. The authoritative parents had the best results with their children in every respect. The authoritarians, however, had the worst record of the four categories.[4] Conclusion: where the rod is not used in love, it becomes counterproductive.

*3. The rod must be used early in life.* "Chasten thy son while there is hope, and let not thy soul spare for his crying" (Proverbs 19:18). There comes a time when the rod ceases to be effective. The parent who avoids corrective discipline to avoid the trauma of using the rod is only postponing sorrow, for the pain of watching a wayward teenager laughing his way toward hell is a hundredfold worse than the pain of holding a sobbing child after a spanking.

*4. The rod must be accompanied with instruction.* "The rod and reproof give wisdom: but a child left to himself bringeth his mother to shame" (Proverbs 29:15). "And, ye fathers, provoke not your children to wrath: but bring them up in the nurture [literally, *chastening*] and admonition of the Lord" (Ephesians 6:4). Notice that both of these verses—one from the Old Testament and one from the New—tie chastening with instruction. Spanking a child does not replace the responsibility of teaching. The two go hand in hand. It is the disregard for instruction which occasions the use of the rod. Even so, it is the use of the rod which makes a child ready and willing to hear instruction. The rebel does not want instruction, but the penitent is glad for it. When the child's heart is hardened against hearing instruction, the rod must be used to bring the child to the place of accepting the instruction of the parent without resistance, either active or passive.

*5. The rod delivers the parent-child relationship from tension.* "Correct thy son, and he shall give thee rest; yea, he shall give delight unto thy soul" (Proverbs 29:17). Where parents attempt to use scolding, threatening, or bribery to overcome the child's bent to disobey, the relationship becomes characterized by manipulation, anger, and frustration. Parents end up obeying their children—their nerves are a wreck, and the children are wild, unhappy, and insecure. On the other hand, where parents consistently meet the child's stubbornness with the rod, they do not experience the buildup of frustration, and the child does not experience the frustration of never knowing what he can get away with. In the modern home where "rest" and "delight" sound like a foreign language, the loving use of the rod needs to be restored.

 **SNAPSHOT FROM LIFE**

*Bethany was her parents' third child, so they were not novices to child training. But they were unprepared for Bethany's high-strung temperament. The "terrible twos" began by the end of the first year and refused to go away.*

*When Bethany didn't get her way, Yeow! on the floor she would go, legs working like pistons, voice screaming full-throttle, nonstop. Spanking didn't seem to work. She could be spanked for a tantrum and five minutes later, Yeow! same story, line for line.*

*Bethany's parents were ready to conclude God's plan for the rod was for everyone except Bethany. There must be another way. They studied the Scripture. They read Christian child training books, and finally decided since this was God's direction, they would continue to follow it in faith.*

"*We won't try to win the war in one battle,*" Bethany's father concluded to his wife. "*But we will continue to meet her challenges to our authority with the consequences God has prescribed—the rod.*"

*Several years later Bethany's father remarked, "Bethany is one of the sweetest and tenderest children we have . . . but she surely didn't come that way.*"

*God's method applied consistently in God's way was working.*

## GUIDELINES FOR THE USE OF THE ROD

1. Be certain you have made your expectations clear to the child and that they are within his ability. (The practice of warning a child [not threatening] can safeguard against spanking where there has been misunderstanding.)

2. Always use the rod in private. (Privacy is necessary in respect to the child's personhood and need for emotional release.)

3. Talk to the child first, asking him to tell you what he did. (Confession is helpful for penitence. It is important to ask *what*, not *why*, and to require a *what* answer before listening to a *why* answer. The practice of talking first likewise safeguards against spanking in a flash of anger.)

4. Explain that such behavior is not acceptable. Explanation should not descend to nagging nor expand into a lecture. The use of a Bible verse related to the offense may help a child accept the justice of discipline.

5. Use a "rod" on the buttocks. An instrument which causes more than surface stinging is unsuitable.[5]

6. Use the rod according to the child's need. (The purpose is to bring the child to surrender and willing obedience, not to hurt the child or to provide an outlet for the parent's anger. Excessive use of the rod is as damaging as no use.)

7. Permit the child to cry, but not to scream or thrash about. (Some children try to control the spanking session. A spanking should subdue anger and bring the child back under the parent's control, not give opportunity for further rebellion.)

8. Comfort the child. (Comfort should come from the same parent who gave the discipline.) While this is an important time of bonding in the parent-child relationship, ideally the child should seek the comfort of the parent, rather than the parent immediately after discipline initiating large doses of affection. Comfort is in order; a smothering kind of affection may create emotional confusion. In some instances, especially for certain misdemeanors, this may also be a time to pray with the child.

By instruction, example, and the rod, parents should train their children to obey promptly their verbal instructions spoken in a normal tone of voice. A child who delays or who obeys in his own way or who obeys only when he is told why is exercising a passive form of rebellion. The parent who fails to train his child in prompt obedience, actually trains by default various forms of disobedience. In effect, he is telling the child:

●You don't need to obey until I have repeated my instructions several times.

●You don't need to obey until I raise my voice, threaten, or scream at you.

●You don't need to obey until I go for the rod.

●You don't need to obey until I have answered all your objections and arguments.

●You don't need to obey if you can distract me or cause

196

me to laugh.
- You don't need to obey if you beg, whine, or cry enough.
- You don't need to obey if you throw a tantrum.
- You don't need to obey if you make a scene in front of people.
- You can obey but strike back with the words, looks, or posture of rebellion.

All that we have considered on the use of the rod does not mean the rod is the only form of correction to be used with children. It is the form suited to meet rebellion in children, to bring them to submission, back under the control of the parents' will. But there is much shaping necessary for a child's behavior even when that child is submissive. A child needs to learn manners, carefulness, good work habits, etc., and this part of training requires both reward and punishment.

Suppose, for example, a child needs to improve his hygiene habits. You might make a chart of good and bad things. On the "good" side, you might list such things as "Brush teeth after breakfast," and on the "bad" side, such things as "Leave sink dirty." You could set appropriate rewards when the child has met a certain standard of behavior.

Punishment is also necessary in training children's behavior. Punishment is distinct from using the rod in that it is not for rebellion, but demonstrates just and due consequences for wrong behavior. For example, if a child is careless and spills milk at the table, his punishment is to apologize and clean up the mess (provided, of course, he is old enough to understand the wrongness of care-lessness and spilling milk). If a child disrupts other children's play, he might be punished by apologizing and sitting quietly by himself.

Punishment requires the exercise of wisdom and common sense. The following principles may help to clarify the use of punishment:

1. The punishment should be related as closely as possible to the misbehavior. Make a mess—clean it up. Break or damage items—restore or fix them (as able, of course; a child may need to help a parent with the task of repairing). Infringe on others—lose privileges.

2. Punishment should be neither excessive nor trivial. Punishment is based on God's laws of justice. A child should not be crushed under it, but be taught by it.

3. Children should not be punished if the standards of behavior are not clear. God's Word makes a difference between wrongs done in innocence and wrongs done knowingly. Parents should also.

4. The rod may be used as punishment where children have inflicted pain or where the misbehavior seems significant enough to merit it. There is justice in feeling pain when causing pain. A child who takes advantage of a younger child's innocence or who mocks a handicapped person may do little apparent damage. But the emotional pain caused may well deserve the rod.

5. Children should acknowledge their wrong before receiving punishment. Confession paves the way for justice to have its desired effect.

God holds parents responsible to train their children to obey because He wants those children to become His obedient servants in the years ahead. The behavior patterns of one's childhood become the base for behavior patterns of adulthood. And thus, parents who fail their children fail God as well.

## APPLYING THE PRINCIPLES OF CHILD TRAINING

Knowing that children need teaching, correction, and example does not answer all the questions parents have.

The following pages present specific characteristics of children at different age levels and provide some practical pointers for child training. It also gives suggestions for activities which are wholesome for children at the different age levels.

### First Year

*Characteristics*

- Baby is dependent and cuddly.
- Communication is simple—facial expressions, sounds, and tone of voice are especially prominent.

*Training Tips*

- Babies need plenty of love, handling, caring, and cuddling in the first year (from fathers as well as mothers). This is the year to cultivate trust.
- Spanking may be necessary in the latter part of the first year, but only where there can be clear communication of the parents' wishes, where there is clear resistance to those wishes, and where there can be a clear surrender on the part of the child. Spanking before this time is apt to create insecurity rather than train effectively.

*Guidelines for Wholesome Activities*

1. Activities which include parental touch, comfort, and care are important.
2. Children respond to activities which involve communication—talking and singing.
3. Parents should care for and communicate with the baby firsthand, rather than turning the baby over to a baby-sitter. Lack of touch can be damaging emotionally, mentally, and even physically.[6]

### Second Year

*Characteristics*

- Baby begins walking.
- Walking almost invariably accompanies a shift toward greater independence.
- This is the age of exploration and experimentation.
- Toddler may begin saying words.

*Training Tips*

- Toddlers need to be taught the meaning of no. During this training period, some of the more breakable items may need to be moved out of reach.
- During the second year, the child continues to need plenty of closeness and holding by parents, but begins to need directions and reproofs as well. He should learn to follow simple, one- or two-word instructions such as "come," "sit," "lie down," "sh-h-h," etc., and should experience discipline when he resists. Instructions, of course, must be clearly understood. (See "Guidelines for the Use of the Rod.")
- Enter into the child's natural exploratory ventures— warning of hot or dangerous items, introducing the feel of grass, water, etc.

*Guidelines for Wholesome Activities*

1. Encourage activities which require simple motor skills—motion songs, cobbler's bench, building blocks, etc.
2. In reading to toddlers, use books with pictures to aid both comprehension and attention.
3. Talk to toddlers—it is vital to the development of their own communication.

## Third Year Through Age Six

*Characteristics*

- Exploration tendencies are usually followed by testing tendencies. The "terrible twos," however, are not so much the result of children trying to be bad as children needing to learn their limits.
- The child does a lot of imitating and role-playing as a preschooler—imagination seems to run nonstop; energy seems boundless.
- The child is very believing—a parent's instructional opportunities are prodded by countless questions.
- Thinking is concrete rather than abstract. Thus, while the child views God in quite human form (sometimes amusingly so), the unseen is as real to the child as the seen.
- While children can be taught much at this age, they are closer to adults emotionally than intellectually. They probably learn more from what they feel and sense than from what they are told.

*Training Tips*

- The main part of the correcting work in children occurs from the second year to the sixth year. Parents must require prompt, respectful obedience. While tantrums and outright rebellion should be met with the rod, parents should avoid turning every incident into a confrontation.
- Do not resort to scolding, threatening, or bribing to get a child to do what you want. These methods will train a child to manipulate rather than to obey.
- Children can and should be introduced to work appropriate to their age and ability—picking up toys, dusting, dishwashing, making beds, etc.
- Politeness policies should be taught—table manners, playtime courtesy, and conversational politeness such

as "please," "thank you," and "excuse me."

●Children continue to need plenty of affection and encouragement. Corrective work should not only punish negative tendencies, but reward positive behavior. A chart setting realistic goals and rewards for appropriate behavior can be effective.

*Guidelines for Wholesome Activities*

1. A child needs consistent teaching about spiritual realities. Family worship, bedtime prayers, Bible stories (on the child's level of understanding), and Sunday school build a reality base for the rest of life.

2. Active participation is preferred above passive participation. Thus, a sandbox is far better than a VCR as an activity center.

3. Activites which stimulate creativity are good—modeling clay, finger paints, and role-playing (playing school, church, shopping, camping, etc.). Sometimes the whole family can enter into this—have a camp-out in the basement.

4. Children should be encouraged in activities which develop coordination and provide exercise—hide and seek, coloring, family walks, tag, learning to ride bike, catch, etc.

5. Beware of toys which distort reality or tend toward sin. Many dolls are fashionable adult models rather than babies. Grotesque television characters and toys designed to imitate violence trigger wrong imaginations in the child.

### Age 7-12

*Characteristics*

●This is often the age most neglected by adults. The child is no longer a little child, but is far from an adult.

●Sometimes silly, teasing, and quite irresponsible; yet he/she wants to do adult things, use adult tools, etc.
●At this age the child is very hero/heroine minded—admires and imitates favorite young men and women.
●Often this child is sensitive and has many fears, but may not express these except to a trusted parent.

*Training Tips*

●Parents need to make conscious effort to be sensitive and affectionate to the child this age. Although the body is becoming more adult, the child inside needs tangible evidence of being loved and accepted.
●Respect the emerging personhood of this child—beware of causing embarrassment by laughing or remarking about oddities, especially in front of others.
●Give time to this child. The quantity and quality of time spent in these years become foundational to solid parent-teen relationships.
●Place confidence in this child. This takes wisdom, of course. Children should not be burdened with adult responsibilities, but let them do what they can. Beware of scolding them for failure or inefficiency in something you allowed them to do. Helpful pointers work better than irritable criticism.
●Talk to this child and listen—give him freedom to express himself. Beware of attempting to force open doors of communication.

*Guidelines for Wholesome Activities*

1. Children this age will likely move toward activities suited to their gender. During this age, girls will likely want to cease rough-and-tumble activities, but boys will gravitate even more toward wrestling and feats of strength.
2. Activities should be avoided which force early self-awareness (such as mixed swimming).

3. Humor should be kept wholesome. Guide away from activities which are suggestive or which make light of the sacred. Everything from music to reading to parties should be wholesome.

4. Beware of activities which pressure adult life on the preadolescent. It is one of the plagues of our day. At this age children need time with their parents, working, talking, and playing, rather than, for example, competing on junior leagues. Entertainment media are major culprits in pressuring the childhood out of children.

5. Entertaining activities should stimulate the mind creatively rather than enslave it. Games of skill or planning are better than games of chance. Beware the electronic games which BEEP, beep, BEEP, beep, beep their way through hours of intellectual monotony.

6. Hikes, camping, gardening, baking, cookouts, crafts— these are all ways to spend time productively with children.

7. Reading materials should provide exemplary characters, particularly as the child moves into the hero era. The secular market is loaded with the sensational and the mysterious for ten-to-twelve-year-old readers. Even "Christian" literature often follows this pattern. There are stirring biographies, however, written for this age group which can provide Christian role models.

8. Private talk time continues to be important. Praying together at bedtime may provide for some of this, but it may be necessary to schedule special times, especially as the child approaches adolescent changes.

### Teen Years

*Characteristics*

•This is the time of transition: physically, changing from

boy to man, from girl to woman; socially, moving from being dependent to being responsible; spiritually, emerging from innocence to accountability.

●Teenagers ask questions, present challenges, and use logic—answering their questions becomes more difficult, but especially so where the relationship with parents is strained.

●Young people see the world idealistically and react to inconsistency, hypocrisy, and formalism, even when they have the same in their own lives.

●Teenagers have a growing attraction for the opposite sex.

*Training Tips*

●Youths need to be guided without feeling forced, understood without being threatened, instructed without feeling crammed, loved without feeling babied, heard without being belittled, and trusted without being abandoned.

●Generally, the time of spanking should be past by the teen years.

●Parents are most effective when they clearly demonstrate love and integrity. Their firmness and frankness should be tempered with kindness, consideration, and consistency.

●Communication continues to be important. This age presents many opportunities for instruction, but the effectiveness of the instruction depends first upon how well the parents have exercised control in former years (it is virtually impossible to teach a rebel), and second, on their willingness to listen to youthful ideas and be considerate of the emerging personality (it is difficult to gain a hearing without giving a listening ear).

●Privileges should be accompanied with accountability. Although teenagers sometimes complain about restrictions, they are happier and more secure when they know their boundaries.

●Teenagers need to be taught principles of responsibility and stewardship in the handling of finances. This is such a necessary and neglected area, that several practical pointers are given at the close of this section.

●Teenagers should be instructed how to respond to overtures from the opposite sex, including requests for dates. Parents should expect to provide guidance and counsel in this area and should be clear in communicating their expectations.

●As personalities emerge, parents should be sensitive to the unique qualities and interests of each child and should openly discuss possibilities for the future, providing encouragement and guidance.

*Guidelines for Wholesome Activities*

1. Activities should be intellectually stimulating and enjoyable and should provide for healthy social interaction.

2. There is danger in activities where entertainment becomes an end in itself. Inevitably the quality of the activity degenerates, and conflicts with authority figures develop.

3. There is danger in activities which consume or tie up resources without justifiable returns such as the use of recreational vehicles or other expensive recreational pursuits.

4. Social activities should be structured to preserve youths from moral danger and to strengthen home interests and loyalties. Highly organized youth groups with excessive activities easily do just the opposite, making the youth group a rival to the home. Relationships between youth and their parents are stronger where activities are directed by parents from their

home rather than by youth sponsors from outside the home.

5. A family should do things together as a family, as an extended family, and as groups of families, encouraging a mingling of age levels. Such activities could include picnics, hikes, camp-outs, ball games, and tours of museums, science centers, nature centers, etc. Christian service activities as a family are also appropriate—visiting shut-ins, singing and holding Bible studies for shut-ins or the elderly in nursing homes, and handing out Christian literature.

6. Teenagers should be encouraged to develop hobbies which expand skills, knowledge, or creativity—hobbies such as insect collecting, stamp collecting, rock collecting, painting, music, sewing, basket weaving, knitting, etc. (Note: Collections which accumulate through purchase rather than by observation or discovery tend to be less beneficial.)

## Guidelines for Teaching Financial Responsibility to Children

1. Parents must understand and practice Biblical principles of stewardship and responsibility themselves if they are to pass this on to their children.

2. Children should be taught that everything we have is the Lord's—we are but managers of His goods. The tithe is a tangible reminder of this.

3. Parents should teach children the difference between needs and wants and the priority of needs over wants in purchasing.

4. Parents should not give children and young people the privilege of spending money without giving them guidelines for spending it responsibly. A common mistake parents make in an affluent society is providing their young people with spending money "as needed."

Youths love fun and can find endless ways of spending money—driving around, eating out, buying new clothes, snacks, collectibles, sports equipment, sound systems, tapes, and a host of trivia just for the fun of it.

5. Children need to be taught the direct tie between work and money. Parents should avoid, and should teach their children to avoid, the mentality of society which wants much for nothing, which is constantly looking for the quickest, easiest way to riches.

6. As children and youths begin earning money, clear policies should be established for how this money is used. There are various options:

a. Parents receive all the money. The child is taught that his work contributes to the overall family good, and he receives in return the inner security of belonging and the tangible reward of his own needs met. Where this option is chosen, parents often give the child a certain "portion of goods" when he reaches the age where he manages his own affairs.

b. Child receives either a portion or all of the money with budgeting guidelines for how it is to be used. Here the child becomes responsible for tithing and for certain needs, such as clothing, and is taught firsthand the experience of management while still under the protection of his parents' control.

c. The child's money is tithed, a very limited amount is given for the child's management, and the remainder is placed in savings for the future needs of the child.

7. Children need to be taught sales resistance. (Parents usually need to exercise "begging resistance" in the process and, of course, train their children not to beg.) Teach children to weigh purchase decisions, compare products and prices, and avoid purchasing on impulse.

8. Children need to be taught the principles of giving— the joy of sacrifice, sensitivity to the needy, the danger of

giving to be seen, the value of laying up treasure in heaven, responsibility for the needs of the church, and responsibility for family members in need.

9. Children need to be taught the dangers of credit. Buy now, pay later is not the teaching of the Bible. It is the encouragement of people who offer credit cards, collect phenomenal interest rates, and keep the people of this generation in perpetual bondage to payments. Children need to learn the discipline of saving money, of making do with what they have, of repairing and servicing rather than throwing away.

10. If parents commit themselves to teaching their children wise use of finances, they must accept, and teach their children to accept, that they will be different from many of their friends. They will not cater to their appetites and desires. They will not have the latest fads. They will not buy and spend and waste after the manner of many people around them.

## CONTROLLING ANGER

If the responsibility of child training were to be narrowed down to one word, that word would be LOVE—not so much the feeling kind of love as the commitment kind, the kind that says, "I am resolved to doing all in my power for your well-being."

On the other hand, one of the most destructive things in child training is uncontrolled anger. There is, of course, a correct anger which parents may feel when their children do wrong, a clear and firm displeasure. But it must never act against the commitment of the parents to their children, never attack the personhood of the children, never override the parents' wisdom. In parents, destructive anger comes in varied forms, from quiet disdain to general irritability to cutting criticism to biting sarcasm to red-faced shrieking. Following are seven reasons this kind of anger in parents is wrong:

1. An uncontrolled temper destroys trust.

2. An uncontrolled temper cuts off communication.

3. An uncontrolled temper creates an atmosphere of tension.

4. An uncontrolled temper lets loose unbridled actions.

5. An uncontrolled temper damages self-image in children.

6. An uncontrolled temper gives the devil access (Ephesians 4:26, 27).

7. An uncontrolled temper grieves the Holy Spirit (Ephesians 4:30, 31).

Many parents struggle with habits of peevish anger. Unfortunately, instead of increasing a parent's control of a situation, such anger decreases control. It projects the parent's weakness and inadequacy to the child, lessening the force of what the parent says and undermining his authority.

Once patterns of destructive anger are entrenched in a parent's words, looks, and reactions, they are difficult to remove. But removal is a must if parents wish to regain the trust and respect of their children. Following are several pointers for overcoming destructive anger patterns:

*1. Acknowledge the problem specifically before God.* It may be best to write out the problem, how it is commonly expressed, and what effect it is having on the family. "He that covereth his sins shall not prosper: but whoso confesseth and forsaketh them shall have mercy" (Proverbs 28:13).

*2. Recognize this as an expression of the self-life which grieves the Holy Spirit.* "And grieve not the holy Spirit of God, whereby ye are sealed unto the day of redemption. Let all bitterness, and wrath, and anger, and clamour, and evil speaking, be put away from you" (Ephesians 4:30, 31).

3. *Find verses about anger and paraphrase them to specifically fit your situation.* Write these out, read and reread them, and put them in a place where you are reminded of them often. God's Word has a cleansing, correcting effect in our hearts and minds. "The law of the LORD is perfect, converting the soul" (Psalm 19:7).

4. *Pray daily to experience the life of Jesus in place of this stronghold of self.* "But we all, with open face beholding as in a glass the glory of the Lord, are changed into the same image from glory to glory, even as by the Spirit of the Lord" (II Corinthians 3:18). "I am crucified with Christ: nevertheless I live; yet not I, but Christ liveth in me" (Galatians 2:20).

5. *Confess the problem to your family.* Discuss steps you are taking for victory and pray together. Ask for continued prayer support. If the problem persists, schedule regular family meetings to encourage a sense of accountability. "Confess your faults one to another, and pray one for another, that ye may be healed" (James 5:16).

6. *Look reasonably at the things which commonly anger you and search for more constructive responses.* If a particular person irritates you, for example, you might begin to focus on positive things about that person which you can appreciate. If a messy house, a messy garage, or a messy room gets your blood pressure rising, discuss ways you or the family could improve the situation. If the situation is beyond your power to change, consider ways you can accept it or adjust to it. In all situations, you can ask yourself, "How would Jesus view this?" He said, "Learn of me; for I am meek [controlled and gentle]" (Matthew 11:29).

7. *Refuse to justify your anger.* "How many times have you heard 'He made me mad'? That's nonsense. No one

211

*makes* us angry."[7] Anger is in one way an involuntary emotion, but our responses, the way we express our anger, and our control or lack of control depend upon our own choices. Consider how easily anger is controlled if the telephone rings. Presto. We can be as calm as if we had just read Psalm 23. Unfortunately, the carnal mind can devise an excuse for anything if we allow it to. We need to follow the instruction of Paul. "Put ye on the Lord Jesus Christ, and make not provision for the flesh" (Romans 13:14).

## WHAT ABOUT DAY-CARE CENTERS?

About 50 percent of the mothers of preschool children in the U.S. have jobs. The result is that little ones are being trundled out of the house at increasingly early ages to day-care centers. Many "experts" have tried to assure parents that such centers are designed to meet the needs of children and that children easily adapt to changes and new environments. The following observations, however, should direct Christian parents to other conclusions.

1. Day-care centers decrease a child's attachment to their natural parents. The head of Harvard's Preschool Project, who researched preschool care for more than 30 years, said he would not think of placing his infant or toddler in any substitute-care program. Wisely, he warned, "Babies form their first human attachments only once."[8]

2. Day-care centers offer depersonalized care. Children in group settings simply cannot be treated like children in a home. One writer spent hundreds of hours observing day-care firsthand. She noted that while care centers do not abuse children, the children's lives were "frighteningly empty." She gave specific examples, but the bottom line of her report was that there is a fundamental

problem at day-care centers: Mommy is gone.[9]

3. Day-care centers do not provide the teaching and training which God asks of Christian parents. Studies have demonstrated that children who spend early years in substitute care are later more prone to aggressive misbehavior and are poorer in academic performance than children cared for by their parents.

This is not to say that all who provide substitute care are doing a poor job. Many are doing their best. It is simply to recognize the realities of substitute care and to say that their best cannot replace the parents.

## THE ADOPTED CHILD

Many couples today are postponing childbearing. This pattern, coupled with increased stress and a variety of other factors, has resulted in an increased rate of infertility, which in turn has resulted in an increased interest in adopting children. Meanwhile, other social factors have decreased the number of babies available for adoption. Abortion, for example, eliminates from one to two million babies each year. So while adoption has become more desirable, it has also become more difficult. The typical waiting time for parents in the U.S. wanting to adopt a child is from five to eight years.[10]

There are three basic ways to adopt a child. The most traditional has been adopting through an adoption agency. A growing trend in adoption, however, is what is termed independent adoption. Here, the birth mother (and at times the father) arrange directly for the placement of the baby. Laws regulating this vary from state to state, but the advantage is that the mother is able to take a more active role, even discussing with prospective parents her wishes and expectations. A third form of adoption is adopting a child from a foreign country. Korea and Latin America have been the most common countries from which to adopt children. The process includes much paperwork and can be rather expensive, but many prospective parents are willing to incur these inconveniences for the joy of raising children.

Adoption is both like and unlike having a child by natural birth. It is the same in that the parents are responsible for the training and care of the child. Adoption has its unique features, however, which can be both negative and positive. The knowledge that these are not the "real" parents can be used knowingly or unknowingly to drive wedges, manipulate, etc. The other side of the same truth is that adoption demonstrates an outreaching, giving love so beyond the call of duty that it is actually an "act of grace" akin to God's love.

While the formality of adoption varies from one locality or agency to another,[11] parents typically have questions about what they can expect with an adopted child and what they should do or not do. Situations vary. Some agencies require counseling for parents both before and after adoption. But the following principles speak to most situations:

1. *The adopted child has normal needs for such things as love, acceptance, and correction and should be treated normally.* In the U.S., most adoption processes include a question to parents which reads, "Do you understand that if your adoption petition is granted, you will be entering into a contract with this state, in which you will be agreeing to treat the child, in all respects, as if you had given birth to him or her, without exception?"[12] The more parents are able to treat the adopted child as though they had parented the child, the more secure the child will feel in the home. Partiality and favoritism are obvious violations of this principle. But some well-mean-

ing parents go to the other side and grant special privileges or exemptions to the adopted child, perhaps to
offset past rejection; but while the child overtly is drawn
to this, the special treatment covertly signals messages
of rejection. It says, "You are different," and in the long
run it increases the child's insecurity.

*2. Parents should honestly answer questions about the
child's past on the child's level of understanding.* Children vary in their curiosity, and a parent will need
wisdom in knowing how much to tell a child how soon,
but generally it is necessary for a child to grow up
knowing he has been adopted. In some cases, the child
can even know the general reason—for example, if
parents have died. Traditionally, the privacy of birth
parents has been protected by law, and even with many
independent adoptions, the birth mother and parents
know each other only by first name. Thus, in most cases,
very few details can or need be told about birth parents.
Honesty about adoption is the point to be acknowledged
and accepted without ado.

*3. Do not permit adopted children to play upon their
situation for selfish advantage.* Children are children. A
child in a pout will grab any lever in sight, including the
sensitive guilt nerve of his parents. "You don't love me.
You're not my real mom." There is no better way to give
such a child security than quietly but firmly to correct
his rebellion, for that is what it is, an attempt to gain
control. There are times, of course, particularly for the
child who has been adopted after the infant stage, when
he may grieve for past memories. Such feelings should
certainly be permitted and should be sympathized with
just as sincerely as one would with any other person. The
point here is that such feelings should never be the
grounds for a child getting his own way.

*4. A parent should not assume the mentality of a*

*"rescuer" of the adopted child.* This is the counterpart of a child manipulating his parents. While we noted that adoption is an act of love and "grace," if parents use "what all we've done for you" as a lever to manipulate the child, it creates resentment, not gratitude. The adopted child needs parents, not rescuers. It is only by taking the normal role and responsibility as parents that parents can expect an adopted child to take the normal role and attitude of being their child.

5. *The earlier a child is adopted, the less adjustments are necessary in the new home.* An older child certainly may be adopted, but he will need to be accepted as he is before he can be led effectively to being a member of the new family. Such a child will need to learn the expectations of the new home, but at the same time will need a certain amount of freedom in expressing responses, including negative responses to his new environment. Much of the success of adjustment depends on the quality of communication between the child and members of his new home.

6. *Racial differences between parents and adopted children are more significant outside the home than in the home and are more apt to cause difficulties in adulthood than in childhood.* In the home, parents are usually able to provide an atmosphere of love and acceptance suitable for any child. Outside the home, however, they have not as much control. Even so, in childhood racial differences seldom pose a problem, except perhaps the problem of too much attention. Thoughtless adults easily spoil a "special" child. As a child nears adulthood, however, and experiences normal social desires, racial differences may become more significant. Reluctance from the opposite sex to build more than casual relationships is often interpreted as rejection and attributed rightly or wrongly to racial prejudice.

216

7. *Each adoption has its unique twists, and each adopted child his unique personhood, so that parents must avoid trying to make either the process of adoption or the child fit predetermined expectations.* There will be surprises. There will be mistakes. Parents must be willing to learn and adjust personally in the process of receiving and training their children (whether theirs by parentage or by adoption). Those parents who lean on the Lord and His Word for wisdom have a base for working through their difficulties.

## SUMMARY

Christian parents face the responsibility of preparing their children to serve God. They must instruct, example, and correct their children, showing them the right way to live and delivering them from wrong ways. When they use the rod, they must do so in love until children are trained to obey their instructions promptly and willingly. Different stages in a child's development prepare him for different stages in the training process. Instruction begins at an early age and continues through adolescence, but the rod is necessary in the early years of childhood to deliver the child from rebellion and make him receptive to instruction. Parents need to communicate, show personal respect, and be consistent throughout a child's life, but especially when children reach the teen years. Children who are adopted should be treated like children of natural birth. All children need the security provided by love, acceptance, and godly training.

## THINKING TOGETHER

1. What are some practical ways to make family worship meaningful? What might hinder worship from being

meaningful? How ought worship practices to change as children grow older?

2. What are advantages and disadvantages of home schooling?

3. How might the family work together at service projects?

4. Are there practical things a Christian can do to oppose abortion without overstepping Biblical principles?

5. What are some typical situations which present parents with the opportunity of teaching their children God's ways? What are typical hindrances to such teaching?

6. What are the typical problems which result from failure to use the rod? From overuse of the rod? What is the difference between warning and threatening?

7. How might parents appropriately help a child in the following matters?
   - in developing habits of neatness
   - in overcoming poor eating habits
   - in avoiding becoming sidetracked when given responsibilities

8. List suitable and unsuitable activities for children in each of the following age brackets: 3-7, 8-12, 13-15, 16-19.

9. If parents need to leave children with a baby-sitter, what guidelines should they follow? (i.e., frequency, length, phone numbers, sitter's character, etc.)

10. What Biblical guidelines are there for the intermarriage of people from different cultures or races?

## WORKING TOGETHER

1. As parents, discuss the quality of your child training and teaching. Make a list of weaknesses. Discuss

specific ways to improve, and plan for periodic times to assess your progress.

2. Assess your use of the rod, rewards, and punishment. Is there need for improvement? Are there areas which need a more clear reward/punishment system? Again discuss specific improvements, and take positive steps to implement them.

3. Are there activities in your home which are unwholesome? Discuss as a couple, then as a family, how you might improve your activities. Consider children's interests and skills, and then discuss a number of creative hobbies which might be started or encouraged.

# 7

# THE HOME AND THE CHURCH

## INTRODUCTION

The home and the church are both social units designed by God for His glory and for man's well-being. When ordered according to God's design, the two function in harmony, not in opposition. As each has swung into step with modern pace, however, the home and the church have sometimes jostled each other as strangers or even antagonists rather than co-laborers.

Pace, however, is not entirely to blame. Both the modern home and the modern church have strayed from God's design, and such straying always leads to trouble. In this chapter, we will consider how the home and the church, when functioning according to God's directions, are mutually supportive of one another.

## WHAT IS THE CHURCH?

"But ye are a chosen generation, a royal priesthood, an holy nation, a peculiar people; that ye should shew forth the praises of him who hath called you out of darkness into his marvellous light: Which in time past were not a people, but are now the people of God" (I Peter 2:9, 10).

The Greek word for *church* literally means "the called out." In the New Testament it refers to the assembled believers who have responded to the call of God. Thus, the church is not a building made of stones, mortar, and plaster, but the assembly of Christians. Believers do not really "go to church." They ARE the church—the church meets whenever and wherever believers come together.

Several figures of speech are used in the New Testament to describe the church. It is Christ's "body" (Ephesians 1:23); He is the head. It is Christ's "wife" (Ephesians 5:23-27); He is the husband. It is God's "building" (Ephesians 2:19-22); Jesus is the foundation and the chief cornerstone. It is Christ's "kingdom" (Colossians 1:13); God's "dear Son" is the King.

In each picture of the church, Jesus is in the forefront. He is the director, the provider, the very life of this assembly of believers. Each member receives forgiveness through His work, receives direction through His Word, receives unction and enablement through His Spirit, and is brought to maturity through interaction and service in His body.

The work of Jesus in the church is a work which will continue until the "fulness of times" when "all things in Christ, both which are in heaven, and which are on earth" will be gathered together (Ephesians 1:10). While each member of this assembly enters on his personal confession and faith, the work of redemption is a collective work. Through Jesus, God is calling out an assembly, "a great multitude, which no man [can] number, of all nations, and kindreds, and people, and tongues" (Revelation 7:9). The assembling is going on now and will continue "until the redemption of the purchased possession" (Ephesians 1:14).

Saints of all ages have looked forward to the culmination of this great work of God. Paul described it in vivid terms. "For the Lord himself shall descend from heaven with a shout, with the voice of the archangel, and with the trump of God: and the dead in Christ shall rise first: Then we which are alive and remain shall be caught up together with them in the clouds, to meet the Lord in the air: and so shall we ever be with the Lord" (I Thessalonians 4:16, 17). This is the final calling out, the triumphant ingathering, the great homecoming of all believers of all time to the King of kings and Lord of lords.

The church, then, is not the building on the street corner. It is the assembly of believers in whom Jesus lives and for whom He is coming again.

## MEMBERSHIP IN THE CHURCH

A proper understanding of the church is necessary for a proper understanding of church membership. Where the "church" is the building on the corner, church leaders are free to set their own entrance standards, and membership is usually little more than having one's name on a register and attending according to one's liking. If, on the other hand, we understand the church in the Biblical sense as the assembly of the redeemed, we must likewise look to the Bible for a description of membership. In the New Testament the concepts of the church and the concepts of membership are inseparable.

223

| · Church Concepts | Membership Concepts |
|---|---|
| 1. The church was purchased by Christ and belongs to Him. | ●"Ye are not your own" (I Corinthians 6:19). |
| 2. The church is the collective recipient of Christ's redemptive work. | ●If I am going to be saved, I must be in union with the redeemed people of God (Ephesians 1:10-14). |
| 3. The church collectively is the temple of God's glory. | ●My spiritual condition is not my private affair (I Corinthians 3:16,17). |
| 4. The church is the earthly executor of Jesus' purposes. | ●I cannot fulfill Christ's will alone; I need the help of the other members (I Corinthians 12:14-27). |
| 5. The church experiences collective strength, wisdom, and growth. | ●I cannot stand properly alone, see properly alone, or grow properly alone (Ephesians 4:11-16). |

It is an unfortunate reality that most "churches" today know little about the true church, proper membership, and real brotherhood. Church is something of a Sunday club, with a president who gives weekly lectures and pep talks. The rest of the week the "members" go on with life, giving little thought to and having virtually no accountability to this Sunday club.

In contrast, the Scriptural view of the church and membership carries with it an all-the-time, all-of-life involvement. The work, the play, the education, the activities of the members are engaged in as citizens of heaven. There is even through the week a gravitation toward interaction with other members for mutual encouragement, instruction, prayer, and fellowship. Overall, there is a recognition that each member is a kingdom builder, and that he will engage in nothing out of character with his membership in the assembly of the redeemed. Rather, he will attempt to make everything a blessing and contribution to it.

A Scriptural view of the church causes members to view themselves as spiritually interdependent. They consider themselves members of a working unit, and therefore the spiritual health of every member is necessary to the overall health of the whole body. They exhort each other. They pray for each other. They encourage each other. And when necessary, they rebuke each other. Being "members one of another" (Romans 12:5), they treasure their interdependence and jealously guard one another's spiritual well-being in love. "Take heed, brethren, lest there be in any of you an evil heart of unbelief, in departing from the living God. But exhort one another daily, while it is called To day; lest any of you be hardened through the deceitfulness of sin" (Hebrews 3:12, 13).

The church is a called out assembly. The "citizenship" of its members is in heaven. Followers of Jesus have heavenly loyalties and purposes which forbid the use of force (Matthew 5:39-44), stand above participation in earthly warfare (John 18:36; II Corinthians 10:4), and refuse such methods as litigation to protect personal interests (I Corinthians 6:1-7; Hebrews 10:34).

 — **SNAPSHOT FROM LIFE**

*Brian grew up in an unbelieving home. He learned to know Jackie, a Christian young woman, and through her was introduced to a group of believers and led to the Lord. Brian later began dating Jackie and eventually married her.*

*Brian's work took him to another locality, and there they joined an evangelical church. The group was in many ways a "normal" evangelical group—the pastor preached fundamental messages. But as Brian and Jackie learned to know the members, they saw that things were going on in the church which were not right. There was ill will and gossip. There was rivalry and political maneuvering. Some members were indulging in worldly practices. Some justified divorce and remarriage. Most seemed to feel it was no one else's business to try to "meddle" in these things.*

*Brian and Jackie learned of another group in the area who believed strongly in brotherhood. They believed when one member had something in his life which was not according to the Bible, the other members were responsible to confront him and help him to obedience. At first Brian and Jackie were fearful—they felt that such a group would likely be "all eyes" for anything wrong in their lives. But they decided to begin attending the new group, and they were surprised to learn that the underlying spirit of this group so minded to holiness was not criticism and finger-pointing, but love. True brotherhood, they learned, operates with concern for the well-being of each member. The members of such a brotherhood are not content with a once-a-week meeting and a touch-me-not sort of relationship. They enjoy seeing each other through the week—visiting, praying, studying the Bible, asking counsel, and exhorting each other in the ordinary affairs of living.*

*"That," Brian and Jackie concluded, "is Biblical brotherhood."*

## THE HOME AND CHURCH WORKING TOGETHER

Such a view of the church and church membership has a direct bearing on the home. The church is the assembly of the redeemed, but the home is where the people spend much of their time. The quality of home life, then, is foundational to the quality of church life. Where there are godly homes, there will be godly congregations. Where there are home problems, there will be church problems. Where Christians succumb to the breakdown of the home in Western culture, the result can be nothing but trouble and apostasy in the church. The health of the home and the health of the church are inseparably interdependent.

While the home and the church should work together, they do not always do so. There are times when family loyalties become so strong as to disrupt church unity. On the other hand, many congregations today become so heavily organized that they nearly pull families apart. Following are some guidelines for keeping the home and the church in healthy cooperation:

1. *Church involvement should strengthen the family unit.* The church should instruct men in the Biblical pattern for husbands and fathers. It should instruct women in God's order for wives and mothers. It should instruct children in the principles of honor and obedience. Given vision and proper oversight, the Sunday school can be a tremendous asset to the home. So also can the Christian day school. The teaching program of the church should encourage wholesome family interaction and warn, even specifically, against that which is harmful or dangerous. In short, as a direct result of church interaction, the family should be more loving and godly.

*2. Church activities should not undermine family unity.*
This may seem to be but a restatement of the first
guideline. The organization of church activities, however, presents a problem which needs special attention.
In the name of "ministry" special activities are being
created for every age level and special interest group
possible—youth, juniors, preschoolers, singles, young
marrieds, senior citizens. . . . Underneath the chaotic
schedules, this super-activity is creating loyalties and
interests which rival the unity of the family. Who wants
to sit at home with big brother and little sister when "all
my friends" are practicing for the Easter play? The more
the family has imbibed the spirit of the times, the less
they will question either the hubbub of schedule or the
quality of the activities. But one thing they will experience is a disquieting tension in the family.

*3. Activities organized by the church should be in
keeping with the character and calling of the redeemed.*
The Western world is infatuated with entertainment and
fun, and the germ has spread into the church. The
schedule of events for youth groups, junior clubs, and
kiddies for Jesus clubs are jammed with excitement.
When these activites are planned by the church and
include a few Bible verses and songs, few parents pause
to evaluate. But unfortunately, under the artificial halo
of "church activity," the world has entered the church,
elbowing worship into an unattractive corner and bringing entertainment to center stage. It doesn't take much
discernment to observe that when interest in dramas,
films, and concerts rises, interest in preaching and
prayer dwindles. The modern church likes its fun
throughout the week as well. Its agenda is replete with
banquets, barbecues, fund raisers, and a whole lineup of
practices and play-offs for its sports teams. Does this
mean that the church should never plan a supper or a

social event? Not necessarily. But every church function should be in character with a meeting of the redeemed, and the overall focus of church-planned activities should be upon worship, service, and evangelism, in keeping with the church's nature and mission. We could surely gain heaven's perspective of the present fun-focus by paraphrasing a short statement of Jesus. "My house shall be called a house of prayer, but ye have made it an entertainment center."

*4. The church should not usurp or replace parental responsibilities.* Many homes are run wrongly today, and many are the consequences. The temptation, especially to church boards and church leaders, is to step in and take responsibilities which are not theirs to take. Pastors, for example, may bypass parents or husbands, in giving counsel to children or wives. Some church-run schools operate as though the educational responsibility of children were theirs alone, rather than viewing themselves as servants to the parents.

*5. Parents should train children with a view to servanthood in the church.* All Christian parents want their children to follow Jesus. The reality of this, however, does not come simply by taking them to church. It comes by home training as parents guide their children toward a kingdom-building mindset. "Seek ye first the kingdom of God and his righteousness" is an important motto for every home. Such values are basic to training children for service in the church.

*6. Families should regularly support gatherings of the church for worship, prayer, ministry, and outreach.* Where the church is a body of believers, a brotherhood of the redeemed, its gatherings are primary activities for the family. Children should be as welcome here as they were in the earthly ministry of Jesus. While the meetings need not necessarily be geared to children, neither should they be so academic and formal that they are altogether irrelevant to children.

7. *Family loyalties should not disrupt or override church unity.* It can be a tremendous joy to have grandparents, uncles and aunts, brothers and sisters, and plenty of cousins in the same fellowship. A large family, however, can become a large problem if loyalties are wrong and if church protocol is ignored. Where a large family is represented in a congregation, they should beware of the potential of each of the following:

●Favoring family members for positions in the church.
●Shielding family members from church discipline.
●Railroading church decisions in the interests of the family.
●Spreading news through the family so that trust is betrayed or that issues are discussed with people whose involvement is secondary rather than primary.
●Being so absorbed in family interests that newcomers feel left out.
●Developing such a set pattern of doing things that people with new ideas or ways are made to feel cheap or second rate.

The potential for the above to occur is increased where the lead pastor is also patriarch of the family, and increased still more where several from the same family are in the ministry. This does not mean that father-son ministry teams are unworkable, but perhaps that special precautions need to be taken.

8. *Families should take the initiative in planning for and providing for the social interests of children and youths.* This guideline will surely cut across much church-planned activity. But consider what would result if such things as ball games, camp-outs, sight-seeing, and socials were planned by parents and families instead

of being scheduled by the designated church committee or sponsor. First, there would likely be more mingling of age levels in these events, giving them additional long-term benefits. Second, they would be planned with a view to family needs and schedules, rather than the family trying to accommodate an activity schedule (or a half a dozen activity schedules). And third, there would be less pressure on each family to conform to a preset activity norm. Some families may feel a need for more activity than others. Or for some families, certain times of the year are more suited to extra activities than other times of the year (or month, or week, or even day).

The danger of family-planned activities is that cliques may develop. Some may have repeated involvement in activities while others are neglected and feel snubbed.

Where the church and home function as co-laborers rather than rivals, there is mutual benefit. Parents are actively involved in training, teaching, and preparing their children for conversion and entrance into the assembly of the redeemed. The church receives the converted by baptism and becomes the place of further training and an outlet for service.

Homes vary. Parents vary. Children vary. And the process of bringing young Christians into the assembly, if not handled wisely, can create confusion. Here church leaders should have clear, Biblical guidelines for parents. Consider, for example, the following general guidelines. (Church leaders may be more specific, of course, in view of local situations.)

## GUIDELINES FOR RECEIVING YOUNG CHRISTIANS INTO THE CHURCH FELLOWSHIP

1. Parents should not pressure or bribe their children into the church.
2. Church leaders are responsible to require evidence of a true conversion.
3. True conversion requires the knowledge of sin, the experience of repentance from sin, and the confession of faith in Jesus Christ as Lord and Saviour.
4. While children can easily be taught the Word in preparation for salvation, such basics as the awareness of sin, repentance, and commitment to Jesus can be experienced only beyond the innocence of childhood.
5. In discerning the reality of conversion prior to baptism, church leaders may meet with young Christians, discussing with them the fundamentals of faith.
6. Where applicants are insincere, they should not be baptized, but warned to repent.
7. Where applicants are sincere but uncomprehending of basic spiritual truths, they should receive further instruction. If they do not seem ready for this instruction, they should be encouraged to continue in openness to Jesus and His call in their lives.
8. Sincere applicants should be baptized and welcomed into the church fellowship.

As parents understand the guidelines of church leaders for receiving new Christians, they can work with them in preparing their children for membership. Without guidance from church leaders, parents may discourage young children by "leading them to Christ" before they are spiritually ready and then holding them off from church membership.

Just as the home and the church must work in cooperation in bringing new Christians into the church, so they must work in cooperation in their ongoing membership. Probably the most difficult part of this cooperation is where members grow spiritually cold and require rebuke or discipline. Church members who still live at home under the direction of parents are responsible to the leadership and instruction of both the home and the church. Obviously, home leaders and church leaders should be in harmony, but there can be conflict.

Suppose, for example, a young man begins listening to wrong music and catering to some of the fads and practices associated with this music. His minister in concern may wish to address the problem, both for the young man's sake and for the sake of the other young people in the church. But suppose he finds the young man's parents defensive.

To avoid locking horns in a situation such as this requires several things. First, it requires a commitment by those in authority to work together rather than in opposition. Church leader in open conflict with home leader is as dangerous as Father in open conflict with Mother. In the minds of those under this conflicting authority, it undermines respect for all authority. It sets up sides which can then be used as an escape from doing what God wills. Again, the first step in avoiding conflict is a mutual sense of commitment to work together.

The second requirement for church leaders and home

leaders to be united is respect for one another's position. In view of this, it is best for church leaders to discuss with parents concerns they have for those still under the parents' direct authority. This is similar to a father-mother consultation regarding a problem. With a united position, both can address the problem as necessary. Parents show respect for the position of church leaders by being open to advice and by demonstrating healthy attitudes in discussing and resolving the problem with their young people.

The third requirement for unity between church and home authority has been implied in both of the former— good communication. Church leaders and parents need to be open with each other, honest, kind, and Biblical. Of course, for dialogue to be healthy when resolving problems, it must be healthy otherwise as well.

Even when church leaders try to follow the above guidelines, they sometimes meet up with parents who defend their young people in waywardness. They must, of course, properly discern the nature of the problem in the young person. But if sin is being defended, church leaders must deal with the defensiveness of the parents before they can deal effectively with the waywardness of the young person.

The other side of the picture is that church leaders are sometimes carnal and mistaken in judgment. If a parent is convinced this is so, he should appeal to the church leader. For such an appeal to be effective, it must come from a pure and righteous heart (consider Daniel 1:8). If this appeal is unheard, the parent might ask the minister if together they could arrange a meeting with another minister or bishop to discuss the situation. (This is one of the values of a congregation working in unity and fellowship with other congregations.)

No matter how convinced a person is that a leader is

carnal, however, he must be respectful in his own speech and actions (Acts 23:5). And he must avoid the natural tendency to accuse. The minister's life is in many ways exposed to public view, and he needs the careful and loving regard of his brothers and sisters. Fellow ministers as well as all members do well to follow the caution Paul gave to Timothy. "Against an elder receive not an accusation, but before two or three witnesses" (I Timothy 5:19).

The final authority is God. Sometimes a parent may need to accept a less than perfect decision, trusting his situation to the hand of God. Such acceptance is Biblical and right, provided, of course, the parent is not violating God's direction.

## THE LORD'S DAY

Instruction for a Sabbath (rest) day came on the heels of Creation. "And God blessed the seventh day, and sanctified it: because that in it he had rested from all his work which God created and made" (Genesis 2:3). In the Law given to Moses, God gave further instructions and restrictions for this day. The Mosaic Law, of course, was fulfilled in Christ. From the New Testament, however, and from history we learn that the early church came to honor the first day of the week (on which Christ rose from the dead) as the Lord's Day, and many of the principles of the Sabbath were applied to it. Consider the following New Testament Scriptures regarding a day of rest.

*1. Jesus verified that the day of rest had been made for man's well-being.* "The sabbath was made for man" (Mark 2:27).

*2. On this day, even under the Law, it was right to give emergency help in times of accident or injury.* "What man shall there be among you, that shall have one sheep, and

235

if it fall into a pit on the sabbath day, will he not lay hold on it, and lift it out?" (Matthew 12:11).

*3. It was within the intent of the Law to do acts of kindness and compassion on this day.* "Wherefore it is lawful to do well on the sabbath days" (Matthew 12:12).

*4. The Sabbath was a day for collective worship.* "And, as [Jesus'] custom was, he went into the synagogue on the sabbath day, and stood up for to read" (Luke 4:16). The early church was encouraged not to miss this type of gathering. "Not forsaking the assembling of ourselves together, as the manner of some is; but exhorting one another: and so much the more, as ye see the day approaching" (Hebrews 10:25).

*5. At the time of Jesus, the Sabbath had become regulated by tradition in such a way that its purpose and benefits were obscured.* The Pharisees had so focused on the rules and rituals of the day that they had lost sight of the Lord. "But I say unto you, That in this place is one greater than the temple. But if ye had known what this meaneth, I will have mercy, and not sacrifice, ye would not have condemned the guiltless. For the Son of man is Lord even of the sabbath day" (Matthew 12:6-8).

*6. After Jesus' resurrection, the first day of the week was observed as a day of rest.* The early Christians met on this day for preaching (Acts 20:7). They took collections (I Corinthians 16:1, 2). And they referred to the first day of the week as "the Lord's day" (Revelation 1:10).

While the ceremonial observance of the Sabbath was fulfilled in Christ (Colossians 2:16, 17), many of the principles of the Sabbath are in keeping with the intent of the Lord's Day as practiced by the early church. The day is for our good, specifically for our spiritual good, and it is proper therefore to worship, rest, and do good on this day. It is also in keeping with this day to refrain from manual labor (except for necessary chores such as feeding animals or caring for the sick, as well as emergency work). Activities related to pleasure, business, and such things of this present life ought to be set aside in favor of focusing on the Lord.

The home plays a major role in properly keeping Lord's Day concepts. The attitudes of parents guide the attitudes of children. Where children see parents setting aside a day to seek God for spiritual fellowship, and for the good of the kingdom, they will develop a proper view of the day.

Developing such a view, however, certainly has its challenges. Today's pleasure-seeking, fast-paced society is not geared to Sabbath concepts. In the interests of production, workers are pressured into round-the-clock, round-the-week schedules. In the lust for fun and recreation, the weekend becomes a time for outings, games, and pleasure. Christian parents must draw the line somewhere. In doing so, they should be aware that the line is not necessarily between what is right and wrong, but between what is more conducive or less conducive to the principles of rest, worship, and doing good.

With this goal, parents should question activities on the Lord's Day which:

●are physically exhausting and void of spiritual benefit. (The degree of physical activity may well vary with the age of children. The above guideline would be particularly for older children.)

●deprive the family of collective worship.

●depend upon the labor of others on the Lord's Day.

●are business related.

●are intended primarily for temporal pleasure.

On the other hand, parents should encourage activites on the Lord's Day which:

●stimulate awareness of God.

●refresh the mind and spirit and give physical rest.

●reflect the kindness, mercy, and love of Jesus.
●spread the Gospel and disciple believers.
●strengthen faith and relationships between believers.

Again, these things are encouraged primarily through home standards and values. Stringent and detailed legislation of Sabbath rules easily becomes counterproductive. For Christian families, the Lord's Day should be a day to be enjoyed for its refreshment, not a day to be dreaded for its restrictions. Much of this is dependent upon the attitude and planning of parents.

## SUMMARY

The church is God's family for eternity. The Christian family has present ties which should be maintained in such a way as to strengthen and support the ties in God's family. By working together, the church and the home can mutually benefit one another—the home supporting the church, and the church providing spiritual guidance and stability for the home. A good working relationship between the home and the church is maintained by mutal respect and wholesome communication between parents and ministers.

## THINKING TOGETHER

1. What are some common misconceptions concerning the church, and what Scriptures provide a correct view?
2. How should the church relate to members who do not have a correct view of their membership—who wish to be rather detached from accountability?
3. What are some practical ways a family can preserve unity and healthy interaction when the pressure is on to go, go, go? What kinds of activities should be a

priority for Christian families?

4. How should a church leader respond to parents who are defensive of their young people's misbehavior? (The youths are church members.)

5. How should parents respond when they believe their young people are being dealt with unfairly or unwisely by church leaders?

6. In view of the guidelines for the Lord's Day, how would you look at each of the following activities?
   - mowing lawn
   - going for an afternoon drive
   - having an outdoor picnic
   - distributing Christian literature
   - shopping
   - helping a widow with property upkeep
   - playing softball, tennis, etc.
   - going boating, fishing, golfing, etc.
   - weekend camping
   - taking cookies to shut-ins
   - eating out
   - visiting neighbors or friends
   - baking cookies
   - taking a quiet walk as a family
   - reading
   - doing bookwork or phone work for a job
   - knitting or sewing
   - fixing broken items

## WORKING TOGETHER

1. As a family, evaluate the activities which split up the family. Are you spending enough time together? If not, what guidelines could you come up with to correct the situation?

2. Do you regularly support preaching services, prayer

meetings, and evangelism activities? What is the nature of your church activities? Are any of these activities out of character for a group of people whose life-focus is the kingdom of God? (Or is the overall emphasis of these activities improper?)

3. As parents, are there any ways in which you improperly protect your children from responsibility for their behavior?

4. As a family, are your Lord's Day activities conducive to rest, worship, and kingdom building? How might you make improvements?

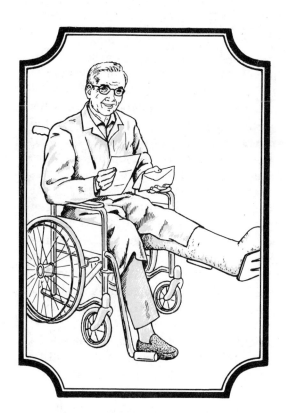

# 8

# WHEN TROUBLES MULTIPLY

## INTRODUCTION

God's people have not been exempt from injury, trials, sickness, and death. Isaac grew blind in old age. His son Jacob was made lame by the angel who wrestled with him. Hezekiah was "sick unto death." Job lost herds, house, family, and health. David lost an infant son. Anna was a widow, as was the woman who cast in her "two mites." Paul had a "thorn" in his flesh—some unnamed physical problem. He testified to being in Corinth "in weakness, and in fear, and in much trembling." At one point he left Trophimus "at Miletum sick."

Sometimes in moments of anguish and despair, the

righteous have questioned God's goodness and providence. Job complained, "Man that is born of a woman is of few days, and full of trouble. . . . Know now that God hath overthrown me, and hath compassed me with his net. . . . He hath also kindled his wrath against me, and he counteth me unto him as one of his enemies" (Job 14:1; 19:6, 11). Asaph confessed, "But as for me, my feet were almost gone; my steps had well nigh slipped. For I was envious at the foolish, when I saw the prosperity of the wicked. . . . They are not in trouble as other men; neither are they plagued like other men" (Psalm 73:2, 3, 5). The writer of Ecclesiastes in frustration wrote, "All things have I seen in the days of my vanity: there is a just man that perisheth in his righteousness, and there is a wicked man that prolongeth his life in his wickedness. . . . Time and chance happeneth to them all" (Ecclesiastes 7:15; 9:11).

In the middle of pain, trouble, or frustration, however, we do not always retain a very clear picture of reality. What seems to be at such a time, we see later was distorted and even untrue.

In this chapter we will honestly look at such problems as pain, sickness, injury, old age, and death. And we will consider the guidance God has given for coping with these troubles.

## PAIN IN PERSPECTIVE

There are differing opinions about such troubles as sickness, accidents, and untimely deaths. Some believe all such things are of the devil. They declare that God intends Christians to enjoy good health and prosperity all their days. Others, however, recognize that we are yet in a sin-cursed world and that our redemption is not yet complete. To them, whether Christians experience sickness or health, poverty or prosperity is not as important as whether or not their lives are bringing glory to God.

The following principles help to put this in Biblical perspective:

*1. Man is mortal.* "Wherefore, as by one man sin entered into the world, and death by sin; and so death passed upon all men, for that all have sinned" (Romans 5:12).

*2. The earth is under the curse.* "For we know that the whole creation groaneth and travaileth in pain together until now" (Romans 8:22).

*3. In his body, man is subject to the pain, trouble, and sickness of this present order.* "And not only they, but ourselves also, which have the firstfruits of the Spirit, even we ourselves groan within ourselves, waiting for the adoption, to wit, the redemption of our body" (Romans 8:23).

*4. Some sickness, pain, and trouble is the direct result of sin.* "Jehoram . . . had the daughter of Ahab to wife: and he wrought that which was evil in the eyes of the LORD. . . . Moreover he made high places in the mountains of Judah, and caused the inhabitants of Jerusalem to commit fornication, and compelled Judah thereto. . . . And after all this the LORD smote him in his bowels with an incurable disease. And it came to pass, that in process of time, after the end of two years, his bowels fell out by reason of his sickness: so he died of sore diseases" (II Chronicles 21).

*5. Some sickness, pain, and trouble is the attack of Satan.* "So went Satan forth from the presence of the LORD, and smote Job with sore boils from the sole of his foot unto his crown" (Job 2:7). "And lest I should be exalted above measure through the abundance of the revelations, there was given to me a thorn in the flesh, the messenger of Satan to buffet me, lest I should be exalted above measure" (II Corinthians 12:7).

*6. Some sickness, pain, and trouble is neither the result of personal sin, nor the attack of Satan, but is simply part of the present imperfect world order.* As noted earlier, Isaac grew blind in old age. Paul left Trophimus sick at Miletum. Jesus seemed to refer to this principle also when He said, "Suppose ye that these Galileans were sinners above all the Galileans, because they suffered such things? . . . Or those eighteen, upon whom the tower in Siloam fell, and slew them, think ye that they were sinners above all men that dwelt in Jerusalem? I tell you, Nay" (Luke 13:2, 4, 5).

*7. It is proper and right to pray for healing and deliverance, provided we pray in faith and submission.* "Is any sick among you? let him call for the elders of the church; and let them pray over him, anointing him with oil in the name of the Lord: And the prayer of faith shall save the sick, and the Lord shall raise him up; and if he have committed sins, they shall be forgiven him" (James 5:14, 15). "For this thing I besought the Lord thrice, that it might depart from me. And he said unto me, My grace is sufficient for thee: for my strength is made perfect in weakness. Most gladly therefore will I rather glory in my infirmities, that the power of Christ may rest upon me" (II Corinthians 12:8, 9). "Father, if thou be willing, remove this cup from me: nevertheless not my will, but thine, be done" (Luke 22:42).

## HAVING RIGHT ATTITUDES

Some of the most distressing troubles we face are things we have little or no control over. A child may die of leukemia. A young father may be crippled for life in an accident. Parents may give birth to a Down's syndrome baby. A mother may be widowed and left with a large

244

family. Aging parents may deteriorate physically, mentally, or emotionally.

Sometimes these troubles seem to come all at once, and life seems to be falling apart. God and His promises may seem to be nothing but wishful thinking.

At such times, certain attitudes become extremely important for the Christian, and certain other attitudes become extremely dangerous. We will look first at proper attitudes and then at improper attitudes.

### Right Attitudes

*1. In times of trouble, Christians need the attitude of faith.* We need not understand what God is doing to express our faith and trust in Him. In the midst of his trouble, Job said, "Though he slay me, yet will I trust in him" (Job 13:15). It is precisely when we do not understand that faith is most needful. God says, "For as the heavens are higher than the earth, so are my ways higher than your ways, and my thoughts than your thoughts" (Isaiah 55:9). God's people, time and time again, have found that their troubles and misery were but gateways into God's grace and goodness in ways they could not have imagined beforehand.

Faith is not easy. It means not only believing God in times of trouble, but giving Him the freedom even to increase that trouble; not only trusting Him when our plans are disrupted, but trusting Him when our plans are crushed out of existence. Faith is believing that whatever comes into our lives is never beyond the sovereign control of the Almighty, and that, in His hands, it can be turned into our eternal benefit and blessing. "And we know that all things work together for good to them that love God, to them who are the called according to his purpose" (Romans 8:28).

*2. In times of trouble, Christians need the attitude of*

245

*meekness.* The natural tendency in difficulty is to react. Meekness, in contrast, is an attitude of submission. It is the Spirit-directed response to those things we cannot change as opposed to the ranting and murmuring and bitterness of the flesh.

Meekness is rooted in faith. The eyes of meekness rest upon God and in that confidence accept the good He sends and the trouble He allows. Job's wife reacted to their calamity, but Job, in the spirit of meekness, replied, "What? shall we receive good at the hand of God, and shall we not receive evil?" (Job 2:10).

The attitude of meekness gives us the freedom to look objectively at trouble and to distinguish between what must be accepted and what can be changed. To be meek does not mean to be altogether passive. It does not mean to cease resisting evil powers. It does not mean to quit in the determination to overcome a handicap. Meekness, in fact, gives freedom to do what must be done because it ceases to spend energy bucking what must be accepted. Meekness delivers us from irrational anger and opens us instead to seeing things from God's perspective. The psalmist says, "The meek will he guide in judgment" (Psalm 25:9).

*3. In times of trouble, Christians need the attitude of prayer.* Prayer, certainly, is an action, but it is also an attitude. When troubles multiply, we need to be minded to seek the Father. The natural man in trouble will plan and figure, squirm and struggle, worry and fret. As a last resort, he may cry out to God. The children of God can save themselves much inner anguish by developing the attitude of prayer. "Be careful for nothing [do not be full of care about anything]; but in every thing by prayer and supplication with thanksgiving let your requests be made known unto God" (Philippians 4:6). The heart that continually brings its cares to the throne room of heaven

246

does not become weighed down with them. The mindset of confident request changes our focus from frustration over earthly trouble to anticipation of heaven's reply.

*4. In times of trouble, Christians need the attitude of thanksgiving.* This is perhaps the most difficult of attitudes to maintain, and it is impossible without the attitudes of faith, meekness, and prayer. But the focus upon God makes the attitude of thanksgiving both possible and proper. Thanksgiving in times of trouble is not a mindless, irrational, "Praise the Lord anyhow" sort of response. It rests in realities. "Rejoice in the Lord alway: and again I say, Rejoice" (Philippians 4:4). God in Himself is cause for joy, and the trusting Christian cannot look long at God, no matter what his situation, without coming to the attitude of thanksgiving.

### Wrong Attitudes

*1. In times of trouble, Christians should beware of a complaining attitude.* When the Israelites faced hardships in the wilderness, their complaining attitude not only cut them off from God's blessings, but also brought upon them further trouble. Complaining challenges God's sovereignty. It ignores His power and goodness. It focuses on present trouble and hinders God's people from experiencing His grace for deliverance.

*2. In times of trouble, Christians should beware of a defeatist attitude.* This attitude goes right along with an attitude of complaint. The more we focus on our troubles negatively, the darker we view the situation. Shortly we begin describing not only actual trouble, but probable trouble. The present picture grows worse in the shadows of pessimism about the future. Such an attitude further cuts us off from the power and goodness of God. "God hath not given us the spirit of fear; but of power, and of love, and of a sound mind" (II Timothy 1:7). Christians

247

must, like Caleb and Joshua, view the giants from the solid ground of faith in the Almighty. To wallow in the mire of self-pity feels good to the flesh, but it is ruinous to the spirit.

*3. In times of trouble, Christians should avoid an attitude of presumption.* Faith rests upon the reality of God; presumption pulls God's words out of context and begins to demand things from God in the name of faith. A father whose diabetic son died when they withheld insulin, presuming he had been healed, wrote, "A major flaw exists in the *positive confession* principle that is so popular today. The practice encourages people to incorporate selected verses from the Bible as their own record or promise from God. Passages concerned with many spiritual principles can have general application. But not all verses necessarily will apply to your circumstances or God's plan for your life. . . . Arbitrarily claiming the general promises of the Bible for specific needs opens the door to presumption. *Out of balance,* many of the teachings of the Bible can have heartbreaking consequences."[1] Understanding this in times of sickness and difficulty is important lest faith descends to presumption.

*4. In times of trouble, Christians must beware of an attitude of bitterness.* Essentially, bitterness is a pattern of blame. Troubles in life are usually tied somehow to other people. Joseph was a slave in Egypt because of his brothers. David was a fugitive for years because of Saul. Samson was tricked by Delilah. Esau was outwitted by Jacob. Jephthah's daughter was never married because of the rashness of her father. But if we study the above examples, we discover a direct tie between the success or failure in overcoming trouble and the attitude of the one who was wronged. Bitterness turns people into unforgiving, unrepentant Esaus. Forgiveness and faith, on the other hand, produce Josephs and Davids. "Looking dili-

248

gently . . . lest any root of bitterness springing up trouble you, and thereby many be defiled" (Hebrews 12:15). Bitterness not only ruins relationships, it sours one's own personality. It shuts people off from God and His enabling grace. And thus, the very things needed to cope with trouble—friends, character, divine aid—are the things bitterness destroys.

5. *In times of trouble, Christians should beware of developing selfish attitudes.* In the Christian family and in the church community, times of trouble are times of sharing. Different people respond in different ways when they find themselves in a condition of need. Some are humiliated and angry, some are grateful and gracious, and some seem to play on their helplessness and need. When we are in a condition of need, we do well to train our minds to think of others too. Ours are not the only needs and troubles in the world. We must not demand service. We must not monopolize conversation with our tales of woe. We must sympathize, understand, reach out, care, and listen, lest we allow our troubles to turn us into receivers only and we lose the joys of love and giving. The other side of wanting to receive is refusing to receive. This, too, is rooted in self. It takes humility to receive graciously. The point here is that attitudes centered around self make us unhandy when we are in trouble, and we therefore should avoid letting our life become focused on our woes.

## PHYSICAL HANDICAPS

Physical handicaps vary both in kind and degree. *Handicap* is a general term referring to any physical problem which hinders normal participation in ordinary functions of life. Thus, handicaps include such things as the loss of a physical sense, such as sight or hearing; the loss of limbs—arms or legs; or the loss of use (or impairment of use) of certain parts of the body, due to such things as paralysis, arthritis, and injury.

Some people are born with handicaps. Many others are handicapped through accidents or sicknesses. No matter what the cause, every handicap presents its own challenges, difficulties, and opportunities. Those who are handicapped from birth face the continued challenge of fitting in with a world which is not geared to their level of ability. Those who become handicapped through accident or injury face the trauma of adjusting suddenly from being able to do certain things to not being able.

### General Guidelines for Coping With a Physical Handicap

1. Face the situation realistically. Take mental, emotional, and spiritual steps toward accepting what is.

2. Pray for grace and wisdom to experience Christ in new ways (see II Corinthians 12:9, 10).

3. Learn appropriate ways to handle frustration. This means neither denying one's emotions, nor being controlled by them. We usually need to learn how to talk about our frustrations, when to talk, and to whom to talk.

4. Become acquainted with others who have successfully coped with similar problems. This can be through books, tapes, or personal friendships.

5. Give Christ freedom to mold attitudes and open your eyes to the needs of others. A spirit of cheer, goodwill, thoughtfulness, and gratitude is anyone's pass to friendship and acceptance. A healthy sense of humor is invaluable.

6. Accept the reality that some people will be unthoughtful. Generally, people are not intentionally rude, but even when they are, avoid taking it too personally—these people likely are rude to others also.

7. Live as normally as possible. Develop positive attitudes and look for ways to expand your skills, overcome obstacles, and do your best at whatever you are able to do.

Christian parents need to teach their children proper

 — **SNAPSHOT FROM LIFE** —

*Alvin was a normal, healthy ten-year-old boy, but an accident in school one day left him partially paralyzed. He spent the next several years in rehabilitation programs both in the hospital and out, but he never regained the normal use of his legs and right arm.*

*As a teenager, he was unable to go like the other young people his age. As a young adult, he was unable to consider most of the work opportunities of his peers.*

*Instead of growing bitter, however, Alvin determined to do what he could. He read. He studied. He developed journalistic skills. He learned to repair watches and clocks. Eventually, he married and reared a family, writing and teaching for a living.*

*As an adult, Alvin came to be known as a devout Christian, a man of keen understanding, and one who knew his Bible well. Many people began seeking out his counsel for various problems and difficulties they were facing.*

*By accepting his limitations, refusing to grow bitter, and turning his heart and mind over to the Lord, Alvin lived a very meaningful and productive life.*

ways of relating to the handicapped. Following are some general guidelines for relating to someone with a handicap and then guidelines for specific handicaps. These guidelines could be discussed in a series of family worship times, using Leviticus 19:14 as a springboard. Children could even practice various of the pointers. One child, for example, could take the part of a blind person by being blindfolded, while another tries to describe what is going on outside. Or children might practice lipreading. Scriptures and songs relating to kindness, love, respect, or proper speech could also be read and discussed.

### General Guidelines for Relating to Someone With a Handicap

1. Show a genuine interest in the person. Everyone shares the need for acceptance and friendship.

2. Ignore inappropriate attitudes or behavior unless you have a close enough relationship to confront knowledgeably and considerately.

3. When a handicapped person is with a group, arrange for at least some activities in which all can participate. (But avoid a condescending "we're doing this for you" approach.)

4. As a friend, avoid pressuring or prodding a handicapped person into things which cause him anxiety or embarrassment. Everyone needs prodding at times, but we accept it better from those who understand us and are responsible for us.

5. If the handicap is discussed, show courtesy. Most people with a handicap do not mind discussing it, provided there is genuine interest. But avoid being sentimental, curious, or inappropriately humorous.

6. Teach children proper responses to handicapped people. They should not stare, point, whisper, mock, or

play pranks (Leviticus 19:14; I Thessalonians 5:14). They should have awareness, show kindness, build friendships, and be patient toward those with handicaps.

7. Be encouraging and supportive. Help the handicapped person reach his goals rather than forcing your expectations. Be positive and upbeat, but not pushy.

## Guidelines for Particular Handicaps

### Relating to the blind

1. Give your name when speaking, unless your voice is so well-known, that there is no question to the blind person who is speaking.

2. Do not become silent when a blind person is walking toward you. His ears need to know where you are.

3. Be ready to make the first move in starting a conversation—a blind person does not want to interrupt or disturb you if your attention is elsewhere.

4. Courteously signal when you leave. A silent departure after conversation has waned could cause embarrassment.

5. If a blind person needs to be led (in unfamiliar or crowded places) and you have never led a blind person, ask how to do it. Proper leading is easy to follow, but a blind person does not like to be pushed or pulled along.

6. If a blind person seems to be lost, make yourself known and ask if you can help. Everyone needs help at times.

### Relating to the deaf

1. If the deaf person lipreads, speak distinctly, but don't overdo lip movement.

2. Avoid turning away when talking. If you draw attention to something away from you, wait until the attention is back to continue the conversation.

3. If you are in a public meeting and you sit beside a

deaf friend, take notes so your friend can follow the main points.

4. In a group where chatter goes too fast for a deaf person to follow, occasionally summarize the conversation for the deaf person. (You may do so silently to avoid drawing attention to what you are doing.)

*Relating to a person in a wheelchair*

1. When carrying on a conversation, sit if at all possible, to be on eye-level with the person.

2. If you operate the wheelchair, be sure you know what you are doing, especially on inclines or steps. Avoid excessive speed and beware of catching footrests or wheels on furniture or on people in passing.

3. Offer to carry extra items (books, Bible, notebook, etc.) if the person is operating his own wheelchair and has no storage compartment.

4. Do not permit children to use an unoccupied wheelchair as a plaything unless friendship is such that you have mutual understanding. Sometimes, however, a person in a wheelchair may demonstrate the use of it to children (perhaps even allow them to operate a motorized wheelchair). This can help to expand children's awareness. But it should be owner-supervised.

*Relating to someone using crutches or a walker*

1. When walking, let the handicapped person set the pace. Sometimes walking is necessary for exercise. Companionship may be more significant encouragement than conversation.

2. Watch for hazardous walking conditions. Spilled water, toothpicks, buttons, scraps of paper, even throw rugs, can cause a serious fall, especially for those using crutches.

3. Do not insist on giving help, or on your own way of

giving help. In some conditions, a handicapped person may need to be carried (up or down stairs). Usually he or she knows the method most suitable for the occasion. Follow instructions. Nobody enjoys the embarrassment of a fall.

*Relating to someone who is bedfast*

1. If your visit is more than a few minutes, sit to provide a more relaxed atmosphere.

2. Be sensitive to needs—water, tissue, a book, etc. You can be legs for one who cannot be up and about.

3. Often a person confined to bed finds such things as flowers and cards meaningful reminders of friendship.

4. Be sensitive to the time, the duration, and the nature of your visit. Sometimes your presence is more needful than conversation. Reading or singing is usually appreciated. Older people often enjoy reminiscing.

## MENTAL HANDICAPS

Like physical handicaps, mental handicaps vary greatly. There are learning disorders so slight that they go undetected for years, and at the other end of the spectrum are mental handicaps so severe a person needs complete care.

The general guidelines for relating to someone with a handicap (given earlier in this chapter) apply here. We should note, however, that mental handicaps seem to tempt people to inappropriate humor more than any other human disorder. Learning proper responses to those with mental handicaps depends much upon home training. Parental attitudes are important. The goals should be to help children respect the personhood of all people. Those with mental handicaps are often quite normal emotionally. Like all people, they need love and acceptance, and they are hurt by mockery, unkindness, and rejection.

To help children accept those with mental handicaps, parents should build awareness. They can do this by visiting those with such handicaps (explaining appropriate behavior beforehand), by discussing proper and improper terms (Down's syndrome, Alzheimer's disease vs. moron, idiot, etc.), and by reading stories or articles about people with mental handicaps.

While many physical handicaps are caused by accident or injury, mental handicaps are often due to genetic factors—children are born with the problem. Parents who have a child with a mental handicap, especially where the handicap is profound, usually go through a period of adjustment. Some parents feel humiliated. They struggle with anger, with "why" questions, with feelings that life is not fair. Nearly all parents of handicapped children grapple with fears. They wonder how they will ever manage to give the proper care. These feelings of inadequacy sometimes continue through life. Some parents also assume personal guilt for the handicap of their child, or for the child's failure to achieve. Parents of handicapped children may find the following pointers helpful:

1. Take steps mentally and emotionally to accept that which cannot be changed. For the Christian, this is always linked to faith in a sovereign God who is devoted to our eternal well-being.

2. Talk to others who have faced similar situations. This can help both in verbalizing your own feelings and in receiving helpful advice.

3. Read up on the problem. Many struggles of parents are related to fear of the unknown.

4. Where it is possible, provide care in the home, rather than in an institution. Studies have repeatedly

shown that the mentally handicapped do better with home care than with institutional care, though certainly home care can be supplemented.

5. Arrange for breaks where care is demanding.

6. Consciously tally things to be grateful for and express your thanks to God.

7. Arrange for appropriate expression of your innermost feelings. Confide in a trusted friend, pray, and possibly keep a diary or journal.

8. Treat the handicapped person as normally as possible. Beware of smothering with affection or overmuch care. This can both hinder progress and create tensions for others in the family.

9. Share responsibilities among family members. Other children in a family usually profit by being included in responsibilities.

A child with a handicap such as Down's syndrome usually requires more care. Life expectancy may be shorter, particularly where other complications exist. Sometimes parents and family members are not prepared for the emotional shock of an early death. Any time someone requires extra care, however, special ties are being formed. Those ties broken in death produce a singular grief, poignant beyond words. Those who have felt it know and understand. Pointers for coping with death are given later in this chapter.

## CARING FOR AGING PARENTS

"Honour thy father and thy mother: that thy days may be long upon the land which the LORD thy God giveth thee" (Exodus 20:12). "But if any widow have children or nephews, let them learn first to shew piety at home, and to requite their parents: for that is good and acceptable before God. But if any provide not for his own, and specially for those of his own house, he hath denied the faith, and is worse than an infidel" (I Timothy 5:4, 8).

The Scriptures are clear that children are to honor their parents. Jesus' definition of honor included not only the attitude of respect but material and financial help as well (Matthew 15:3-6). Many parents in old age come to a point where they need care. They are no longer physically able to provide for themselves or care for their property. Someone needs to help them. The Bible says children and relatives are first responsible. Then, where needs are beyond their resources, the church should provide.

Parents' needs in old age vary greatly, and those who give care are often ill-prepared for the demands and adjustments involved. We will first consider some preparatory factors which make parental care easier to accept and adjust to and then look at practical pointers for caregivers.

### Preparing for Effective Care

Traditionally, the family unit among the Mennonite and Amish people has been strong. Older parents in rural settings have often moved into the *daudy haus,* a cottage on the home place specially built for Grandpa and Grandma. As they came to the point of needing more care, they either moved into a home of one of the children or had a single daughter or niece move in with them.

Although other care procedures, such as retirement centers, have become more common among mainstream Mennonites, many older people, especially among the more conservative groups, are still being cared for in the homes of family members. Home care of the elderly can yield great blessings, but it can likewise place tremendous strain on a family. This is sometimes beyond the control of anyone involved. Some care, in other words, is difficult no matter how it is approached. Sometimes, however, the difficulty is the result of negative factors in motion long before the actual care. The following points demonstrate some prerequisites for healthy and effective care of elderly parents.

1. *Parents in many ways are preparing for the quality of their own care in old age by the quality of care they give to their children.* Children who have been cared for in an atmosphere of love and acceptance are better prepared to provide such care. This is not to excuse anyone from loving and honoring their parents, but to recognize that many tensions in later years are the direct result of unresolved tensions in former years of the parent-child relationship. Anger patterns, control tactics, cynicism, criticism, and put-downs, if left unresolved, return when children are called upon to care for their parents. Unfortunately, bad habits usually grow worse with old age.

2. *The more Christlike the relationship between siblings, the better they will be able to cope with the difficulties of caring for their elderly parents.* Cold wars in a family easily erupt into active fighting when care of parents becomes a necessity. Rivalries, jealousies, grudges, and all suchlike attitudes between children hinder the working together necessary for caregivers.

3. *Open communication in the family is necessary both in planning for care and in providing it.* All the children should be aware of such things as the physical condition of the parents, the ways each family member can help, the financial situation, and the stresses on those giving the immediate care. Lack of communication results in overload for some and thoughtlessness in others. Communication regarding parental care should take place before such care is necessary. Sometimes parents have suggestions or requests. Where these can be honored, they should be. In any case, an important key to working

together as a family is good communication.

*4. Any family who takes a parent into their home should be united in the decision.* Lack of unity is certain to spill out in tension and frustration, adding to the normal difficulties of such an arrangement.

*5. The more interaction a family has had with an aged parent prior to a live-in arrangement, the more likely the compatibility.* Where a family is considering taking in a parent who lives in a different community, they may wish to begin with a trial period—one or two months, for example—to better assess the adjustments necessary. Of course, sometimes the need for care rises suddenly and no trial time is possible.

*6. Christian families should develop and maintain the mindset of care for aged parents.* Western culture is generally not minded to respect and care for the aged, much to the surprise and disappointment of visitors from Eastern cultures. If Christians are to maintain a mentality of care for the aged, they should consider the factors in Western culture which erode such thinking. Consider the following:

### Factors in Western Culture Negative to Elderly Care

*1. Fast pace.* The Western world is on the run. Schedules are timed to the second. For people in a hurry, wasted seconds are irritating. Wasted minutes are exasperating. A wasted hour is utterly intolerable. But old people are slow. They don't fit into modern schedules. Western culture, instead of accepting the realities of old age, tends to push the elderly out of the way so the pace can go on uninterrupted.

*2. Change.* Closely related to the rapid pace in the West is the change going on continually. The new is scarcely out until the improved hits the market. Older people don't keep up. They do things as they always have done them. The older they grow, the more they tend to resist change. Their minds simply function best in the familiar. The younger generation often grows exasperated at the "stubbornness" of older people and at the same time often loses touch with their wisdom.

*3. Independence.* "As a society, [we] have made a fetish of independence. We almost worship it. It's time to ask ourselves whether dependence is really so awful."[2] The independent way of thinking is, "I don't want to be tied down to anyone, and I don't want anyone tied down to me." Such thinking is threatened by frail, old parents. It needs to be threatened. One lady who cared for her parents suggested that the dependency of the elderly is actually a gift to their families. Certainly there is the abuse of dependency, where a person tries to control by "helplessness." But the dependence of old people challenges our self-centeredness and shows us what needy human beings we really are.

*4. Fear of reality.* The modern "civilized" world is in so many ways artificial. Life, people imagine, should be fun, pain-free, and youthful forever. In reality, it is not. The mindset to take an aspirin for every difficulty doesn't know what to do with old age. Realities such as the brevity of life, the frailty of the body, and the certainty of death are sometimes too sobering, too solemn, too weighty for the plastic world view of the present generation.

If the Christian family is to maintain a respect for the elderly and a commitment to their care, they must recognize and resist the thinking which finds old people such a bother. The Christian family, therefore, should avoid always living in a rush, should develop respect for old ways, changing only in accord with wisdom, should treasure the interdependence of the generations, and should fully accept realities of life, death, and eternity.

Such a way of life will gladly make room for old people.

If we accept the pace and values of our day to the exclusion of our elderly parents and to the neglect of their care, do we not come under the rebuke of Jesus? "Full well ye reject the commandment of God, that ye may keep your own tradition. For Moses said, Honour thy father and thy mother; and, Whoso curseth father or mother, let him die the death: But ye say, If a man shall say to his father or mother, It is Corban, that is to say, a gift, by whatsoever thou mightest be profited by me; he shall be free. And ye suffer him no more to do ought for his father or his mother; making the word of God of none effect through your tradition" (Mark 7:9-13). We might paraphrase Jesus' comments thus for our day: "The people of this age attempt to nullify the instructions of God. For the Word says, 'Honour your father and mother,' but you say, 'I can't afford it. The time and money required to care for my parents would take away my extra job, my vacation money, my privacy, and my freedom.' Thus, by your life-style and your values, you empty God's instructions of practical meaning and shove off the responsibility of caring for your parents onto the state."

### Providing Effective Care for Elderly Parents

As noted previously, the needs of elderly parents vary greatly, and there are a variety of ways being chosen to meet those needs. Some parents' need for care develops slowly. Others are disabled suddenly by a stroke, heart attack, or accident. Some develop a terminal disease such as cancer, Alzheimer's, or Parkinson's disease and deteriorate slowly or rapidly as the case may be. Usually one parent requires care ahead of the other. In some cases, parents need care before they are willing to receive it— they are no longer competent to drive, cook, or care for themselves, but they insist they are well able. How do children provide effective care for their aging parents?

There are no pat answers. Specific care is as varied as the needs and personalities of people. The following pointers, however, apply generally to the care of elderly parents.

*1. Be knowledgeable about your parents' condition.* Read up on any disease or physical problems your parents may have. Know the symptoms, the prognosis, and the available treatment.

*2. Be aware of available help and support both for your parents and for yourself as you give care.* Family members, as they are made aware of needs, can provide care and arrange for breaks in the routine. Where care is too heavy for the family, local church groups may organize supportive care. Receiving this help requires the humility to ask for it, but without such a request, many willing-hearted people have no idea how to give needed assistance. In addition, there are often home health services available for the elderly, particularly those with certain disorders.

*3. Keep your parents surrounded by the familiar as much as possible.* Most elderly people resist change. Radical changes, even when they are obviously for your parents' good, may be met with extreme ingratitude. Change increases in the elderly their natural yearning for the past. Thus, it is best to keep parents in their own home as long as this is possible, and when they need care, to provide it as a family. Sometimes, of course, parents enter a retirement center well ahead of their need of care, and that center itself provides care in later years. If this is the parents' choice, so be it. But often such centers have waiting lists. Furthermore, the cost is beyond what many can afford.

*4. As your parents age, focus on what they can do rather than on what they cannot do.*

When parents lose the ability to do things—drive, knit, cook, sew, garden, etc.—they will naturally tend to dwell on those things. If Grandma can no longer hang out clothes, she may still be able to cook a meal. If she cannot cook, perhaps she can set the table. If Grandpa can no longer garden, perhaps he could grow a number of indoor vegetables. Be generous with appreciation, encouragement, and praise. Focusing on negatives often narrows the vision and stifles creative ideas.

*5. Avoid circular communication.* Older people sometimes grow negative in their thinking and speech. They often are fearful, lonely, and grieving over their losses in life. Sometimes they chafe under restraints. Every day, for example, Grandpa might ask, "Why can't I drive? Don't you trust me anymore?" And every day, you may respond, "I've told you again and again, it's not safe. Your reflexes are slower, and we feel you just shouldn't." Grandpa replies, "Who's we?" And so round and round the conversation goes. A parent in such a conversation normally does not want reasonable answers. He is grieving over a loss. One lady who cared for her aged mother for six years suggests what she calls "active listening."[3] Active listening picks up on what a person is feeling. It often rephrases what the person says. In the above situation, for example, an active listener might reply, "I suppose it is rather difficult to give up something like driving. Are you struggling with feeling kind of useless?" Such responses empathize with the feelings of the older person and redirect the conversation away from pointless argument.

*6. If a parent moves in, establish and respect lines of territory.* This is usually more easy to talk about than to do. Everyone has a personal "territory" which is his. Furthermore, each family has its territory. Inviting a parent into a home easily becomes an invasion of this territory. Negative feelings associated with this invasion are sometimes the more frustrating because both the territory and the invasion are only vaguely understood. Children may feel their territory is invaded if Grandma walks freely into their bedrooms. And another territory, less visible but just as real, is invaded if she freely orders them about. For older people, however, moving in with someone amounts to giving up a territory, and sometimes they assume privileges without realizing the effect it has on others. Parents move in, of course, at different levels of mobility and care needs. Normally, however, it is best to have a certain section of the house, or at least a room, which the older person can call his own. The arrangement, upkeep, and limitations for this territory should be as much in the hands of the occupant as possible. Further guidelines for respecting territory can be worked out as the need arises, but it often includes the nitty-gritty, such as opening mail, operating a kitchen, and training children.

Territorial respect is often complicated because of the role reversal—the child is now caring for the parent in the child's home. Some caregivers struggle with reverting to a childhood relationship, letting the grandparent dominate the household. Where there are problems, the general rule is to talk about them. There must be honesty, frankness, and respect. If Grandma is dominating the kitchen, a territorial rule may be, "I'll plan the meals. You prepare them." Or, "You prepare lunches. I'll take care of breakfasts and dinners." A grandparent who moves in with a family commonly complains that the children are too unruly. Sometimes they are right. It must be recognized, however, that an underlying competitiveness is common between grandparents and children where three generations live under the same roof. Usually this competitiveness has its roots in territorial violations. The more clearly everyone understands the lines of territory, therefore, and respects them, the more compatible the relationship will be.

7. *Take care of yourself.* When an aged parent needs care, the person most involved in giving the care makes tremendous sacrifices. This is right and proper. Self-sacrifice is both Christian and rewarding. Under the load of caring for an older person, however, one can become improperly neglectful of personal and family needs. "Everybody's needs must be balanced, including the needs of the caregiver. . . . The most important thing you have to give to your parent is yourself."[4] To take breaks, to relax, to read the Bible and pray, to do things with the family, to do something you enjoy personally—these things, as they refresh you and keep you physically, emotionally, and spiritually in shape, are in the best interests of your loved one. Sometimes this will mean asking for help. Sometimes it will mean not pleasing the one needing help. Sometimes it may mean being misunderstood by others. Where the caregiver is driven by guilt or by pride, asking for help or not meeting others' expectations can be agonizing. Often the decisions about personal needs can be made best and wisest in consultation with other family members or with a pastor or pastor's wife. To help assess personal needs, you may periodically ask yourself the following questions:

- Am I continually tired?
- Do I have any recurring ailments such as headaches, heartburn, chest pains, etc.?
- Do I eat and serve balanced meals?
- Do I find myself frequently depressed?
- Have I been able to laugh in recent weeks?
- Are there things which have bothered me for some time which I have not discussed with anyone?
- Do I feel resentful toward other family members?

- Do I hear frequent complaints from my family about things I am neglecting?
- Is my relationship with my spouse warm and open?
- Have I gained any spiritual insight recently?
- Am I able to find inner peace when I pray?
- Do I sing or do I commonly have songs running through my mind?

As noted earlier, caring for parents presents problems for which there are no easy answers. With these problems, however, as with all problems, the Christian can claim the promises of the Bible. God promises to give wisdom to those who ask in faith (James 1:5), to provide strength for the weary who wait upon Him (Isaiah 40:31), and to personally accompany those who do His will (Joshua 1:9).

 **SNAPSHOT FROM LIFE**

*Ilene was 64 years old and dying of cancer. Her husband Lester cared for her with help from their daughter Sarah who lived nearby. Ilene suffered very little pain, but she needed increasing care as the cancer progressed. When the care load became too heavy for Lester, Sarah and her family moved in with them.*

*Ilene was rational and comprehending most of the time, but on occasion she did things or thought things which didn't make sense. Sometimes her sentences simply trailed off, and she couldn't remember what she had been saying. Physically, she was deteriorating as well, losing strength as well as body functions. The family found these losses the more pathetic because Ilene had always been robust and healthy, the kind of person to help others, not to need help. The strain of constant care was compounded by the emotional strain of watching this competent loved one grow more and more incompetent.*

*Lester and his daughter found the strain more than they would have anticipated. Loss of sleep, high-intensity care each day, new signs of deterioration almost every day. . . . At times their own inner tensions spilled over into impatience with Ilene. Then their consciences berated them for their thoughtlessness and lack of love. Friends offered advice and encouragement, but no one really knew what they were giving each day. Working together, however, had its great advantages. They could give each other breaks, and they could also talk over their frustrations with each other.*

*After Ilene passed away, they wondered how they had been able to keep the schedule and endure the strain of the last month. Had they been able to look ahead and see it all in advance, they would likely have said it was an impossible burden. But looking back, they were so grateful they had done it. The joy of knowing they had honored a wife and mother who had loved them, that they had stood by her in the deepest crisis of her life, that they had faced the reality of sickness and death head-on, and that they had left an example of honor and commitment to Sarah's children were well worth the sacrifices they had made.*

## FACING DEATH

Death is never easy. It is the part of our existence, however, probably more than any other one thing, which brings us face to face with certain realities. We are not secure on earth. We do not have promise of tomorrow here. Human life is fragile and limited. Earthly ties we have with anyone we know may be terminated at any given time.

Death comes in different ways. Sometimes we have warning, sometimes none at all. Some deaths are sudden and traumatic, others quiet and peaceful. Some people die in old age, some in mid-life, some in childhood, and some before even the first breath is taken.

Every death presents its singular heartache because every person is unique and has his own ways, his own problems, his own triumphs, his own relationships. The death of a lifelong companion is difficult because of all the years of working together, the fond memories, and the strong bonds. The death of a child is difficult just the other way around—the anticipation of life, of what might have been, of bonds fresh and new. A sudden death seems especially painful because there was no warning. An expected death, on the other hand, seems especially painful because of the emotional strain of watching a loved one deteriorate. The truth is simply that death has its sting. While some deaths may be more grief-filled than others, there is little point in comparing grief. It always hurts.

For Christians, of course, the real sting of death has been taken away by the resurrection of Jesus. We have the sure hope of eternity with God. Sometimes, however, Christians assume that this hope should shield us from the necessity of grief. This is not so. Christians weep too, though not "as others which have no hope" (I Thessalonians 4:13). The knowledge of heaven and eternity with God provides stability and even an underlying joy as we experience the pain of parting with loved ones. We, of all people, can weep freely because we have a solid hope and a sure understanding.

Although death comes in a variety of ways, and people have different emotional character, there is a fairly regular emotional pattern for those who lose loved ones. First there is shock, then grief, and finally healing.

*Shock.* Being brought face to face with death is usually traumatic. The more sudden and unexpected the death, the greater the shock. Emotionally, there is such an upsurge of feelings that one scarcely feels anything distinctly. Shock is actually a buffer against the poignant pain of initial grief. There is often a sense of disbelief, of feeling this can't be, of indistinct fears. Mentally, the time of shock is likewise characterized by numbness. There is often an experience of confusion, of forget-fulness, of thoughts running from one thing to another. Spiritually, a person in shock often experiences near panic. God, faith, Bible verses, the church—the spirit moves from one to the other for assurance, comfort, and help. Often "why" questions surface during the shock period, but the mind and spirit are seldom calm enough or collected enough to hear answers.

*Grief.* Often the period of shock lasts through the time of the funeral. Friends are sometimes amazed at the peace and composure of the family, while the family members sometimes feel guilty for not grieving more. The truth is, they can't grieve properly until the shock wears off. But sooner or later, the reality of parting comes, and so do the tears.

The period of grief varies both in length and in intensity. It has several elements—loneliness, questions, hurt, a sense of loss, and sometimes feelings of anger and guilt—each of which has its own flavor. The grieving one sometimes feels tossed back and forth from one feeling to another.

For Christians, probably the more difficult feelings to understand and cope with are those which we know are reactionary and wrong. Feelings and thoughts of anger, resentment, blame, self-railing, self-pity, and discouragement may churn unbidden in the grieving heart. We may or may not recognize these feelings. If these negative feelings are not arrested, if we deny them, and if we do not find proper alternatives to them, we not only prolong the grieving process, but hurt both ourselves and those close to us.

The more honest and understanding we are with ourselves and God about our true feelings, the better off we are. Some people find that a journal helps. Writing out the thoughts and feelings of grief brings relief to the heart and clarity to the mind. Some find similar blessings in talking to a friend, others in praying. At any rate, verbalizing our deepest feelings is generally needful and good for us.

*Healing.* While grieving is normal and right, there comes a time when we need to move on to healing. One can grieve too much and begin to savor the bitter flavor of tears. This does not mean that tears will never fall again, but that we can learn to put meaning to the death, experience faith in our trials, and begin to look at the past, the present, and the future with new awareness.

Healing comes harder for some than for others. Some people find themselves caught in a guilt trap when they begin to forget their sadness. They feel they are betraying their departed loved one. Some find it hard to give up little reminders—toys, books, clothes, crutches, a chair, etc. When the time is right, however, a family needs to sort through things. Continuing reminders are not all wrong, provided they permit us to move onward and do not trap us in the past.

The pain of parting with a loved one who is not saved is perhaps the bitterest of grief. There is no comfort in such a death, except as we look to God. We can know that much as we grieve, God must grieve also. He allowed the body of His precious Son to be broken to save sinners. Most assuredly, then, He is "not willing that any should perish, but that all should come to repentance" (II Peter 3:9). We can also rest in the knowledge that God is just and right, that when all is over, there will be no unfairness with Him.

## PREPARING FOR DEATH

The most important preparation to be made for one's death, of course, is getting right with God. What many Christians fail to consider, however, are the practical issues their loved ones must deal with after their death. To make no preparations for one's death means that loved ones must make many decisions on short notice, at a time when grief makes decisions difficult. Planning and foresight can make a significant difference.

*A will.* Anyone who is married or has property or goods of their own should have a will. The will designates what to do with property in the event of the death of the owner. Wills also can give direction for the care of children. In the absence of a will, the disposal of property and the care of children are matters decided by the state. In some states, a simple will can be written privately, provided it is witnessed and notarized. The help of an attorney is usually needed for larger estates.

*Funeral plans.* Christians, especially as they grow older, can often help their families by making certain funeral plans and requests ahead of time. The service arrangements including minister, pallbearers, music, and even such things as type of casket can be described. These things should be written down. With these requests should also be information about the location of the will and other documents and records. Often, funeral homes make available booklets designed for such plans and requests. These arrangements can be very helpful to a grieving family.

*Ethical issues.* Modern medical science is making advances which sometimes present families with agonizing decisions. It is possible to keep a body "alive" even after brain activity has stopped. Trauma centers and hospitals in fact can make dying very difficult. Decisions can become especially painful when the patient is old or terminally ill. Should life-support systems be continued? Should consent be given for surgery which will at best extend the life of a dying person another few weeks or months? Should treatment be given which itself presents high risks and has a low ratio of success? Sometimes older people prefer to die at home and request not to receive certain treatment for terminal illnesses. Some older people fill out a "Living Will," which requests not to receive life-sustaining procedures which artifically prolong life when they are dying. Discussing these issues before they rise can be helpful for those who need to make the decisions.

 — **SNAPSHOT FROM LIFE** —

*Ilene, the lady who was cared for by her husband and daughter, chose not to receive chemotherapy for her cancer. For one thing, the success ratio was low for her type of cancer. Furthermore, she had observed the trauma of others taking this kind of treatment, and she felt she would only be prolonging her suffering.*

*Lester, her husband, kept in touch with the doctor as her condition grew worse.*

*"There is little more we could be doing for her in*

> *the hospital," the doctor acknowledged.*
>
> *Ilene passed away quietly one morning with her husband, daughter, and grandchildren gathered around her bed. There was no flurry of resuscitation techniques, no beeping and blinking of machines, no white-clad strangers whisking about. Just a few closing breaths for Ilene and then a quiet togetherness for the family for tears, reflection, and prayer.*
>
> *Obviously, there is a place for lifesaving gear, hospitals, and operations. Not everyone can choose where they will die or under what conditions. But Ilene had chosen to accept her death as it came, without attempting to postpone at all cost what was only inevitable eventually.*

Medical technology will likely continue to present us with decisions which are not merely procedural, but ethical. The following principles will not answer all questions, but should be considered by Christians when faced with such decisions.

1) It is wrong to take life willfully, even when death would seem desirable. (See Exodus 20:13; compare Job 3 with Job 42.)

2) It is proper to take reasonable efforts to preserve life and health (Ephesians 5:29).

3) It is proper to accept death when it comes (II Timothy 4:6-8; Psalm 90:10). In light of this, should we sometimes reconsider the all-out efforts of man to preserve life artificially, particularly when age or terminal illness make death inevitable?

4) It is wrong to use any methods to preserve health or life which involve occult powers or procedures (Deu-

teronomy 18:9-14). The family of someone with a terminal illness will often be amazed at the host of "miracle" cures recommended to them by friends and acquaintances. Some of these are harmless. A few may be helpful. But others are associated with questionable forces or powers such as energy zones, mind energy, body fields, meditation, invisible rays, magic boxes, etc.

5) The preservation of health or life should not be considered an end which justifies all means (Romans 3:8). Medical science considers what it CAN do; Christians need to consider further what they OUGHT to do. Just because something is possible does not necessarily mean it is right, even when the result seems good. In the 1980s, for example, researchers found that Parkinson's disease could be treated with tissue from aborted fetuses. As another example, biological engineers have proposed eliminating such things as Down's syndrome through genetic "repair." They have even suggested the possibility of custom ordered babies. While this seems far-fetched, already in 1969, one author said such things are a matter of when, not if. He made these bold statements: "Coming: the control of life. All of life, including human life. With man himself at the controls. Also coming: a new Genesis—the Second Genesis. The creator, this time around—man. The creation—again man. But a new man. In a new image. A whole series of new images."[5] The affront to God is clear. Again, in medical issues, Christians must consider not only what is possible, but what is right.

## LOSING A COMPANION

Probably the most traumatic event in one's life is the death of a companion, particularly if the death is sudden and leaves the remaining spouse with many responsibilities. Besides the grief, there are questions innumerable and tasks seemingly insurmountable. Situations vary, and advice is far easier to give than to implement, but the following pointers usually apply.

*1. Make no major decisions in the midst of grief or discouragement.* Such decisions as disposal of property, moving to a new location, and marrying a new companion have far-reaching effects. They require wisdom, and wisdom comes through the Word, prayer, counsel, and careful thought.

*2. A widow should look to her father, father-in-law, older brother, or some male relative as a source of counsel.* This is not because women are less competent, but because it gives them added protection against such things as intimidation, emotional pressure, and misunderstanding.

*3. A family with a father or mother gone usually needs more interaction with the extended family but also needs to function as a family unit.* Each family will need to work out a suitable balance.

*4. A widowed parent who contemplates remarriage should carefully consider the following points:*
- A new companion can never restore the old relationship. A completely new relationship must be formed.
- A new relationship should not be initiated until children have worked through their grief sufficiently. Otherwise, they are apt psychologically to associate the step-parent with the cause of their sorrow.
- Where two families, each with a deceased parent, are brought together, special wisdom is needed. There are always more problems than anticipated, especially where children are of similar age and gender. It is wise to counsel with a family which has gone through a similar situation.

● When bringing a new companion into old surroundings, it is usually wise to make some changes, especially in places where strong memories linger, such as the kitchen, shop, or bedroom. (Rearrange furniture, get a different bedroom suite, etc.)

● Do not make this move without the support of those who are close to you (family, church, close friends). You will need their support in the months ahead.

5. *Those who lose companions and do not remarry will have certain unmet needs which the Lord alone can supply.* Needs for such things as companionship, wisdom, and protection can be intense to say the least, but so also can be the grace of God. It was a single man who heard the Lord say, "My grace is sufficient for thee: for my strength is made perfect in weakness" (II Corinthians 12:9).

6. *Parenting inevitably seems overwhelming to the surviving parent.* The lack of a father image or mother image leaves a vacancy. Frequent interaction with grandparents or uncles and aunts can be helpful here. A widowed parent, however, must consider his or her own needs also. He (she) is wise to have a trusted friend or couple in whom to confide and seek counsel. A widowed parent should beware of the following common traps:

● Purposelessness.

● Reclusive behavior.

● Hanging on to the past (trying to live in the past).

● Denying the past.

● Self-pity and despondency.

● Overprotection of children.

● Resentment toward responsibilities.

Most widowed parents struggle with the above to a greater or lesser degree. To be characterized by these things, however, is the result of being "swallowed up" in grief, of not allowing oneself to go on to experience the healing which the Lord can bring. Following is a list of positive steps one can take to avoid the above traps.

●Face reality squarely.

●Allow yourself to grieve.

●Throughout your grief, verbalize to God your faith in Him.

●Regularly express gratitude to God, to people, and to your children.

●Ask God to show you things He wants you to do. Jot them down, especially if you regularly struggle with the feeling that life is pointless.

●Find God's promises to widows, orphans, and the needy. Write them down, read them, paraphrase them, claim them.

●Develop the habit of bringing your needs, cares, and problems to the Lord.

Following are some Scriptures which speak to various needs of families when losing a loved one.

### God's concern for our grief:

"Precious in the sight of the LORD is the death of his saints" (Psalm 116:15).

"But I would not have you to be ignorant, brethren, concerning them which are asleep, that ye sorrow not, even as others which have no hope" (I Thessalonians 4:13).

"A man of sorrows, and acquainted with grief. . . . Surely he hath borne our griefs, and carried our sorrows" (Isaiah 53:3,4).

"Mine eye is consumed because of grief. . . . The LORD hath heard the voice of my weeping. The LORD hath heard my supplication; the LORD will receive my prayer" (Psalm 6:7-9).

"He healeth the broken in heart, and bindeth up their wounds" (Psalm 147:3).

"Come unto me, all ye that labour and are heavy laden, and I will give you rest" (Matthew 11:28).

"And I heard a voice from heaven saying unto me, Write, Blessed are the dead which die in the Lord from henceforth: Yea, saith the Spirit, that they may rest from their labours; and their works do follow them" (Revelation 14:13).

"And God shall wipe away all tears from their eyes; and there shall be no more death, neither sorrow, nor crying, neither shall there be any more pain: for the former things are passed away" (Revelation 21:4).

### God's love for children:

"And the streets of the city shall be full of boys and girls playing in the streets thereof" (Zechariah 8:5).

"Suffer the little children to come unto me, and forbid them not: for of such is the kingdom of God. Verily I say unto you, Whosoever shall not receive the kingdom of God as a little child, he shall not enter therein. And he took them up in his arms, put his hands upon them, and blessed them" (Mark 10:14-16).

"Take heed that ye despise not one of these little ones; for I say unto you, That in heaven their angels do always behold the face of my Father which is in heaven. . . . Even so it is not the will of your Father which is in heaven, that one of these little ones should perish" (Matthew 18:10, 14).

### God's care of widows and orphans:

"Thou art the helper of the fatherless" (Psalm 10:14).

"A father of the fatherless, and a judge of the widows, is God in his holy habitation. God setteth the solitary in families" (Psalm 68:5, 6).

"The LORD preserveth the strangers; he relieveth the fatherless and widow" (Psalm 146:9).

"For thy Maker is thine husband; the LORD of hosts is his name; and thy Redeemer the Holy One of Israel" (Isaiah 54:5). (This refers specifically to Israel, but application can be made to widows.)

### God's commitment to the needs of His people:

"For the eyes of the LORD run to and fro throughout the whole earth, to shew himself strong in the behalf of them whose heart is perfect toward him" (II Chronicles 16:9).

"But seek ye first the kingdom of God, and his righteousness; and all these things shall be added unto you" (Matthew 6:33).

"Be careful for nothing; but in every thing by prayer and supplication with thanksgiving let your requests be made known unto God. And the peace of God, which passeth all understanding, shall keep your hearts and minds through Christ Jesus. . . . But my God shall supply all your need according to his riches in glory by Christ Jesus" (Philippians 4:6, 7, 19).

### God's promises for the future:

"For if we believe that Jesus died and rose again, even so them also which sleep in Jesus will God bring with him" (I Thessalonians 4:14).

"Behold, I shew you a mystery; We shall not all sleep, but we shall all be changed, in a moment, in the twinkling of an eye, at the last trump: for the trumpet shall sound, and the dead shall be raised incorruptible, and we shall be changed. For this corruptible must put on incorruption, and this mortal must put on immortality. So when this corruptible shall have put on incorruption, and this mortal shall have put on immortality, then shall be brought to pass the saying that is written, Death is swallowed up in victory. O death, where is thy sting? O grave, where is thy victory? . . . Thanks be to God, which giveth us the victory through our Lord Jesus Christ" (I Corinthians 15:51-55, 57).

"Beloved, now are we the sons of God, and it doth not yet appear what we shall be: but we know that, when he shall appear, we shall be like him; for we shall see him as he is" (I John 3:2).

"For I reckon that the sufferings of this present time are not worthy to be compared with the glory which shall be revealed in us. . . . For we know that the whole creation groaneth and travaileth in pain together until now. And not only they, but ourselves also, which have the firstfruits of the Spirit, even we ourselves groan within ourselves, waiting for the adoption, to wit, the redemption of our body" (Romans 8:18, 22, 23).

"For we know that if our earthly house of this tabernacle were dissolved, we have a building of God, an house not made with hands, eternal in the heavens. For in this we groan, earnestly desiring to be clothed upon with our house which is from heaven" (II Corinthians 5:1, 2).

"Nevertheless we, according to his promise, look for new heavens and a new earth, wherein dwelleth righteousness" (II Peter 3:13).

## SUMMARY

"Man is born unto trouble, as the sparks fly upward" (Job 5:7). Trials, problems, sickness, and death are part of this present order. They cause us pain and tears. But the grace of God is effective to deliver those who trust in Him and to bring them through all their troubles, even through death itself, to victory. For those facing trouble, the Word, the brotherhood, prayer, and the extended family become precious recourses from which to draw strength, counsel, and encouragement.

## THINKING TOGETHER

1. Right and wrong attitudes toward trouble are given in this chapter. What additional attitudes could be added to each list?

2. What are the indications that one has not accepted unchangeable aspects of a difficult situation?

3. How should one respond when he observes someone mocking or taking advantage of a person with a handicap?

4. What are some group activities in which a blind person could or could not participate? A deaf person? A person on crutches?

5. As aging parents become increasingly incompetent, how can their children take responsibility for decision making with a minimum of strife and resistance from their parents?

6. What are the advantages and disadvantages of a grandparent living in the home of a son or daughter? How can grandparents be assured of their welcome?

7. Define *active listening* in your own words. What does it help to avoid? In what situations might it not help? In what situations might it be effective other than with the elderly?

8. How might men and women typically grieve differently? How might children and adults grieve differently?

9. What are the legal guidelines in your state when a person dies without a will?

10. What ethical dilemmas have Christians in your acquaintance faced in the medical field? What principles would apply?

11. Do you know families which have merged in marriage after the death of companions? What difficulties have they faced?

## WORKING TOGETHER

1. As a family, list troubles which you have experienced. Evaluate your attitudes. Have you accepted situations realistically? What steps might you take to develop such attitudes as faith and gratitude?

2. Discuss ways you could develop more awareness and sensitivity toward the handicapped. Do you know someone with a handicap different from those discussed in this chapter? What suggestions would be appropriate for relating considerately?

3. As a family, do you have parents or grandparents who may need care in later years? Have you discussed your options among yourselves and with your grandparents? Do you have a healthy view of older people, their characteristics, and their problems? Are there things you need to alter or plan for in view of issues discussed in this chapter?

4. As a parent, have you made adequate preparations in the event of your death, so that your companion and children would not be left with unnecessary decisions and problems? If not, what steps ought you to take?

# 9

# WHEN THE HOME BREAKS DOWN

## INTRODUCTION

God's design for the family is such that, correctly followed, it provides a deep-rooted sense of security and well-being to each family member. There is love and respect for all. There is leadership, support, and a harmonious working together. When people depart from God's ways, however, just the opposite results. Waywardness brings fear, rejection, anger, and pain. It tears at the family and often leaves family members broken, hurting, and overwhelmed with problems.

In this chapter we wish to look at waywardness, at what it does to the family, and at proper responses.

## WAYWARD CHILDREN, HURTING PARENTS

All Christian parents want their children to grow up to serve the Lord. And most children in Christian homes make a beginning of some sort. There is a time when they sing, pray, attend church, and believe what their parents teach them. Later on, some teenagers turn to their own ways, rejecting their former faith. The relationship between them and their parents may deteriorate to the point of open rebellion. Sometimes, however, there is a more passive "Christianity just isn't for me" kind of waywardness. Still other children become unfaithful after they have left home, sometimes after they have families of their own.

The immediate question which Christian parents ask is, Why? For concerned parents, the question can become an agonizing self-analysis. The sense of failure, the tension from confrontation, and the fears for the future drive sleep away at night and rob peace during the day.

Why? The answer to that question will vary with each case. Causes overlap, and, furthermore, although parents know the situation firsthand, objective evaluation of causes becomes extremely difficult because of the emotional hurt involved. Even so, we will look at some of the most basic causes of waywardness in children.

*1. Sin.* In every person the principle of sin makes waywardness a possibility. This indwelling sin cannot be trained out of a person. It cannot be commanded out. It can be rendered powerless only by the indwelling Holy Spirit upon a personal surrender to Jesus Christ. "Our old man is crucified with him, that the body of sin might be destroyed, that henceforth we should not serve sin" (Romans 6:6).

This does not negate the place of parental training. Training should equip the child with the proper under-

286

standing, the right attitudes, and such a pattern of obedience that surrender to Christ is readily chosen at the proper time. Even while recognizing the importance of training and the accountability of parents to train by God's principles, we must recognize the principle of sin in every person. Ultimately, in spite of all other influences, each person will be held accountable for his own choices. A wayward son or daughter will perish in hell unless he repents because he personally said yes to sin and the path of waywardness.

*2. Parental failure to restrain.* As noted above, personal responsibility does not take away from parental responsibility. Children are wayward sometimes because parents have not disciplined them properly. Concerning Eli, God said, "I will judge his house for ever for the iniquity which he knoweth; because his sons made themselves vile, and he restrained them not" (I Samuel 3:13). Although parents can receive forgiveness for this failure, they can never turn back the clock of time and retrain their children. Failure to restrain amounts to honoring the naughtiness of children above the holiness of God (see I Samuel 2:29). The result is always grief for parents.

*3. Harshness in parental authority.* "Fathers, provoke not your children to anger, lest they be discouraged" (Colossians 3:21). While discipline, including spanking, is proper in restraining children, it must be exercised in love if it is to be effective. Harshness is counterproductive. It stirs reaction rather than submission. The authority vested in parents was never intended to be a privilege for venting selfish anger. When parents shout, demand, and strike in anger, they are attempting to batter their children into submission. This immature and dangerous concept of authority adds resentment to resentment in their children and predictably erupts later in teenager rebellion.

*4. Patterns of independence.* "But I would have you know, that the head of every man is Christ; and the head of the woman is the man; and the head of Christ is God" (I Corinthians 11:3). "Remember them which have the rule over you, who have spoken unto you the word of God: whose faith follow" (Hebrews 13:7). Sometimes parents undermine their children's concept of authority by trying to be independent of authority God has placed over them. When parents show disrespect for authority, they are greatly increasing the risk of their children becoming wayward. This can be a very deceptive process. A mother who resists the authority of her husband may have the children on her side and only later experience their anger and disrespect toward her. Parents may be critical of the church and its leaders and later reap a harvest of disrespectful, wayward children. Unfortunately, such parents sometimes view the waywardness of their children as yet another reason to blame the church.

*5. Inconsistency.* "Woe unto you, scribes and Pharisees, hypocrites! for ye shut up the kingdom of heaven against men: for ye neither go in yourselves, neither suffer ye them that are entering to go in" (Matthew 23:13). Differences between what we profess and what we really are become obstacles for those entering the kingdom. This seems to present a special hurdle for young people because of their inclination toward idealism. Parents and church leaders who are not genuine, who set double standards, who show partiality, who wrest judgment, who in any way practice and justify inconsistency make waywardness easy for young people. The carnal mind loves to hide personal sin behind the sins and faults of others. Consistency in attitudes and actions at home seems to be particularly important to young people. Husband and wife must be genuine in their love for each other and in their commitment to God in ordinary living. This holiness at home preserves the integrity of parents and gives them credence with their children.

*6. Materialism.* "They that will be rich fall into temptation and a snare, and into many foolish and hurtful lusts, which drown men in destruction and perdition. For the love of money is the root of all evil: which while some coveted after, they have erred from the faith, and pierced themselves through with many sorrows" (I Timothy 6:9,10). One of the many sorrows of materialism is wayward children. Parents who accumulate treasures on earth or who indulge their children with the things of this earth find it very difficult to convince their children to have heavenly interests.

*7. Worldliness.* "Ye adulterers and adulteresses, know ye not that the friendship of the world is enmity with God? whosoever therefore will be a friend of the world is the enemy of God" (James 4:4). "Love not the world, neither the things that are in the world. If any man love the world, the love of the Father is not in him. For all that is in the world, the lust of the flesh, and the lust of the eyes, and the pride of life, is not of the Father, but is of the world. And the world passeth away, and the lust thereof: but he that doeth the will of God abideth for ever" (I John 2:15-17). The world has its fashion, its music, and its entertainment.[1] Parents only deceive themselves when they believe they can accept certain things of the world without harm. For each friendly step one generation takes toward the world, the next generation seems willing to take several more.

*8. Overinvolvement.* God tells parents to teach their children His ways "when thou sittest in thine house, and when thou walkest by the way, and when thou liest down, and when thou risest up" (Deuteronomy 6:7). Unfortunately, some parents seldom sit in their houses, and fewer yet walk by the way. Parents today easily get caught up in the rush of living, even in the rush of serving, to the point that they do not have proper time for their children. One father remarked that children spell love T-I-M-E.[2] Intended or not, overinvolvement sends messages of rejection to children. Waywardness is sometimes the child's reaction to the pain of this rejection.

*9. Exposure to ungodly counsel.* "Cease, my son, to hear the instruction that causeth to err from the words of knowledge" (Proverbs 19:27). Sometimes children are wayward as a result of exposure to wrong instruction. The instruction given in public schools and colleges and even in some "Christian" colleges deviates from God's Word. Ungodly counsel need not be formal, however, to wield a negative impact. Interaction with other children can be a means of receiving the counsel of the ungodly, especially interaction in homes where television and videos operate freely. Parents who wish to avoid the pain of wayward children will jealously guard the social and educational input in their children's lives.

Because of the tremendous influence of parents on their children, waywardness in children should always call for introspection in parents. This is painful, but necessary. Introspection, of course, should be wise. It sometimes requires the help of someone less emotionally involved, such as a pastor. Without wisdom, self-examination easily descends to self-railing and increases emotional confusion rather than spiritual understanding.

Where problem areas are discovered, parents need to acknowledge these honestly before God. The goal in such repentance, however, needs to be clearly understood. It is not primarily to effect a turnaround in one's wayward child, but to get right with God. Where waywardness in a child is traceable to wrong in a parent, the wrong must be viewed as something which grieves the heart of God. The waywardness in the child is God's reproof. The erring parent should be motivated to repent of his wrong primarily because in this area his life is not bringing glory to God.

Parents who are sensitive and teachable will find God and His truth precious in new ways. They will seek God's direction for correcting things in their lives, such as schedule, values, and relationships. The blessings of repentance and obedience will not take away all the pain of having wayward children. Parents will, however, develop deeper spiritual roots and find themselves closer to God.

The ongoing questions for parents with wayward children are, "How do we relate?" and, "What can we do?" There are no easy answers. Sometimes the children are still at home. Sometimes they have left home. Sometimes they already have homes of their own.

In considering how to relate to wayward children, let's look at several important don'ts.

*a. Don't nag or beg.* Wayward children need to hear the Spirit of God. Sometimes with good intentions parents repeatedly scold and plead with wayward children. By placing themselves so much in the forefront, however, parents actually may hinder their children from hearing the voice of God.

*b. Don't compromise principles to maintain harmony.* This is the other side of the above guideline. While parents should not nag, neither should they try to accommodate the waywardness of children. The simple reality is that where people differ in response to God's truth, there will be tension. That tension is actually necessary. While it should not be aggravated by nagging, neither should it be naively hidden in some back closet as though everything were all right. In those situations where the

291

tension surfaces, parents should honestly, kindly, and courteously discuss the issue and make their position clear.

c. *Don't use emotional pressure.* Emotional pressure is the attempt to get someone to do something by making them feel bad if they don't. Because it focuses on feelings, it is somewhat roundabout in its approach. Such comments as, "You're going to put your mother in her grave early," or, "Go ahead and die young if you want to," create emotional pressure, but such comments almost invariably cause reaction rather than remorse. People who use emotional pressure usually do so without realizing it. When emotional pressure is a habit, it can be exerted not only by comments, but also by such means as facial expressions and silence.

d. *Don't protect the wayward one from the consequences of his behavior.* The path of disobedience always has reproofs. God sees to that. Knowing this should free Christian parents from the urge to coerce or pressure their wayward children back into the way of faith. The 19-year-old who wrecks his car after a party should not be loaned money for another. Parents should not post bail for their delinquent teenager. This sometimes stirs anger in the wayward one, but it is the anger of selfishness. The temptation to cater to that anger is almost invariably amplified by the parents' sense of guilt. When parents allow themselves to be driven by guilt to try to rescue their errant children, they may actually be getting in the way of God's chastening rod. The prodigal "came to himself" in a pigpen. His father gladly took him back as a penitent, but very wisely he did not try to rescue him before that.

e. *Don't permit the wayward one to control the home.* Where a wayward son or daughter lives at home, parents should maintain limits which protect other children and the integrity of the home. Obviously, establishing the limits requires discernment, and maintaining them may create tension. In the Old Testament a rebellious son who would not submit ultimately came under civil jurisdiction and was stoned (see Deuteronomy 21:18-21). This was certainly a stern measure and one we would not carry out today, but it demonstrates the necessity of not allowing a wayward youth to control his parents.

When parents have searched their own lives, repented of wrong, and submitted to the purging of God's Word and Spirit, the most powerful thing they can do in behalf of wayward children is to pray. This is a work in which the teachable Christian experiences growth. Early prayers are often tainted with fleshly desires and reasoning. Learning to intercede in the Spirit is a personal growth process the Christian learns primarily on his knees. The following principles of praying for the lost can be profitably discussed, but they can be learned properly only through exercise.

## PRAYING FOR THE LOST

*1. Prayer is spiritual battle.* The Holy Spirit is not the only spirit. In Ephesians 6:12 we are told we wrestle against spiritual powers of evil.

*2. We must stand in the strength of the Lord.* Effective praying is never done on our own merits, never for our selfish interests, never by our own might. True prayer is offered in the name of Jesus. Its aim is to accomplish His purposes. It operates by His own power.

*3. Through prayer the strongholds of the enemy must be cast down.* "(For the weapons of our warfare are not carnal, but mighty through God to the pulling down of strong holds;) casting down imaginations, and every high thing that exalteth itself against the knowledge of God, and bringing into captivity every thought to the obedience of Christ" (II Corinthians 10:4, 5). By faith we should name specifically the areas where the enemy has built resistance to the truth of God. On the authority of Jesus' name, these strongholds must be cast down.

*4. Prayer for the wayward must be persistent.* Prayer must be persistent, not because God is reluctant, but because the enemy is persistent. We know that God "will have all men to be saved, and to come unto the knowledge of the truth" (I Timothy 2:4). But we also know that the enemy "as a roaring lion, walketh about, seeking whom he may devour" (I Peter 5:8). Him we must continually resist by prayer in the name of the One who "spoiled principalities and powers . . . triumphing over them in it" (Colossians 2:15).

 — SNAPSHOT FROM LIFE

*To his parents, Steve was a clown—a hot-tempered one at times and not always obedient, but with such a sense of humor that he seemed harmless enough. But underneath Steve's funny ways was a growing waywardness. In the local high school he was becoming increasingly involved in extracurricular activities. He was planning by his senior year to make an out-and-out break with the church and enter full-barrel into the life he wanted—fun.*

*Steve's church had special meetings that fall, however, and for some time ahead of the meetings God placed a burden for Steve on the heart of another young man in Steve's church. Joe prayed for Steve ahead of the meetings. As the meetings progressed, he continued praying. The Lord began moving in the hearts of other people, but Steve resisted. He hated the meetings. He didn't want to go, but neither did he have much choice.*

*The last night of the meetings, with the burden for Steve weighing heavily on him, Joe decided to talk to Steve directly. Prayer had made his own heart rich with the presence of God. Prayer and the preaching each night had softened the hardened areas in Steve's heart. The resistance crumbled.*

*Steve's bid for repentance and peace, however, met with unexpected struggle. Satan had a strong hold on Steve. Steve prayed. Joe prayed. The evangelist prayed. Others prayed. Those praying with Steve actually saw his physical features distort as the devil yielded to the power of Christ. Out of Steve's heart came confession of sin, lying, pornography, cursing, and involvements Steve's parents had not been aware of at all.*

*Steve was rescued that night. He was saved from the misery of guilt and from the eventual consequences of his waywardness. His parents were spared the grief of further alienation from him. His congregation was spared the pain of seeing a young man go into the world. All because someone was faithful and persistent in praying.*

## WAYWARD PARENTS, HURTING CHILDREN

As we have seen, many parents today are hurting because of waywardness in their children. Unfortunately, the reverse is also true. Sometimes children and young people want to follow the Lord, but their parents are unbelievers or have backslidden.

The tragedy of this sort of situation is amplified because so many things are backwards. Instead of parents being concerned and praying for their children, it is the other way around. Where normally parents are struggling with what to say or what not to say by way of direction to their youths, the youths are struggling with how to talk to their parents. Spiritual perception may be stronger in young children than it is in a wayward parent. While all of these incongruencies are painful to observe, they are worse to experience.

We noted earlier that it is common for parents with wayward children to blame others. Where parents grow wayward, however, it is common for their children to blame themselves. Consciously or unconsciously, they feel they are responsible for their parents' waywardness. Although these feelings are almost always unfounded, children sometimes need special guidance to verbalize and resolve their guilt feelings.

Why do parents depart from faith? Many of the reasons given earlier in the discussion on wayward children apply here as well. Besides the root cause of indwelling sin, probably the two main causes in parental waywardness are marital problems and worldliness—the business of the world, the cares of the world, the fashion of the world, etc.

For children, however, understanding the cause of parental waywardness is not as important as knowing how to cope with it. There are two basic principles which guide those who are under non-Christian authorities:

*1. The principle of honor.* Christian young people who have unbelieving parents are not free from the responsibility of honoring their parents. Honor, in fact, has even more implications in this sort of situation because it is often the channel through which God works most powerfully.

Suggestions for how to honor parents (particularly "imperfect" parents) were given in Chapter 1. We should note here, however, that those young people whose parents depart from faith face special struggles. There are several pitfalls into which young people can easily fall, even when the desire is to honor parents. Here are a number of helpful don'ts for relating to parents who are wayward.

*a. Don't try to correct.* Unbelief makes people do foolish things. Looking at a wayward parent through Christian eyes, there are plenty of things that just aren't right. Usually underneath, the wayward one's conscience knows this, but on the surface he isn't willing to admit it, and further, he resents someone under him telling him he's wrong. God has His own ways of bringing correction on an errant authority (consider, for example, Saul's rejection as king, I Samuel 15:22, 23).

*b. Don't use parents' wrongs for personal justification.* This is a common tactic of the carnal mind. We tend to hide our own inconsistencies behind those of others, to feel even that others are responsible when we do wrong. A young person, for example, may decide to leave for the evening without asking for permission because the last time he asked, his father just shouted, "Do whatever you want. You will anyway!"

*c. Don't argue.* "Not answering again" (Titus 2:9). This instruction to the way servants relate to their masters surely applies to children and youths relating to their parents. Argument seldom settles issues; rather, it usually entrenches people more determinedly in their own ways. Where argument has become a way of life, the Christian young person should begin to explore new, more Christ-honoring ways of responding. Consider, for example, the suggestions for "active listening" given in Chapter 8.

By avoiding the above pitfalls, the young Christian in a non-Christian home is more likely to be respected and heard. It gives more freedom to wield a positive Christian influence through such things as obedience, kindness, and prayer.

*2. The principle of faith.* The second principle for young people with wayward parents is the principle of faith in God. Since God stood above Pharaoh and delivered the Israelites from Egypt, since God stood above Saul and protected David from Saul's jealous anger, since God raised up Timothy to be an early church leader in spite of an unbelieving father (presumably), surely God can take care of young people today.

Faith in God has several specific applications for those with wayward parents. First, it means entrusting one's life entirely to God. By faith, the difficult situation is viewed as in God's hands. It is not out of control. The wayward parent even in his waywardness is subject to a sovereign God. The young person, therefore, need not fret about how things will work out. He needs, rather, to faithfully bring the situation to God, to give God the freedom to bring about His purposes and His solutions. God's ways invariably extend beyond what we can see. Israel, for example, simply wanted out of Egypt; God purposed to bring judgment on Egypt at the same time. David simply wanted protection from Saul; God's intention was to prepare both David and Israel for David's rulership.

The second way faith applies here is that the person under non-Christian authority lives in obedience to God. He honors his parents whether they are deserving of honor or not because God has told him to, and he is committed to honoring God. Thus, the principle of honor actually rests upon the principle of faith. Should his earthly parents attempt to usurp God's authority, however, and command that which God has forbidden or forbid that which God has commanded, the young person, according to the example of the apostles, "ought to obey God rather than men" (Acts 5:29).

Such confrontations can sometimes be averted by entreating the one in authority to consider an alternate decision which would be mutually acceptable. Probably the clearest example in the Bible is Daniel, who purposed not to eat the king's meat, appealed to the prince of the eunuchs to accept an alternative, and thus averted a confrontation. Daniel, of course, had laid a good foundation for this appeal. He was committed to honoring God, which gave God full liberty to work in his behalf, preparing the heart of the prince. Furthermore, Daniel was apparently obedient and cooperative otherwise. Then when he actually approached the prince, he came in humble request, not with a defiant attitude (see Daniel 1).

Those who find themselves in situations where they must obey God rather than men must be willing to suffer. The three Hebrews who obeyed God were thrown into the fire. The apostles who obeyed God were put into prison. A young person who obeys God contrary to his parents' commands may be ridiculed or punished. God attends to such, however, with a peculiar grace and glory. "For this is thankworthy, if a man for conscience toward God endure grief, suffering wrongfully. For what glory is it, if, when ye be buffeted for your faults, ye shall take it patiently? but if, when ye do well, and suffer for it, ye take it patiently, this is acceptable with God. For even hereunto were ye called: because Christ also suffered for us, leaving us an example, that ye should follow his steps" (I Peter 2:19-21). An attitude of complaint, on the other hand, destroys the opportunity to bring glory to God.

## WAYWARD PARTNER, HURTING PARTNER

Because the bonds of human relationship are nowhere more intimate than in marriage, the joy of that relationship is more bright and the pain more dark than anywhere else. Waywardness in a companion brings a singular heartache which only those who have experienced it can understand fully. "Can two walk together, except they be agreed?" the Lord asks (Amos 3:3). Many today can testify to the anguish of that question.

Christians do well to notice that the Lord is fully acquainted with the pain of waywardness in a loved one. The people of Israel were adulterous in their relationship with Him, and we can almost hear divine sobs in some of God's words: "My people are bent to backsliding from me. . . . How shall I give thee up, Ephraim? how shall I deliver thee, Israel? . . . Mine heart is turned within me" (Hosea 11:7, 8). So it feels to the husband or wife whose companion turns wayward.

How does one respond to a wayward partner? We should recognize first how variables can affect the situation. Someone who departs from faith is different from one who has never believed. Whether the unfaithful one is the husband or the wife makes a significant difference—a Christian wife struggles with how much she can follow a non-Christian husband, while a Christian husband struggles with how much he can expect from a non-Christian wife. Marital fidelity plays a big role in

300

determining proper responses—unfaithfulness widens the hurts and the implications of the waywardness. Whether the unfaithful partner stays at home or leaves bears significantly on how one responds.

While direction for specific situations needs to rise from an understanding of those situations, there are guidelines which apply to most cases. Sometimes knowing what not to do is as important as knowing what to do.

*Don't nag, beg, or scold.* These tactics tend to further alienate rather than draw the wayward one back. They usually rise from desperation and thus are generally more controlled by the flesh than by the Spirit.

*Don't use love as a lever.* Love is a commitment to the well-being of another. When it is offered only on certain conditions, it loses its integrity. When, in other words, such things as cheerfulness and goodwill are given or withheld to get one's way (no matter how righteous that way may seem) love is being used as a bargaining tool. Such "love" has grown selfish. It is no longer the love of God. Admittedly, unselfish love is beyond the ability of man in his own strength, but God produces it in us if we are willing to love.

*Don't deny or hide a wayward partner's sin.* Sometimes a wayward partner wants to hide his waywardness from the church, the family, or the community. There are two sides to this, of course. No one should want to publicize sin, least of all a companion. But neither should a Christian try to hide in a companion's life such sinful behavior as drunkenness, child abuse, fraud, and adultery, particularly from those who ought to know.

*Don't become absorbed in self.* There are hurts innumerable in problem marriages, and rightly these problems receive the focus of the Christian's attention and prayer. As the Christian finds God's grace and leading, however, he should likewise be developing greater sen-

301

sitivity to others and their problems, lest such attitudes as anger, resentment, and self-pity mire him permanently in his problems.

Friends of those with wayward companions play a significant role. Comments which express pessimism, project blame, or give superficial answers may be given thoughtlessly, but they can haunt the mind for days. Likewise difficult to handle is the advice which forcefully expresses personal opinion but rests upon human judgment.[3]

Those with wayward companions need friends who will listen, friends who sincerely care, friends who are sensitive to the whole range of human needs. They need friends who know the Word of God and who rely upon the Spirit of God. They need friends who know how to pray. They need friends who can lift spirits without being flippant or trite, who can offer encouragement and counsel without sounding superior, and who can correct without condemning.

Many times the waywardness of a companion is associated with unfaithfulness in the marriage relationship. This is a double heartache, but the relationship between backsliding with God and unfaithfulness in marriage is very obvious when we consider that both represent the breaking of covenant. Unfaithfulness in one relationship easily moves to unfaithfulness in another. (This is especially clear in Malachi 2:11 ff. where God exposes the spirit of treachery as the cause underlying both divorce and backsliding.)

The implications of this are actually more important for groups to understand than for particular couples. It does not mean, in other words, that every backslider will be unfaithful to his companion. In the larger setting, however, we may be sure that the more lukewarm a group becomes, the more instances of unfaithfulness there will be.

Where unfaithfulness is involved in a companion's waywardness, the issues can become very tangled, and consequently, advice can be extremely conflicting. Old Testament marriage laws, although permitting divorce, were very strict concerning fidelity. Adulterers were to be stoned (Leviticus 20:10). In the New Testament, Jesus forbids divorce (Mark 10:11, 12). The instructions concerning those who are immoral is that they be put out of the church until they repent (see I Corinthians 5). Where there is clear repentance, there is to be genuine forgiveness, love, and reconciliation with the church. "Sufficient to such a man is this punishment, which was inflicted of many. So that contrariwise ye ought rather to forgive him, and comfort him, lest perhaps such a one should be swallowed up with overmuch sorrow. Wherefore I beseech you that ye would confirm your love toward him" (II Corinthians 2:6-8).

Christian spouses, then, whose companions are unfaithful should practice forgiveness and work for reconciliation, difficult as that may be. If the unbelieving companion departs, according to I Corinthians 7:11-15, so must it be, but the remaining companion is not to remarry.

Perhaps a more agonizing problem exists when the unfaithful partner wishes to remain but persists in unfaithfulness. Some believe, in such a situation, the faithful partner may separate, but of course, remain unmarried and work for reconciliation. Others say a Christian companion should accept whatever the non-Christian does.

The following thoughts may not answer all questions, but they should be considered in situations where a spouse wishes to maintain conjugal relations and continue an adulterous relationship also. Love does not

## SNAPSHOT FROM LIFE

*Bill and Cindy were already in the process of divorce when Bill decided to talk to a minister about their marriage problems. Shortly after, Bill confessed his sins and placed his faith in Jesus as his Lord and Saviour.*

*Although he had had some religious training as a child, Bill was unlearned in many of the teachings of the Bible. The minister became a constant source of counsel and encouragement. Bill's wife was living with another man off and on. She had sued for divorce and custody of the children. Bill's "only alternative" had been to countersue.*

*When Bill learned that divorce was wrong, that fighting for rights was the world's approach to marriage problems, that remarriage was not a Biblical option, and that God wanted him to focus on loving Cindy and rebuilding their marriage, his whole perspective was changed.*

*The steps were slow. Old patterns of relating were much more natural than the new way of sacrificial love. Cindy's unfaithfulness, her stubbornness, her lies, her temper were all tests to Bill's newfound faith. And she did not respond kindly when he "preached" to her about her need of God.*

*But Bill had become convinced that come what may, the course he had chosen was love for life. He could not push Cindy into the kingdom. He could not force her to love him. He could not keep her from following other men. But Bill knew he had his part to do. And he knew he had to do it with all the grace of God. Fighting, divorce, remarriage—all the options commonly chosen—would not solve his problems or Cindy's. Sacrificial love—true, honest, constant, holy love—this was what God had chosen for him.*

304

necessarily mean doing what another wants, but doing what is right and what is good with a view to eternity. Is it right for the family and for the integrity of marriage to concede to an ongoing three-way relationship? Such a situation certainly would not have been tolerated by God's laws in the Old Testament. Furthermore, does not God's own relationship with Israel speak to this point? When they repented of their adulterous affairs with heathen idols, He forgave them and received them back. But He did not permit a three-way relationship to continue. He required either faithful love, or He withdrew His presence. Finally, does not God's response demonstrate what is in the best interests of a wayward companion? Certainly, one's manner and methods of objecting to a three-way relationship must be in keeping with godliness, love, and the Biblical roles of husband and wife. But how loving is it in the Biblical sense of love to be party to that which even the ungodly recognize as wrong?

The challenges facing a Christian with an unfaithful companion are immense to say the least. Only the support of God's people and the supply of His grace can enable such a person.

Of course, to give God the freedom to work in our behalf, we need to be faithful in what He asks of us and leave in His hands the things that belong to Him. We frustrate the eternal purposes of God when we refuse to be what He wants us to be and try to interfere with His work.

The wife with an unbelieving husband should be concerned about being as godly a wife as possible. Her godly life and submissive character, apart from any word of testimony, is the most powerful witness God will use to save her husband. "Ye wives, be in subjection to your own husbands; that, if any obey not the word, they also may without the word be won by the conversation of the wives; while they behold your chaste conversation coupled with fear" (I Peter 3:1, 2).

Likewise, the husband with an unbelieving wife should be concerned about being as godly a husband as possible. The Biblical instruction to husbands is to love. Husbands should learn about Biblical love, pray to understand more, and open their lives to the Holy Spirit's molding and promptings in practical expressions of love. Such love is all opposed to the self-life. It is sacrificial, pure, strong, committed. "Husbands, love your wives, even as Christ also loved the church, and gave himself for it; that he might sanctify and cleanse it with the washing of water by the word" (Ephesians 5:25, 26).

No one should minimize the problems of those with wayward partners. There are, however, positive things which can result. God is able to work ALL things for our eternal good as we commit our lives to Him. As noted earlier, the New Testament church leader Timothy was from a home where the father apparently was an unbeliever. The godly woman Abigail had a wayward husband. The Prophet Hosea had an adulterous wife. Only God knows what He can do both in the present and in the future when those in difficult straits yield their problems to Him.

## RESTORING A MARRIAGE

Marriages do not fall apart overnight. A broken marriage is the result of destructive factors at work for some time. At any stage of deterioration, where there is sincere repentance, there can be restoration. But inasmuch as the deterioration was a process which occurred wrong step by wrong step, restoration is a process of right steps. Broken marriages do not fall together of their own accord, even for repentant people.

Where there have been marriage problems large or small, the following principles need to be considered in the process of restoring the marriage:

*1. Both husband and wife need to be committed to being what God has designed for their role in the marriage.* This means first that as long as a partner is wayward, there will be problems. These problems are the very pressure points God has designed to motivate to repentance. Secondly, this principle requires that for solving marriage problems, each must focus first on fulfilling his own role and responsibility rather than on the shortcomings of the other. A husband's shortcomings put added pressure on his wife, and a wife's shortcomings put added pressure on her husband. So each partner focusing on fulfilling his personal role makes it easier for the other. It is well for the husband to verbalize to his wife his commitment to love her, provide for her, and lead her in Christlikeness. It is well for the wife to verbalize to her husband her commitment to be submissive, supportive, and encouraging in the marriage.

*2. Restoration of a marriage requires the exercise of Biblical love, which in turn requires the renunciation of self.* As noted earlier, Biblical love means commitment to another's well-being. There is also in marriage, of course, the affectionate kind of love, but some people have so sinned against each other in marriage that all affection is gone. Only the commitment kind of love can carry such a marriage forward to solid footing. Such love is all opposed to self. Self focuses on hurts, feelings, rights, and personal desires and refuses to go on until its demands are met. Love does not ignore how it feels, but love holds high the well-being of the other, and renounces all selfish thoughts and feelings that stand in the way of doing what is right and good in the other's behalf.

*3. Restoring a marriage requires wholesome commu-*

*nication.* A husband and wife must talk and listen attentively to understand one another's feelings, needs, and problems, and to find the proper steps for meeting the needs and resolving the problems. Such toxic patterns as accusing, belittling, scorning, shouting, and pouting must be resolutely done away with. Talking in carnal ways will add problems, not solve them. Sometimes this requires the help of a minister or counselor as a third party to keep the communication healthy.

*4. Each partner must establish and maintain integrity in the relationship.* Marriage is intimacy, and intimacy demands trust. Falsehood in any form undermines the trust needed for intimacy. Sins of the past and feelings of the present, ugly as they may be, cannot be denied or ignored if integrity is to be reestablished. Each must know where the other actually stands in order to relate honestly, sincerely, and openly as husband and wife. However painful honesty may be, it is never as painful as dishonesty discovered later. If there is ever to be an honesty in righteousness, there must first be an honesty about sin. Honesty is the bedrock of trust.

*5. Restoring a marriage requires the exercise of forgiveness.* Forgiveness, particularly in the event of unfaithfulness, can be extremely difficult. One may believe he has forgiven only to have resentment and anger surface again shortly thereafter. Forgiveness in such cases is a work of brokenness, an act of divine love. The Christian should not consider any other option but to forgive, because it is only in forgiving that we have assurance of being forgiven (see Matthew 6:14, 15). Forgiveness is not accomplished by denying the offense, but in acknowledging it fully. We are then free to focus in faith on the wise hand of God to work all things in behalf of our eternal well-being.

*6. Restoration of a broken marriage must honor God's*

*Word.* There are numerous directives in the Bible both for relationships in general and for the marriage relationship in particular. God's ways are the only ways which will have God's blessing. Guidance for resolving problems must square with His eternal truth, and the contrary reasoning of man must be renounced, no matter how attractive it may sound. We must have the attitude of the psalmist: "Therefore I esteem all thy precepts concerning all things to be right; and I hate every false way" (Psalm 119:128).

7. *Restoring a marriage requires an understanding of one another's needs and taking specific steps toward meeting them.* Many marriages today are suffering because husbands do not understand the needs of wives and wives do not understand the needs of husbands. Some of these basic needs were discussed in Chapter 5. In addition to the general needs, however, each person has needs unique to himself. Marriages are bonded together as each partner becomes the channel through which those needs are understood and met in the other.

Considering all the things which can go wrong in marriages and homes can be depressing. The contents of this chapter should reinforce the importance of following God's ways in home building. There is no substitute for knowing God's Word and following it in faith. The breakdown of the family in our culture and the multitudinous problems and heartaches which result should shout a clear warning against disobedience. It is time for Christian fathers and mothers to take their God-ordained places without apology to a wayward world and train up their children in the Lord's way.

## SUMMARY

The breakdown of the home stems back to waywardness—leaving the directions of the Lord and walking in man's own ways. The result is hurt. Wayward children hurt their parents. Wayward parents hurt their children. Wayward husbands hurt their wives. Wayward wives hurt their husbands. The first step back is repentance—turning back to God's ways. This chapter is not an attempt to make man's ways work. They don't. It is a call to recognize waywardness for what it is and to deal honestly with it. Many are the shallow remedies of our day which treat only the symptoms—they deal with pain, but not with sin. Certainly we must not ignore that people are hurting today, but we must likewise recognize that until sinful man deals with his sin, pain will continue. Where people are willing to obey God, honor parents, train children, and live morally pure lives, home can yet be a place of security and love, a place of refuge for children, and a standard of holiness for our society.

## THINKING TOGETHER

1. What are some of the reasons children depart from faith? Which do you think are the more significant causes?
2. How does disrespect in parents (for authorities over them) affect their children? What are some of the more common ways parents might be tempted to show disrespect?
3. What are some current trends toward worldliness which seem to be especially appealing to young people? How might parents best cope with these trends?
4. What are some things parents ought not to do in

relating to wayward young people? Can you add to the things listed in this chapter?

5. How might Christian youths with wayward parents be tempted to ignore their parents' advice? How do well-meaning Christians sometimes undermine respect for parents in youths whose parents are non-Christian?

6. Describe the need for friendship in a person whose companion is wayward.

7. How might a person with a wayward companion be tempted to use love as a lever? Why doesn't this work?

8. Suppose a person came to you whose divorced companion was taking advantage of him or her—i.e., abusing visiting rights, taking financial advantage, making demands on time, etc. What Scriptural advice would you give?

9. What are the blessings of each partner focusing on his own responsibility in restoring a marriage? What are the results when this is not the focus?

10. What are some needs a wife has which a husband might commonly overlook, and what are some practical ways a husband might meet those needs and vice versa?

## WORKING TOGETHER

1. As a family, evaluate your home. Do you have any of the factors which may result in wayward children? If so, what might you do to correct them?

2. Consider the principles of praying for the lost. Are there any which you need to understand better? Are there some you might add?

3. As a family, do you know young people with wayward

311

parents or people with wayward companions? Could
you take someone as a special prayer concern? Are
there ways you might befriend these people?

4. As a couple, evaluate the quality of your communication. Ask your companion how well you are meeting
his or her needs. How might you strengthen your
relationship?

# ENDNOTES

CHAPTER 1
1. Joan Lloyd Guest, *Forgiving Your Parents* (Downers Grove, Illinois: Intervarsity Press, 1988), p. 6.
2. Guest, p. 19.

CHAPTER 2
1. David Elkind, "Helping the Hurried Child," excerpted from *The Hurried Child* (Menlo Park, California: Addison-Wesley Publishing Company, 1981), p. 2. The pressure to grow up early is certainly broader than exposure to evil, discussed in this chapter. In education, for example, the pressure is to teach students as much as possible as early as possible. In sports, the pressures of adult competition force children into early performance, sometimes to the literal point of breaking.
2. Stephen Olford and Frank Lawes, *The Sanctity of Sex* (LaGrange, Indiana: Pathway Publishing Co., 1963), p. 14.
3. Samuel Yoder, "Accountability and Believer's Baptism" (Taken from a message preached March 1, 1983), used by permission.
4. A special accompanying workbook entitled *God's Will for My Body* is available from Christian Light Publications for parents to use in teaching their children about their sexual development. Each lesson is based on a particular Scripture and guides the parent and the child through a respectful and yet open discussion about physical changes.

CHAPTER 3
1. Ervin Hershberger, *Christian Courtship* (Meyersdale, Pennsylvania: printed by Edgewood Press, 1984), p. 28.
2. Hershberger, p. 29.

CHAPTER 4
1. Evelyn Mumaw, *Woman Alone* (Scottdale, Pennsylvania: Herald Press, 1970), p. 12.
2. Much of what is given in this chapter applies equally to both sexes. To avoid the awkwardness of dual pronoun construction (he or she, him or her, etc.), hereafter the masculine pronoun will generally be used. Where the text relates particularly to women or particularly to men, the context will make this clear.
3. Mumaw, p. 13.
4. The first three in this list are adapted from Evelyn Mumaw's list, pp. 14 ff.
5. Mumaw, p. 17.

6. Mumaw, p. 45.

7. J. H. Horsburgh, "Here Am I—Serve Me," *Christian Focus,* (Birmingham, Alabama: Gospel Publishing Association, May, 1987, p. 8.

## CHAPTER 5

1. Gary Smalley, for example, in his book *If Only He Knew* (Grand Rapids, Michigan: Zondervan, 1988) discusses these differences and says that one of the foremost reasons marriages fail today is because people do not understand male and female differences (see pp. 13 ff.).

2. Lester Miller, *Biblical Financial Guidelines* (Lebanon, Pennsylvania: Sowers Printing, 1988), p. 10.

3. David Showalter, "Helping Those With Financial Problems" (from a message preached December 6, 1989).

4. Where communication is broken down, expressions of love are shallow and cheap. Further help for meaningful intimacy can be found in Chapters 5 and 6 of the workbook, *God's Will for Love in Marriage.* This study guide, recommended for engaged and married couples, is available from Christian Light Publications, Inc., Harrisonburg, Virginia 22801.

5. The divorce discussed here, of course, is the breaking of a legitimate marriage. There are unions which cultures both past and present have permitted which are "unlawful" (that is, are contrary to God's righteous standards) and which should be broken. Consider, for example, incestuous, homosexual, or adulterous unions.

6. Anon., "Scars of Divorce," published by Gospel Tract Society, Inc., Independence, Missouri, pp. 1, 3, 6.

7. Anon., "Out of Adultery," published in *Herald of His Coming,* Los Angeles, California, Sept., 1982, pp. 11, 12.

8. Many are the arguments which hardened hearts can raise in favor of divorce and remarriage. For more Scriptural help on this issue, see *What the Bible Says About Marriage, Divorce, and Remarriage,* by John Coblentz, Christian Light Publications, Harrisonburg, Virginia 22801.

9. The separation of an adulterous marriage, particularly where there are children, seldom has easy answers, but answers can be found when once the commitment is made to return to God's standards. Two basic principles must be observed. First, we must honor the principle of righteousness—discontinuing the adulterous relationship. Second, we must honor the principle of responsibility—arranging as much as we are able for the godly training and care of the children. These principles are important not only for resolving the problems of the adulterous union, but also must be considered with regard to former marital relationships and children.

10. Those who object to separating an adulterous relationship for

righteousness' sake are often the very ones who justify divorce for personal reasons. One man testified to this very thing. He said he received strong opposition from fellow church members when he chose to leave an adulterous relationship, but the same group was "understanding" toward people who divorced and remarried for personal reasons.

CHAPTER 6

1. As quoted by Larry and Nordis Christenson in *The Christian Couple* (Minneapolis, Minnesota: Bethany House Publishers, 1977), p. 101.

2. Commenting from a woman's perspective how contraceptives affect marriage intimacy, Nordis Christenson writes, "I would not go back to using a contraceptive device even if the alternative were having twenty-one children" (Christenson, p. 74).

3. For more specific guidance in this matter, see Chapters 5 and 6 of *God's Will for Love in Marriage*, available from Christian Light Publications, Inc. This study is recommended for engaged or married couples.

4. As reported in Training LIGHTUNIT 4, produced by Christian Light Publications, Inc., 1980, pp. 5, 6.

5. In his book *What the Bible Says About Child Training*, J. Richard Fugate defines the rod as a "narrow stick used on a rebellious child by his parental authorities." (Garland, Texas: Aletheia Publishers, Inc., 1980), p. 114. We would add that God has provided flexible rods on trees. These switches can produce an effective sting without causing bodily harm. Mr. Fugate, with other Christian writers in recent years, raises objection to the use of a parent's hand in spanking because of the psychological relationship to the parent's comforting touch. This is a controversial point. While the Bible refers consistently to the rod, not the hand, as a means of discipline for children, it does refer to the disciplinary "hand" of God (see, for example, Deuteronomy 2:15). Furthermore, emotional damage to children results from the emotional state of the parent far more than from the particular instrument he is using. When a parent has trouble with slapping or spanking in flash anger, however, establishing a policy of not using the hand but rather a rod may give the parent the necessary time to gain emotional control.

6. Evidence for the importance of touch is sometimes disputed, but studies indicate that when infants six to twelve months old are removed from their mothers altogether, they suffer what one researcher called anaclitic depression, the symptoms of which included dejection, weight loss, and susceptibility to sickness. Another researcher gave evidence which indicated that the quality of a mother's touch and attention affected the children's susceptibility to psycho-

315

logical disorders later in life.

7. William Lee Wilbanks, "The New Obscenity," *Reader's Digest,* December, 1988, p. 24.

8. Karl Zinsmeister, "Hard Truths About Day Care," *Reader's Digest,* October 1988, p. 90.

9. Zinsmeister, p. 91.

10. These statistics were for the adoption of normal children in the 1980s. Children with handicaps are far easier to adopt, with less waiting time.

11. Douglas R. Donnelly in his pamphlet *A Guide to Adoption* notes that normally a "home study" is required which typically considers at least four things: criminal record, marriage status, income level, and health (Pomona, California: Focus on the Family, 1988), p. 6.

12. Donnelly, p. 3.

## CHAPTER 8

1. Larry Parker, *We Let Our Son Die* (Irvine, California: Harvest House Publishers, 1980), pp. 160, 161. With compelling honesty, Larry Parker describes factors which led him with his wife to wrongly presume upon the promises of God. He also discusses the heartrending consequences which they subsequently endured on the path to distinguishing between presumption and Biblical faith.

2. Barbara Deane, *Caring for Your Aging Parents* (Colorado Springs, Colorado: NavPress, 1989), p. 36.

3. Deane, pp. 49, ff.

4. Deane, pp. 68, 69.

5. Albert Rosenfeld, *The Second Genesis: The Coming Control of Life* (Englewood Cliffs, New Jersey: Prentice-Hall, Inc., 1969), p. 3.

## CHAPTER 9

1. For a discussion of the contemporary music scene and Biblical principles which guide us, see *Music in Biblical Perspective,* by John Coblentz, published by Christian Light Publications, Inc., 1986.

2. Wilson Grant, *Taking Time Out to Be Dad* (Arcadia, California: Focus on the Family, Inc., 1986), p. 3.

3. In her book *Journal of Tears* (Christian Light Publications, 1984), p. 23 ff., Elizabeth Lapp describes this problem. She writes, "In response to my husband's actions, some people were sure that love was the answer. The advice was to keep the door of reconciliation open and never, never close it. . . . Others were sure I did not need to put up with this. They suggested to give him the 'either straighten up or else' treatment. Both lines of advice were coming from Christian people." To safeguard herself from wrong counsel, she began to use five checkpoints—God's Word, authority figures, circumstances, common sense, and the Holy Spirit's inner promptings.

Christian Light Publications, Inc., is a nonprofit conservative Mennonite publishing company providing Christ-centered, Biblical literature in a variety of forms including Gospel tracts, books, Sunday school materials, summer Bible school materials, and a full curriculum for Christian day schools and home schools.

For more information at no obligation or for spiritual help, please write to us at:

Christian Light Publications, Inc.
P. O. Box 1126
Harrisonburg, VA 22801-1126